Praise for *Broken Scales: Reflections on Injustice*

Even for the most diligent students of our judicial system, Joel Cohen's penetrating examination of injustice in America, and how victims and perpetrators have responded to it, will stun readers and provoke much needed debate. A judicial must read.

—*Judith Miller, Fox News contributor;*
City Journal, *Contributing Editor;*
Tablet Magazine

The thought that ours is a "nation of laws, not of men," lends security, a sense of certainty, and a predictability to our lives. However, Joel Cohen, in his remarkable book, *Broken Scales*, through insightful narrative, interviews, and case histories demonstrates how prosecutors, judges, and manipulators of the system too often lead to injustice and the destruction of lives under the rubric of the rule of law.

—*Sol Wachtler, retired Chief Judge,*
New York Court of Appeals

America's system of justice may be reasonably well understood, but its system of injustice—and the experiences of those unfortunates caught within it—are not. Joel Cohen introduces us to that system and a few of those people—some famous, most forgotten or never known—and, fine lawyer that he is, elicits their stories both clinically and compellingly.

—*David Margolick, Contributing Editor,*
Vanity Fair; *author, including*
At the Bar: The Passions and
Peccadilloes of American Lawyers

Cohen, who has skillfully practiced criminal law from "both sides," writes prolifically about law, social justice, morality, and even the Bible. Against that backdrop, he presents a diverse group of individuals who discuss their very different narratives about injustice. The collage of those interviews provides a unique perspective—reminding us how our justice system can so easily break down into injustice.

—*Barry Scheck, co-founder,*
Innocence Project

A highly readable, intelligent, deeply felt book about injustice: wrongful convictions and sentences; false accusations; shattered lives; destroyed reputations; judges penalized for unpopular decisions. Read these compelling interviews; you'll be glad you did.

—*Ira Glasser, former Executive*
Director (1978–2001, retired),
American Civil Liberties Union

Broken Scales makes pristinely clear that America's justice scales are weighted and extremely imbalanced. This should be required reading for every congressperson, prosecutor, and judge. Maybe, just maybe, it can help change how justice is administered in the United States.

—*Don Siegelman,*
former Governor, Alabama

JOEL COHEN

Author of *Blindfolds Off: Judges on How They Decide*

with DALE J. DEGENSHEIN

BROKEN SCALES

REFLECTIONS ON INJUSTICE

Cover design by Elmarie Jara/ABA Design

Printed in the United States of America.

21 20 19 18 17   5 4 3 2 1

Library of Congress Cataloging-in-Publication Data

Names: Cohen, Joel, 1944– | Degenshein, Dale J., author. | Gertner, Nancy, 1946– writer of introduction.
Title: Broken scales : reflections on injustice / Joel Cohen with Dale J. Degenshein ; foreword by Hon. Nancy Gertner (Ret.).
Description: Chicago : American Bar Association, 2017. | Includes bibliographical references and index.
Identifiers: LCCN 2017002950 (print) | LCCN 2017003487 (ebook) | ISBN 9781634258098 (hardcover : alk. paper) | ISBN 9781634258104 (ebook)
Subjects: LCSH: Justice, Administration of—United States—Case studies. | Judicial error—United States—Cases. | Law—Political aspects—United States— Case studies.
Classification: LCC KF384 .C64 2017 (print) | LCC KF384 (ebook) | DDC 347.73—dc23
LC record available at https://lccn.loc.gov/2017002950

Discounts are available for books ordered in bulk. Special consideration is given to state bars, CLE programs, and other bar-related organizations. Inquire at Book Publishing, ABA Publishing, American Bar Association, 321 N. Clark Street, Chicago, Illinois 60654-7598.

www.ShopABA.org

*He who commits injustice is ever made more wretched
than he who suffers it.*

—Plato

Contents

About the Authors

Joel Cohen is a highly respected white collar criminal defense lawyer in New York. He has practiced in that field, as well as complex civil litigation, at Stroock & Stroock & Lavan LLP for nearly 30 years, after having worked for ten years as a prosecutor with the New York State Special Prosecutor's Office and then with the U.S. Department of Justice's Organized Crime and Racketeering Section in the Eastern District of New York. Joel writes regularly for the *New York Law Journal*, *The Hill*, *Huffington Post*, law.com, and others on criminal law, legal ethics, and social policy. He frequently lectures lawyers, judges, and the public on varied issues, including ethics and religion. He has taught professional responsibility and currently teaches a class at Fordham Law School, "How Judges Decide," based on his earlier book, *Blindfolds Off: Judges on How They Decide*, published by ABA Publishing in 2014. Joel has published several works of Biblical fiction, including *Moses: A Memoir*, *David and Bathsheba: Through Nathan's Eyes,* and *Moses and Jesus: A Conversation*. Finally, he has also authored *Truth Be Veiled, a Justin Steele Murder Case*, a novel that addresses the criminal lawyer's dilemma in dealing with the truth.

Dale J. Degenshein has practiced law since 1984, and has worked at Stroock since 2007. She frequently writes articles on the law and contributed to *Blindfolds Off* as well as Joel's periodic articles over the last four years.

Foreword

by Honorable Nancy Gertner (Ret.)[1]

Joel Cohen has compiled riveting narratives of injustice in the justice system, but not the usual ones—the ones the public has been hearing about far too often. These are not simply accounts of DNA exonerations stemming from botched investigations or official misconduct. The stories he recounts are equally troubling, if that is even possible. These are narratives of injustice imbedded in the justice system and all too often ignored. And they are told through actual interviews with a variety of participants—the wrongly convicted, to be sure, but also the prosecutor whose advocacy blinded him to the unfairness of a conviction, the defense lawyer who battled for a client that everyone agreed should not be in jail, and the judge who is not reelected after ruling for gay marriage.

One story had special resonance for me; I was a U.S. district court judge for 17 years and presided over challenges to state and federal convictions. The writ of habeas corpus, which should have provided a meaningful review of serious charges and substantial penalties, devolved into running the gauntlet of procedural barrier after procedural barrier, too

---

1. Judge Nancy Gertner sat on the U.S. District Court in Massachusetts for 17 years until her return to the practice of law in 2011. She writes and speaks on many issues, including civil liberties, sentencing, forensic evidence, and the jury system. Judge Gertner authored *In Defense of Women: Memoirs of an Unrepentant Advocate* and is currently writing a book about criminal justice. She serves on the faculty of the Harvard Law School, and has received numerous awards, including the Thurgood Marshall Award from the American Bar Association's Section of Individual Rights and Responsibilities.

often masking outcomes that in some cases I strongly believed to have been unjust. It was an Alice in Wonderland of technical trip wires, barring access to the courts for those wrongly convicted and providing opportunities for the prosecutors who happily took advantage of them.

Michael Wayne Haley was one such case, portrayed by Cohen through an interview with his lawyer, Eric M. Albritton. Haley was guilty of stealing a calculator from Walmart, but he was wrongly tried as a habitual offender. Texas's three strikes' law required two prior sequential felony convictions; his record—while surely not admirable—did not fit the statute's requirements so that he was innocent of being a habitual offender. The difference was critical—a petty crime with two years in jail, or a habitual offender sentenced to 16-and-a-half years. Working pro se, Haley read the statute carefully; apparently, no one else did—not the trial judge, the prosecutor, or the defense lawyer. He filed motions claiming that he was erroneously convicted as a habitual offender. The state courts and then the federal court rejected the claim, at the insistence of the prosecutor, not because it wasn't true; everyone agreed it was. But rather because of a "procedural default," which, to lay ears, must surely sound like something out of Heller's *Catch 22*: The procedural default was the failure to raise the issue, but the issue had not been raised precisely because everyone had missed it. Ultimately, the case went to the Supreme Court (argued by Texas's Solicitor General Ted Cruz), and through its procedural machinations, Haley was resentenced to the two years—*after he had served six.*

What the lawyers and judges were doing from the moment they realized that Haley had been wrongly convicted may have looked like justice; the judges in their robes, the lawyers citing to cases, the American flag behind them. But it was not justice, as Albritton said: The State of Texas was "myopically" focused on the principle that no matter how wrong or how unfair, federal courts ought not interfere in state convictions. And he added, "What I find outrageous is that policy considerations eclipsed common sense."

And then there is the opposite, the story of the prosecutor in the Glenn Ford case, A. Martin Stroud III, who took responsibility for Ford's wrongful conviction, not because he hid exculpatory evidence or tainted the investigation. Indeed, at the time of Cohen's interview with him, Stroud didn't even know the facts of Ford's exoneration, only that the then district attorney believed that there was conclusive evidence that the wrong man had been convicted. Rather, Stroud believed he should have done something to prevent the injustice, taking to heart the view that the prosecutor's role is not simply advocacy but to make certain that "justice be done." Stroud knew only that Ford's lawyers were completely inexperienced in criminal cases and were wholly ineffective in his defense. After Ford's exoneration, Stroud worked to oppose the death penalty publicly, and went so far as to turn himself in to the disciplinary committee asking to be disciplined for his role in the wrongful conviction.

And then there are the high-profile and not so high-profile stories that should resonate with all of us. Steven Pagones, an assistant district attorney in Dutchess County New York, was wrongly accused of the Tawana Brawley rape, an accusation that was splashed across New York headlines for years. Kenneth Ireland, wrongly convicted of capital murder in a small Connecticut town, was exonerated by DNA, but only after he had served decades in prison. Miriam Moskowitz was convicted and sentenced in the 1950s for conspiracy to lie about Soviet-related activities, but was never formally exonerated even when grand jury testimony released decades after her conviction established her innocence. Abdallah Higazy, who falsely confessed to having a transceiver device that authorities linked to the 9/11 attacks, after a hotel employee lied about where the device was found, was finally exonerated when an airline pilot staying at the same hotel claimed the device. Their interviews help us understand what it is like to suffer false accusations, to be at risk for extraordinary punishments, even death, and to have the legal system finally recognize their innocence (or not in the case of Miriam Moskowitz) after substantial suffering and sometimes only by happenstance.

Cohen also deals with cases where the issue may not be wrongful conviction but wrongful prosecution or punishment. Jeffrey Alexander Sterling, who had previously charged the CIA with race discrimination, was convicted under the Espionage Act and sentenced to three-and-one-half years in prison for passing secret information to a *New York Times* reporter, when former CIA director David Petraeus received probation for giving his mistress confidential information.

Finally, Cohen interviews those who were not convicted at all, but whose stories tell us something about the extraordinary pressures put on legal system participants who seek to act in a principled manner, or bring diverse perspective to adjudication. Chief Justice Ternus of Iowa lost reelection after she ruled in favor of same sex marriage. Judge A. Ashley Tabaddor, an immigration judge, is recused from hearing cases involving Iranians because she was born in Iran, even though she had lived in the United States for 30 years. Adam Sirois tells of the experience of being the lone juror holdout in a high-profile murder case.

These cases force us to ask, How could this happen? How can these incidents be prevented? And in Cohen's revealing interviews with exonerees, their lawyers, judges, and a juror, perhaps we can find the seeds of an answer.

Introduction

Injustice has been with us since the beginning of time. In Greek mythology, Diké, the goddess of moral justice, is depicted as beating the hideous Adikia, the goddess of injustice. The Egyptians also acknowledge counterparts—Ma'at representing justice, while Isfet the opposite. The Bible teaches that one must "not render an unfair decision" or permit "dishonest scales." It tells the story of Joseph—sold into slavery by his brothers, he resists the seduction of the wife of his master (Potiphar), only to be jailed upon her false accusations of attempted rape.

Yet, lessons are rarely learned and injustice has passed from generation through generation—it is explored by Plato, Aristotle, Voltaire, Shakespeare, Benjamin Franklin, Emile Zola, Thomas Jefferson, Abraham Lincoln, Martin Luther King, Jr., Lyndon B. Johnson, and Nelson Mandela, to name only a few. Perhaps, to put it as only Mark Twain could: "Man was made at the end of the week's work, when God was tired."

One would like to believe that we have evolved, so that our justice system—many believe it the best in the world—has evolved; that it weeds out injustice and people are treated equally and without the imposition of any outside factor. Of course, that is not so. But what is it that contributes to injustice—what prohibits the ideal? Arrogance, laziness, self-dealing, or just plain human failings of those tasked with administering the system have an impact. And we explore, in one interview, just what can happen when no one in the courtroom—not the prosecutor, the judge, or the defense counsel—pays attention. The laziness, or human failing, in that case cost a man a prison term 14 years longer than it should have been.

As we have learned, in certain circumstances the existence of an injustice is an objective fact—there really can be no doubt. We now have DNA evidence, scientifically proving that some who are or have been in jail are "actually innocent." The Innocence Project tells us that 343 people have been exonerated—found to have been improperly convicted based on undisputed scientific DNA evidence. One of those helped (saved, really) by the Innocence Project is Kenneth Ireland—DNA evidence proved, unequivocally, that he was innocent of the crimes for which he was convicted. No question; not a single doubt.

Still, the capacity for an objectively accurate determination is rare. In both the criminal justice system and the social realm, more frequently, the existence of an injustice may "lie in the eyes of the beholder"—viewed through the prism of the individual called upon to characterize the episode. Some are in circumstances patently unjust, and so it is difficult to imagine any disagreement; as to others—perhaps, one reader will be appalled while another will shrug her shoulders. Indeed, I initially contemplated placing the chapters in descending order—the greatest injustice to the least. As I met those I interviewed, and thought about the events in their lives, I of course could not do that—each person's story must stand on its own, with the reader to decide (should he or she choose to) whether an injustice was done and where it falls in relation to the others. Some will question why the ten cases discussed here were chosen of all the cases of injustice that might have been selected for inclusion in this volume. A valid question indeed, but one not totally answerable, aside from the desire to explore injustice from different perspectives.

There may be no better, modern-day example of divergent thoughts on injustice than the criminal prosecution—and acquittal—of O.J. Simpson for the murder of Nicole Brown-Simpson and Ron Goldman. For many, Simpson's play of the "race card" worked; whether or not people saw Simpson as innocent, they saw it extremely possible for a black man to be framed—even for something that he (very possibly) did! From the perspective of an individual who saw Simpson as guilty, his acquittal was the injustice. From the perspective of an individual who saw him as innocent or even simply "not guilty" (which is far different), his very prosecution was an injustice.

How, then, do we look at the life of Steven Pagones? An assistant district attorney, he was very publicly accused of a horrific crime, with racial motives front and center. An eight-month investigation found not only that he was innocent, but that the entire incident was a hoax. Was there injustice? Even though there was no trial, Pagones was, after all, "acquitted." He was found innocent, and his innocence was widely reported. Or is there injustice in his merely having had to live through the hell of the investigation and endure its aftermath? His children, after all, can turn on their computers and see that their father was accused—even though found innocent—of having viciously raped a black teenager, Tawana Brawley, years earlier.

To discuss injustice, we must also look at factors not tied to the "System." How important is public opinion? What are the thoughts and etiquette of the day? Even the best judges—those who scrupulously apply the law even if they vehemently disagree with it—don't live in caves. They read and watch the news; they talk to friends and family; they live in the same world as the rest of us. They hear public opinion and even have their own opinions—opinions that may change, given what is going on around them.

And so all of the interviews you will read, as with all things, must be placed in the context of their time, and in the context of the reader's experience. Miriam Moskowitz was convicted, essentially for being a "Communist sympathizer" as that term would have been understood in the 1950s at the height of McCarthyism. Her story brings to mind the observation of a great Supreme Court Justice, Robert H. Jackson: "The most odious of all oppressions are those which mask as justice." Moskowitz removes that mask, shining a spotlight on a very troubling time in our history.

Abdallah Higazy spoke about a later time—disturbing and ingrained in the memory of many readers. A Muslim man, born in Egypt, he was a guest in a hotel immediately across from the World Trade Center on 9/11. Not surprising that in the immediate aftermath of 9/11, the FBI believed a witness who claimed that Higazy had a transceiver device in his room safe that allowed him to communicate with planes, and thus jailed Higazy. In Aesop's fable of the Wolf and the Lamb, the wolf accused the lamb of wrongdoing, and even though every accusation was proved wrong, the wolf declared that the lamb's family members must have committed the crimes, all to justify killing the lamb. The moral—one can always find an excuse for actions and ignore the reasoning of the innocent. Is that what Higazy's story tells us? Can we believe that a government (our government) is so certain of its position that it may be incapable of seeing beyond its own prejudices, even if it leads to what many would believe is manifest injustice?

Iowa's Chief Justice Marsha Ternus and her colleagues were caught in the tenor of the day when they committed the "offense" of striking down a challenge to same-sex marriage as unconstitutional, causing Iowa to be the first "non-liberal" state to do so. But was their removal from the bench an "injustice"? After all, *the public* voted to remove them. Does the reader question whether Jeffrey Sterling, an African-American CIA operative, was discriminated against in the 1990s because of his skin color? Even if yes, can you then conclude that that treatment—and the government's failure to account for it—caused Sterling to commit a crime by leaking government secrets to a reporter? And, even if you do, was Sterling treated differently from others because he had embarrassed the CIA?

When I began this book, I had no doubt that there would be instances where the injustice was manifest and others where the issue might be grey. As I interviewed the subjects of this book, however, I realized that another theme ran through the interviews—the way in which very ordinary people dealt with the particular injustice thrust upon them or of which they were a part. Some of those interviewed look around every day, hoping no one would know about their past. Others look straight ahead, and shout from the rooftops, "I have been wronged." Still others, perhaps, accept that they have done wrong to another, and try to "make things right," as it were.

Moskowitz spent decades looking over her shoulder. Did the FBI hound her, or leave her to live her life after she served her two-year prison term? Immigration Judge Ashley Tabaddor was told that she was not permitted to hear immigration cases that impacted Iranians, solely because she attended an Iranian-American event sponsored by the White House. She looked at what she perceived as injustice and decided to fight, even though, in practical terms, it made little difference to her cases. Were the famous words of Martin Luther King, Jr. in the back of her mind?—"Injustice anywhere is a threat to justice everywhere."

Marty Stroud was a prosecutor in Shreveport, Louisiana, who, in 1984, aggressively prosecuted Glenn Ford for murder. Thirty years later, when it was determined that Ford was actually innocent, Stroud examined his very belief system and has now dedicated himself to abolishing the death penalty. But when Ford was finally released from prison, did Stroud apologize? Could *you* face the person whom you have wronged and apologize for what you had done? And how would you deal with what your actions had done to the victim?

Abdallah Higazy did something remarkable—although, one suspects, it happens more often than one might think. He confessed to a crime he did not commit. Can you imagine doing that? I myself couldn't when I began this book; I can now understand it, having talked to him. Why did Pedro Hernandez, the subject of juror Adam Sirois's interview, confess to kidnapping Etan Patz decades earlier? How does someone like Sirois, the sole member of the jury who refused to convict Hernandez, address the question of whether Hernandez knowingly confessed?

There is also surprise in the way in which those interviewed addressed their anger. In some, the anger is there. Plain and raw. Stroud is angry at himself. Sirois is angry at his fellow jurors. Moskowitz is angry at the system that allowed her to be convicted (and still stand convicted), and refused to allow her to be exonerated 50 years later.

But others—others whose lives have been forever altered, people one would expect to be fueled with anger—are not, or at least say they are not. They look forward, and have put their past behind in ways somewhat unimaginable. Kenneth Ireland spent 21 years in prison, from the time he was 18 years old. He was exonerated based on DNA evidence—no question that the man who brutally raped and murdered a woman was not Ireland. Could you even imagine being released from prison and *not* being angry? Or did Ireland understand that anger would do nothing for him? Nelson Mandela explained it, perhaps, best: "As I walked out the door toward the gate that would lead to my freedom, I knew if I didn't leave my bitterness and hatred behind, I'd still be in prison."

Chief Judge Ternus—does she believe an injustice was done to her? Or is she disturbed that the people of Iowa were inundated with billboards and advertisements proclaiming that their values, their very way of life, would be forever diminished because of her ruling? Did others stand up for her—to tell the public that she was merely upholding the law? Does it matter to her?

How does Higazy address his anger? Has he moved back to Egypt, denigrating the U.S. every chance he gets? Or does he live with an understanding of why the U.S. government acted as it did toward him? Is Judge Tabaddor angry about her treatment—has the government ever explained the reason for its actions? And what does she do to make sure the government never again demands that a judge step away from cases when there is no showing that the judge is prejudiced in any way? And Sterling—how does he channel his anger as he sits in a cell?

Returning to our premise—injustice(s)—I introduce you to those who were kind enough to allow me to interview them. I say that, but was it kindness that motivated them? Or was there something else? As you read their stories, ask yourself—was there an injustice? How did the periods' public opinions, the public mindset, factor in? And when you look at how they handled their circumstance, ask what you would have done in the same situation.

One final note. In 1965, at the conclusion of the March from Selma to Montgomery, Martin Luther King, Jr., told us: "The arc of the moral universe is long, but it bends towards justice." As you read these interviews, decide if you believe those words ring true.

Author's Note

The ten interviews that comprise this volume—conducted from 2014 through 2016—were recorded and transcribed. Each interview lasted between an hour and one-and-one-half hours. The transcripts were then edited by the author slightly for style and, by prearrangement, thereupon provided to each person interviewed for his or her own comments. Those interviewed made minimal changes, and no one changed the substance of the interview or the responses to the questions asked. While those interviewed knew, in advance, the general subject matter of the interview, none of the interviews was scripted, nor was anyone provided with questions in advance. In short, the interviews were intended to be conducted as extemporaneously as possible.

This project, while conceived by Dale Degenshein and me, was not possible without the kind participation of the ten people interviewed, none of whom we knew before interviewing them. That they were willing to participate in unscripted interviews with a total stranger is a testament to them. We thank and commend each of them.

We also thank the leadership of Stroock—the law firm I have been privileged to be with since 1985, and Dale since 2007—for recognizing the importance of giving back to the legal community (and society in general) by allowing us to use its valuable resources in writing this book. Having said that, any views expressed in this book (aside, of course, from those of the interviewees) are ours alone and, particularly if poorly received, should not be attributed to our thoughtful colleagues, with whom we have been privileged to work.

Finally, Dale and I dedicate this book to the many, both living and dead, and far too numerous to mention, who have suffered over the course of history at the hands of those responsible for injustices.

1

Winning at Any Cost

Glenn Ford discussed by A. Martin Stroud III

*What it has done—the best description I can give—
is that every morning when I wake up I have a hole
in my stomach. A cold emptiness with the north-
wind blowing straight through it. And that's the
direct result of my dealing with the saga of Glenn
Ford. There's no happy ending here that I can see.*

—A. Martin Stroud III, December 22, 2015[1]

One cannot tell the story of A. Martin Stroud III without also telling the story of Glenn Ford. Ford served 30 years on death row for a crime he did not commit; Marty Stroud was the man who put him there. For better or worse, their lives are forever linked.

In 1984, Mr. Stroud was a prosecutor in Shreveport, Louisiana. And when a jeweler named Isadore Rozeman was killed, he put Ford on trial

---

1. This interview took place at Mr. Stroud's offices in Shreveport, Louisiana.

for murder. The evidence against Ford was scant—circumstantial only; there were no witnesses to the murder, no conclusive fingerprints, no solid evidence that Ford fired a gun, and, indeed, no gun. Witnesses's testimony at trial was inconsistent with their own prior statements; and the time of death was put into question (as was Ford's alibi) as a witness first told police—and the prosecution told the defense—that he telephoned Mr. Rozeman at one time, yet he testified the call took place at another. The change in the statement was labeled by the police officer who took the witness's statement as a "mistake."

But Ford was no innocent—he had sold some of the jewelry stolen at the time of the murder, he sold a gun, and he gave five statements to the police, all somewhat different. Perhaps the proverbial nail was that a co-defendant's brother-in-law (and Ford's cellmate while awaiting trial) told police that Ford discussed with him details of the robbery and murder.

Ford was charged and was provided with state-appointed counsel. This was a capital case—one that could send a man to his death. Yet Louisiana's sole requirement was that a defendant's lawyer had to have been admitted to practice for at least five years. There was no need for knowledge of criminal law, no need for trial experience, no need for much of anything. So who was appointed for Ford—a man facing the death penalty on a case built solely on circumstantial evidence? One of his lawyers practiced in the area of oil and gas law and had never tried a single case, civil or criminal, before a jury. The second attorney also had no criminal experience, had never tried a case before a jury, and had met with Ford once—only once—until the penalty phase of his trial. In later motion practice, she conceded that she had no idea how to conduct an investigation. Did Ford receive effective assistance of counsel, as was his right under the Sixth Amendment? Remarkably, or maybe not so remarkably, the answer was "yes" according to the Louisiana courts.

On December 5, 1984, Ford, a black man, was convicted and sentenced to death by an all-white jury who had deliberated less than three hours in a courthouse that had a Confederate flag prominently displayed in front of the main entrance. You see, parties in a criminal trial at the time had the right to exclude certain jurors without articulating a reason, and the prosecution in Ford's case—in the person of Mr. Stroud, a Caucasian—used that right to make sure each and every juror was white. A jury of

Ford's peers? Yes, according to the Louisiana courts (and most of America at the time), but—really?

Ford was committed to the notorious Louisiana State Penitentiary—commonly known as Angola. It is the largest maximum security prison in the United States and, in order to control its population of death-row inmates, including Ford, prisoners were kept in their cells 23 hours a day. The cell? Smaller than an average bathroom. Outdoor activities? They were restricted to three hours a week in an area smaller than a dog run. Ford saw no reason to subject himself to that. In other words, and so there is no confusion on this point, Glenn Ford did not see the sky, the sun, trees, grass, even a dirt road, for seven years.

And through it all, Ford maintained his innocence. He sought relief from the Louisiana and federal courts—he argued that the judge made errors at trial, that the jury composition denied him his right to an impartial jury, and that he did not have the effective assistance of counsel. In each instance, his arguments fell short. But motion after motion kept him alive—at one point he was one week away from death.

But then, in 2013, "credible evidence" came to the prosecutor's office that Ford did not, in fact, kill Mr. Rozeman. Another who had been implicated at the time of the murder was now said to have pulled the trigger. The district attorney—Stroud was long gone from the prosecutor's office—moved to vacate Ford's conviction and sentence and Ford was released in March 2014. Thirty years after he had been sentenced. Remarkably, to this day, this "credible evidence" has not been made public. Could it be information that was available 30 years earlier, had anyone actually looked? It is possible that the public will never know.

Glenn Ford was given $20 as he left prison, barely enough for a meal. He sought compensation from the state for wrongful conviction but again was shot down—the court decided that Louisiana's statute precluded him from receiving any monies because, while he may have been innocent of murder, the court decided he was probably guilty of possessing stolen goods, possessing a gun, helping the actual murderer, and so on. He then brought a suit against the City of Shreveport and the district attorney's office; that suit is pending.

But this is not an interview with Ford—it could not be. Forty days after he was released from Angola, Ford learned of his second, and final, death sentence. He died of lung cancer at the age of 65 in June 2015. He had spent little more than a year "on the outside" wasting his way to a shell of himself.

Now let's return to 1984. Marty Stroud was a prosecutor in the Louisiana district attorney's office. Even then, he had quite a résumé. He had clerked for a federal judge and then worked as an assistant U.S. attorney in Louisiana before arriving at the D.A.'s office.

Stroud was an experienced prosecutor, a trial attorney who knew the law. This was the first capital case Stroud tried, but it would not be his last. And when it came to Ford, Stroud inwardly knew something was not right. The evidence was circumstantial, there were questions, rumors that Ford did not commit the crime that Stroud did not follow up—and that he did not tell the defense about. It turns out, although Stroud did not know it at the time (or perhaps did not want to know it), that a witness was coached, shall we say, by members of the police force, so that her testimony was not quite truthful. The final point—by Stroud's own actions, the jury was comprised of only white people.

And while all of this may have gnawed at Stroud over the years, at the time of trial, he forged ahead. Stroud's interest was in winning—regardless of whether justice was served. And win, he did.

He was, in his words, "arrogant," "judgmental," and "full of myself." He was smug in the knowledge that Ford's state-appointed lawyers had never seen a jury before, much less a criminal trial. Stroud tried his case, obtained a sentence of death for Ford, and, rather than reflect on such a verdict—reflect on the impact it would have on Ford and his family—he went out to celebrate this great win with his team. He was proud. The Ford victory would do great things for his career.

Years after Ford's conviction—30 years later—Stroud learned conclusively from the district attorney himself that he had convicted the wrong man, that he had put someone on death row who did not commit murder. He was devastated.

Could he apologize to Ford—would such a meager act have any real meaning? What of Stroud's career? He left the district attorney's office in 1989 and, in private practice, continues to try criminal cases, including capital cases—now, on the side of defendants. Can he try these cases any longer? Should he be disciplined by the Louisiana Bar Association? Stroud seems to think so, having asked the bar to take action against him.

One thing Stroud has surely done is to speak out. He began with an editorial in the *Shreveport Times* confessing his missteps, the rumors he ignored that, had he pursued them, may have resulted in no charges filed against Ford. He has talked publicly about the broken criminal justice system and his belief that the death penalty should be abolished. But until it is abolished, he implores prosecutors who try capital cases to look carefully at the evidence, to consider alternative theories, and to even spend a day at Angola's death row—all to be able to understand the penalty they are asking a jury to impose. He did this against the backdrop of Louisiana's First Deputy District Attorney Dale Cox—who promptly moved to have Ford released in 2014 when he received the new evidence—but who also responded to Stroud's editorial with the extreme, yet plain, statement that "I think we need to kill more people. . . . I think the death penalty should be used more often."

In 1935, the U.S. Supreme Court wrote of a prosecutor's duty:

> The United States Attorney is the representative not of an ordinary party to a controversy, but of a sovereignty whose obligation to govern impartially is as compelling as its obligation to govern at all, and whose interest, therefore, in a criminal prosecution is not that it shall win a case, but that justice shall be done. . . . He may prosecute with earnestness and vigor—indeed, he should do so. But, while he may strike hard blows, he is not at liberty to strike foul ones. It is as much his duty to refrain from improper methods calculated to produce a wrongful conviction as it is to use every legitimate means to bring about a just one.[2]

These are words Stroud may not have thought about back when he convicted Ford, but he surely thinks of them now.

---

2. Berger v. U.S., 295 U.S. 78 (1935).

The Dialogue

Author's note: During this interview, time gaps between questions and answers were at times quite lengthy. We have timed Stroud's pauses and put the length of time in brackets. When reading, time 15 seconds, 20 seconds to yourself and you will get a sense of just how long he reflected before answering some questions.

JC: Let me preface this interview this way: In 1974 I was a young, inexperienced corruption prosecutor in New York City. I indicted four corrupt detectives in New York, including one sergeant, for stealing money at the scene of a large drug sale. New York law requires that accomplice testimony be corroborated by non-accomplice testimony. The corroboration on one detective was clear-cut. On two, questionable. As for the sergeant, I didn't see it at all.

My boss, the special prosecutor, had extraordinary experience. Faced with my challenges to the case's non-accomplice sufficiency, he nonetheless told me to seek indictment of the four—it would be a big splash. I could have said no. I could have asked off the case. I didn't do either. By the time the case came to trial, nearly two years later, the sergeant had died. I have always assumed that the prospect of facing trial as a police officer led to his heart attack. It was later clear to me from the judge's rulings at trial that he would have dismissed the case against the sergeant. Although I have always believed that the sergeant was guilty, I knew in my heart all along that he wouldn't have been convicted, or that a conviction would have been reversed on appeal. Knowing in advance that that would occur, I was frankly relieved when the sergeant (a guilty man, at least in my eyes) died—sparing me the ignominy of losing a case I knew should and would be lost. I should note, too, that a second defendant also died before trial—maybe the case against him too would have resulted in a loss. I interview you against that background.

* * *

I've read a lot about the Glenn Ford case. You have publicly beaten yourself up, apologizing for having prosecuted him for capital murder. You have publicly and privately tried to apologize or seek forgiveness from a man approaching death who, in his lifetime, was unwilling to forgive you. You have actually tried to turn yourself into the disciplinary committee—asking to be disciplined for your role in the wrongful conviction. You have become something of a poster boy for the death penalty abolition movement. It's to your credit that you have done all that—maybe to teach a lesson to other prosecutors at the edge.

So my question I must ask you—it's a tough question, I'm sure—was Glenn Ford framed?

AMS: [30 seconds elapse] I don't know.

JC: I think the reader should know that you have ruminated for a while, for about 30 seconds.

AMS: I have, because I really have never been asked that question. I've never thought about it in that fashion or from that perspective.

JC: Take your time.

AMS: Others were arrested in connection with the case: a man by the name of George Starks and two men—brothers or cousins—named [Henry and Jake] Robinson. The Robinsons had notorious reputations in the Shreveport area at the time of this killing. They were indicted along with Ford and the indictments against them were later dismissed because of a lack of corroborating evidence—because witnesses did not come forward.

I'll jump forward. Several years later, a couple of years ago, there was a motion to dismiss the case. We had a meeting with the D.A.'s office; the DA's office said had we known in 1983 what they know now there wouldn't have been enough evidence even to arrest Mr. Ford. We were not told—or I was not told—the nature of that evidence. It apparently came from a source who was being used in connection with some current murder cases, one of which involves one of the Robinsons.

Your question brings me to the D.A.'s assertion that had we known what they knew now, we wouldn't have had enough evidence even to arrest the individual. So if you connect the dots, it could very well indicate that Mr. Ford was indeed framed.

JC: The curious thing about the district attorney's statement to you is this: you are saying that you don't know even today what the new evidence is, correct?

AMS: Correct.

JC: Strange. I read the district attorney's motion to set aside the conviction in 2014. That motion refers to the trial evidence that you were of course aware of when you indicted the case over 30 years ago. It refers to Judge [Pascal] Calogero's opinion in the Louisiana Supreme Court dissenting from the affirmance of Ford's conviction and death penalty sentence, arguing that there was insufficient evidence. Curiously, though, the D.A.'s motion doesn't say what the "new evidence" or old—now-uncovered—evidence is. But beyond that, you're telling me, the D.A. didn't even tell you, correct?

AMS: He did not, even though I asked.

JC: What, do you suspect, is the reason why he didn't tell you?

AMS: Well, he indicated that it was an ongoing, highly sensitive, case—and he didn't want the case to be affected by any undue disclosure of this evidence. Now, and at the time, I didn't follow up on that. I didn't ask any more questions. This was the first time that I had heard that evidence had been developed that exonerated Mr. Ford. Or at least I took it that way; because subsequently the D.A.'s office would retreat somewhat, and challenge the claim that Mr. Ford was *truly* exonerated.

But in my mind, when I heard the D.A.'s presentation, I felt that, as lead prosecutor, I had simply participated in a gross injustice. That my conduct led to the conviction of a person who, as a result of my conduct and that conviction, would spend 30 years in a cell—more like being in a cage as an animal—for a crime he didn't commit.

JC: Needless to say, there's a big difference between an "injustice" and a "frame." In the case I told you about in my own experience, I would say that was an injustice but not a frame.

The reason why I use the word frame is that in the *Ford* lawsuit against the City of Shreveport, Caddo Parish, and the district attorney's office, they specifically use the word "frame" in referring to how certain proof was generated by the police who investigated the case. They don't say that about you. The word "frame" is a very strong word. It means a suggestion—in fact, more than a suggestion—that a grand jury was asked to indict an innocent man, with the authorities knowing that he was innocent.

AMS: It is a strong word. [15 seconds elapse] I didn't, *at the time*, have any reason to suspect that Mr. Ford was being framed. I don't say that in an effort to get off the hook; I'm on the hook for other reasons, and rightly should be because of my immaturity at the time. But that's another issue.

But the case was strange in the sense that you had four people indicted for first degree murder. The thought was that the *least* culpable one was Glenn Ford, and that Mr. Ford would be the one to cooperate against the others, which he ultimately didn't do. In fact, he maintained that he had nothing to say and knew nothing about the murder. And so he went to trial and was convicted of capital murder, and given the death penalty. And then there were the other individuals who clearly had violent backgrounds. George Stark was one of them. I don't remember his record but the Robinsons had a history and reputation for being very violent people. Men you didn't want to cross paths with. They walked away from that case, and Glenn Ford went to death row. Imagine!

JC: Why did they walk away?

AMS: The case was "non-prossed"—dismissed for insufficient evidence. Individuals who had told the police about their involvement didn't come forward, didn't give sufficient information that, I saw, would warrant a prosecution; just wishy-washy, "I think he may have been." "I heard he was involved." There was just no strong finger of accusation pointed to those two.

JC: Was Glenn Ford given an opportunity to testify against those defendants?

AMS: Yes. He was asked about what he knew about the case and his position was "I don't know anything about the case. I don't know if they were involved, if they weren't involved. And I wasn't involved." So the case was discussed with him, and from day one Glenn Ford never vacillated in his position.

JC: Was he given that opportunity after he was indicted for murder one with a potential death penalty sentence? I know he was interviewed four times, or so, by the police *before* he was arrested. But, in the arms of a defense lawyer, was he given the chance to cooperate in exchange for leniency—indeed to escape the death penalty?

AMS: [10 seconds elapse] I'm almost certain that that happened. Now the issue there becomes this: the lawyers he had were not experienced in the field of criminal law. I believe they had never tried any case before this one. Certainly not a criminal case. Much less a capital case. And that information was communicated to them and they communicated . . . [10 seconds elapse] I'm not trying to be vague, but I don't think anything was in writing. Maybe there was a writing or a letter somewhere but it was communicated to his attorneys. But that goes right to the heart of one problem among many others in the case.

At the time the only qualification needed to handle a capital case was that you had been admitted to practice law for five years. Nothing else. That was it. If you had five years practice you were eligible to be appointed. Two lawyers were appointed—neither of whom had tried a case, or been involved with a capital case.

Having been personally involved in capital cases as a prosecutor and a defense attorney, when you approach a client about a potential deal or a potential resolution of a case, the way to do that, to me, is learned through experience. You just don't walk off the street, talk to somebody on death row and say "Hey did you have anything to do with it?" That's not going to create a warm and fuzzy feeling for somebody who's never done it before—who has never interviewed a client charged with a capital offense.

So I believe it was communicated to him and we got the message back that he was not, that he did not have any information to provide about the case.

JC: But wouldn't the judge have known how ripe this situation was for an injustice, that is, appointing these lawyers—one of which was, I believe, a gas and oil lawyer—to the case. There were no competent criminal lawyers in or near Caddo Parish, even without death penalty experience, who would been available to defend a man whose life was on the line?

AMS: There were people around who could have been appointed. I believe there was a public defender's office, but for some reason its attorneys had self-recused. There were two attorneys appointed who had private civil practices. I think the reason why the public defender didn't get involved was because there must have been a conflict. There was a book that the judge would go through. Other attorneys could certainly have been appointed. And, looking back on it, that's the absurdity of the whole situation. Here you have a man on trial for his life, and you've got somebody with absolutely no trial experience representing him. And nobody said anything. The judge didn't say anything. I didn't say anything. The question—you're so right—should have been raised. It shows how flawed the whole case was. That's one of the big issues I have with myself—why didn't *I* say something? Why?

JC: But that wasn't your duty, was it? That was how it worked in Shreveport at the time. You beat yourself up about this case. I've seen your interviews and writings. But is this one to beat yourself up about? Did you, yourself, have a duty to come forward and say: "Judge, this lawyer has only handled oil and gas cases"?

AMS: The judge knew that. I just think it's so absurd. Not even a close call. Did I have a duty under the code of professional responsibility? Probably not. I didn't even think about that though. Like most prosecutors I thought about *Brady* and the duty to divulge exculpatory evidence.[3] I didn't think about the procedure itself—the procedure was the procedure. Nobody said anything.

JC: Had you tried death penalty cases before that?

AMS: I think this was my first.

JC: And how many did you try after that?

AMS: I think I tried two more and they both ended up with life sentences.

JC: Why no death penalty in the last two?

AMS: In the last two the jury could not reach a unanimous verdict.

JC: Why in all those years was Ford not executed?

AMS: Appellate delays. I believe also that one judge sat on a motion an extraordinary length of time. When you get into the habeas, collateral relief stage of a capital case in Louisiana, judges tend to sit on them. Nobody's apt to be pushing it. The irony is the case was still in the system when the disclosure by the D.A. of Ford's innocence was made.

JC: So there was no question in your own mind when you indicted Ford, when the case went to trial, and when you sought the death penalty that you were dealing with a guilty man, right?

AMS: None.

JC: But earlier, you used the word "immaturity." You suggested that your immaturity at the time presumably led you to do something that you

---

3. Brady v. Maryland, 373 U.S. 83 (1963).

would do differently today. What was the immaturity? What would you do or not do differently today?

AMS: Number one, I wouldn't have rushed into it so quickly. I was the first assistant but I would have discussed the case more with the district attorney. [10 seconds elapse] I think it would have made more of an impact on me that we were prosecuting the defendant least culpable in the case who could still be convicted as a "principal." There were three others we felt were more culpable—one of whom could have actually been the trigger man—but we couldn't make a case on them. So here we're going ahead with this fourth-string guy and seeking the death penalty.

I didn't realize until many years later what an awesome decision we were making. And that's my whole problem with the death penalty now; human beings making a decision that another human being should be executed. I just didn't think about things like that. There's such a big divide between capital cases and all other cases that I just didn't realize. I just didn't appreciate the extent of that divide. To me now at least, capital cases are very, very serious proceedings. And in the case of Glenn Ford, he wasn't treated as if it was a very, very serious proceeding. It was a murder case, a capital case. And you were asking a jury—my God, *supposedly* of his peers—to render a verdict that says that this man is not worthy of living.

JC: So what would you do differently now? You said you'd think about it more, you'd be more diligent. But I'm sure you were diligent at the time. Would you just not seek the death penalty?

AMS: Oh, I would not seek the death penalty.

JC: But that's the only difference, really. You would prosecute the case the same way. You just wouldn't seek the death penalty.

AMS: Yes, I would have not sought the death penalty. There may have been some political problems and all that, but now . . .

JC: Before we get to the political problems, I know that one of the things you talk about today is that any lawyer prosecuting a death penalty case should visit death row. Did you ever visit Angola? Did you ever see, first hand, the conditions people are asked to live in? What was that like?[4]

---

4. Author's note: This question and answer were given via email after the interview.

AMS: I have been on death row at Angola on several occasions in connection with my representation of a client that I represented through the State Habeas Corpus Proceedings, and at the district court level. The conditions there are horrid. The inmates are in small cages that are dimly lit. Death row is freezing in the winter and scorchingly hot in the summer. The inmates have no privileges; they are not afforded common conditions.

Death row at Angola is a hell hole where human beings all too often are treated as the scum of the earth. I believe that death row is there to deprive the condemned of their humanity while they await their executioner. It is a disgrace.

The reality of death row tears on a man's soul. I find it to be an evil that marks us as a society that cares not for the dignity of every human being.

Yes, I have been there. I have witnessed the pain in the eyes of its occupants. Its harshness is designed to squeeze every ounce of hope out of its occupants. Its continued existence is an indictment of our society. It is a cruel, mean, and unforgiving place, and yet our society condones it. Indeed our blinders are such that we simply do not seem to care that this horror exists among us. God help us.

JC: Do you still try death penalty cases, obviously from the defense side? Has this case changed the way you approach those cases?[5]

AMS: I was involved in my last capital trial in 2014. I found that the stress was simply too much to continue to handle such trials. It finally got to the point that I believed it was time for a younger person to take my place in capital trial battles over the fate of a human being. Glenn Ford did affect the manner in which I attempted to prepare for my last case. I focused more on the weight of the decision the jury was being asked to make *and* the humanity of a client who had been charged with very horrible crimes involving the death of a mother and her child. It was a very tough case for all involved.

I developed a pretty good rapport with the client and I spent many hours with him. I listened closely to what he had to say. Despite the nature of the crime, I focused upon the dignity to which I believe he was entitled as a human being. It helped me better to advocate on behalf also of a client who was charged with horrendous crimes. This process opened up

---

5. Author's note: This question and answer were given via email after the interview.

my ability effectively to communicate with, and understand, the mind of a person who had been demonized and marginalized most of his life. To me, his life, like all life, has value, and killing that potential value is misguided and beyond the scope of the limits of our humanity.

JC: Now, let's go back to the political problems at the time Glenn Ford was on trial. So how much was the decision to seek the death penalty a *political* decision by the district attorney?

AMS: Well, the D.A. actually deferred to us. I was a lead prosecutor and we talked. The position was that when the train left the station—we thought that when Mr. Ford was confronted with the reality of what was getting ready to happen to him, he would flip. That switch didn't flip and the train kept going.

I don't think that at the time there was a big outcry for the death penalty in the Ford case.

JC: Was that because no family advocated for it?

AMS: Correct.

JC: On the other hand you say that the district attorney would defer to his assistants on the death decision.

AMS: Well, he would defer to me—I was the first assistant. I went back and looked at this: Louisiana always has a hard time getting things right. After the *Furman* case[6] in '72 in which the Supreme Court abolished the death penalty, states came back with the "dual procedure." Well, Louisiana was one that came back, because in *Furman*, the Court said you must have "objective standards." Louisiana's answer was to say that if you are convicted of capital murder you automatically get the death penalty—nothing arbitrary in that. The Supreme Court thereupon declared that procedure unconstitutional. Then Louisiana came back with the "guided discretion with aggravating and mitigating factors," and Glenn Ford was the first case where the death penalty was actually returned in Caddo after 1972. Glenn Ford was convicted in 1984 and I believe that Caddo Parish had not had a death penalty case since the '60s. It had been a while in Caddo Parish.

Actually, it was really my belief that the jury wasn't going to return a death verdict. I just didn't think it was going to happen given that it was

_____

6. Furman v. Georgia, 408 U.S. 238 (1972).

a circumstantial evidence case, even though circumstantial evidence can suffice to convict.

JC: I read that after the death penalty verdict you and your colleagues basically celebrated the moment. Were you actually happy, or was that just some sort of fraternal thing in the district attorney's office?

AMS: [15 seconds elapse] To be completely candid, I was happy in the sense that I felt that I had done my duty and that, I'm sad to say, it had enhanced my status within the district attorney's office.

JC: Were you "happy" that you thought that the death penalty for Ford might help as a deterrent against crime in the community.

AMS: I think that was part of it. But . . .

JC: Not happy that you were going to see Ford fry—more that there was public benefit from the work you had done. Fair?

AMS: Yes. But I think that's an example of the problem I now have with capital punishment. I think human beings are simply incapable because of ego to establish a system that is truly fair, truly impartial. We're not God! I don't think we're capable of coming up with a procedure that's legal and proper that can be employed to kill somebody. I think that . . . *celebrating* a death verdict like that shows immaturity—it should be a very somber occasion. There should be no joy whatsoever in obtaining a death verdict.

JC: Did you come to this view after the district attorney called you into his office and told you that new evidence said that Ford was not guilty of the murder? Or did you come to that view having evolved from your days as a prosecutor, now looking at the world from another view?

AMS: I had that attitude several years in advance of the disclosure. In fact, I remember I was interviewed in 1992 about the death penalty generally—I guess, by NBC—and, at that time, I said I had trouble with the case. I had not yet come to the belief that Mr. Ford was innocent, but I had certainly come to the belief that he deserved a new trial and that the death penalty was inappropriate.

JC: Why do you believe that he is innocent, beside the district attorney telling you that he had something new?

AMS: [20 seconds elapse] As human beings, we could probably never be 100 percent certain of anything. But having looked back over the Glenn Ford case; having watched what he did; having watched him spend 30 years on death row and steadily maintain his innocence; having sat down and talked with him and looked him in the eye and gone back and forth with him shortly before he died; I'm as convinced of his innocence as I'm convinced of anything in this world.

JC: I know it's difficult, but tell me about that conversation with him before he died.

AMS: Well he was staying in a place in New Orleans that took care . . .

JC: John Thompson's place.[7]

AMS: Was that it? He was in the Lower Ninth Ward. And I learned that he would meet me. I sat down and said "Look, I'm Marty Stroud." And he said, "You don't have to introduce yourself, I know who you are." I said, "Well, I've come to apologize, to the extent I'm capable of it, for what's happened to you." And he said, "Well, if I had you as a lawyer I would have gotten off."

He said that was the problem. I said, "I don't know if you'd have gotten off, but you certainly deserved better representation." I said, "Those lawyers tried the best they could, it was just, it was not their field." And I said "You know, you taught me something." And he said, "What was that?" I said . . . and I think this is just an example of courts looking the other way when ineffective assistance or counsel is involved—the defense put Glenn Ford on the stand in the penalty phase, obviously without any preparation. His lawyer said "Well, why do you want to live?" He said, "Well, I want to be able to live so I can have the opportunity to show everybody that the jury was wrong."

So, on cross-examination I really got after him about that, and said "You think the jury made a mistake and you're insulting their intelligence." And just really nasty cross-examination that accomplished nothing other than to throw some more dirt and accusations at him that had no basis in fact. And I told him "You know I was wrong and you were right. And I'm sorry for that." And then we were talking back and forth. I asked for his forgiveness. And he looked at me and said "I'm not there yet. I don't think I can get there." And I said, "Well, I understand. I'd probably feel just like you do if our positions had been reversed."

And [10 seconds elapse] we talked a little more and he was on his medication and he was getting tired, sleepy. So that was basically it. Then I

7. Resurrection After Exoneration in New Orleans.

left. It was an emotional experience. When I was first asked by a reporter whether I wanted to see Mr. Ford, my initial inclination was, I guess, to run away from it. I had never thought about trying to see him. But then I said, "Well, if he will see me I would like to see him," and it was set up.

But he had during that meeting a conviction, something in his eyes. Someone said "the eyes are the mirror to the soul," and he just had that. He was focused. He was confident. He knew what he wanted to say. Wasn't any hesitation.

JC: And he knew he was dying, right?

AMS: He knew he was dying, yes. And he had anger. He indicated that he was angry and hadn't worked through all of that yet.

JC: But was he claiming during this conversation that not only was he innocent but that you folks had, to use the word I used before, "framed" him? Or just saying he was innocent—as he had maintained for 30 years?

AMS: He didn't use the word "frame." He was focused more on the system. He said the system gave no justice: "I had no fair trial. I had no counsel. I had no one to assist me. Until later. I was . . . at the mercy of the state. And I spent 30 years in the same cell." And he said, "That hurts. I've been deprived of my life with my children, my family, my friends."

JC: When you talk about the system—I don't know if he raised it— how much did race have a role in the result in this case?

AMS: [20 seconds elapse] Race, particularly in the South in the legal system, is very complicated. [20 seconds elapse] Caddo Parish was once known as "Bloody Caddo." They used to hang people from the oak trees. Or lynch people around the courthouse. Many a black person was convicted by all-white juries. I'm not aware of any white person that was ever convicted by an all-black jury in Shreveport. I don't know that there's ever been an all-black jury in Shreveport.

JC: But, and this is a tough question, how about you individually? Did racism on your part play any role in how this injustice came about?[8]

AMS: I look at who I was 30 years ago and I see a person who was indifferent to race. Did I believe that whites were superior to blacks? No. But that's not the end of the discussion. I didn't empathize with blacks. I didn't understand the effects of segregation; I didn't believe that socio-

---

8. Author's note: This question and answer were given via email after the interview.

economic factors were potential predictions of future criminal conduct. I never gave any real thought to why minorities constituted a disproportionate percentage of the jail population. I had never personally experienced police misconduct. I had never been denied access to a public facility. I had never been turned away because of my race. All of these things I believe factored into my attitude about race 30 years ago. Though, I felt I was treating everyone equally; in reality, I was not because I never considered the effects of life experiences on folks from other races and socioeconomic backgrounds. Is this a form of racism? I think the answer is self-evident, don't you? I believe that I have learned a lot about the parameters of racism over the last 30 years and that I have a better understanding of the nuances of racism. By no means am I perfect in this area, but, again, I do believe that I have worked my way through those prejudices that blinded me to the subtleties of racism that exist in our society.

JC: What was the composition of the jury in *Ford*?

AMS: All white.

JC: And what would have been the percentage of blacks available to serve?

AMS: Back in '84, it would probably have been 40 percent. Today it would be closer to—they may be a majority.

JC: In the *Ford* case, do you remember how many preemptory challenges you used to excuse blacks?

AMS: [20 seconds elapse] I don't remember. I want to say six.

JC: And how many challenges would you have in a capital case?

AMS: I believe 20.

JC: So you use approximately six, give or take, to excuse blacks simply because they were black, more likely be more sympathetic to Ford?

AMS: And that's another reason—but back then I didn't appreciate the subtleties of the race question that I do now. And I have been in the practice for 40 years.

JC: In fairness, how subtle is that? I mean a young, inexperienced student could easily conclude that blacks would be more likely sympathetic to a black, Jews to a Jewish defendant, etc. Not so subtle.

AMS: Well, I for one did not—back when Glenn Ford was first tried, *Swain v. Alabama*[9] was the test standard. I felt that I could properly strike

9. 380 U.S. 202 (1965).

an African-American, unless a pattern could be shown that the office over the years had used a pattern of striking African-Americans. And, admittedly, looking back on it now, that was a hard test for a defendant to meet. I don't think that anybody ever met it.

JC: But if the law allowed it and you thought the defendant you were prosecuting was guilty, you wanted to win the case. If you think that blacks might be *inappropriately* too sympathetic to a defendant simply because he is black, wouldn't it be fair in your mind to peremptorily strike them? They're going to be sympathetic, and you want to win the case. We now know, of course, such strikes are against the law under *Batson*.[10]

AMS: I never thought of it from a standpoint of an individual having a right of citizenship to serve on a jury. I wasn't smart enough to figure that out on my own.

[15 seconds elapse] What I believed at the time was that there was no racial animus there. Although this argument was subsequently discredited, we believed that because we accepted a few black jurors that the defense wanted to excuse, we were okay.

JC: But you as the prosecution accepted them, not because they were black. You sought to seat them because the defense was striking them presumably because they thought they would be antagonistic to Ford's defense, right?

AMS: Shows my naïveté. I was still rather young. My experience with African-American jurors created a naïve stereotype that was just wrong. I mean African-American jurors can be very, very tough on black defendants, and I didn't appreciate that.

JC: Is it also a problem that judges too often give prosecutors the benefit of the doubt even now when exercising peremptory challenges?

AMS: For sure. You say, "I don't like the way he looked at me judge." And the judge basically says, "Okay, that's good cause to strike him."

JC: So you're saying that race is still playing a role?

AMS: I think it is.

JC: In this instance on the part of not only the prosecutors, but judges?

AMS: Right—Caddo Parish was sued for its use of peremptory strikes. It will be interesting to see how that plays out.

---

10. Batson v. Kentucky, 476 U.S. 79 (1986).

JC: There's a lawsuit pending by Ford's representatives against the Parish, the district attorney's office, and the City of Shreveport over this case. When you're deposed I assume you're going to say roughly what you're telling me here. You'll be asked whether there were there *Brady* violations in the case?

AMS: I think there were indeed *Brady* violations because I testified at a post-conviction hearing in state court and was shown some police reports and did not remember seeing these before. And I was asked "If you had seen these, what would you have done?" I said I would have turned them over to the defense.

Now the judge, at that stage, ultimately denied post-conviction relief. But that's another thing. Now this is where I blame myself. I should have been more aggressive in my discussions with the police. Back then when the policeman told me something, I believed it. I bought all this crap on TV, which is just that, crap: policemen didn't lie, there was a thin blue line, that they did their job, that they weren't out to harm innocent people. And if they told me that they didn't have something, I took them at their word.

JC: What you're saying, basically, without using that phrase, is that they did you dirty. They were telling you that material didn't exist that exculpated Ford, but it did?

AMS: I believe that.

JC: Or is it possible that they were telling you what you wanted to hear?

MS: That's possible too.

JC: You never gave off a signal like that, did you? So when the plaintiffs use the word "frame" in this complaint, they don't say that you committed the frame-up. They refer to the detectives on the case.

AMS: I read over the complaint, but I guess I read right over the "framed" part. "Framed" obviously means to me that you know you have the wrong person, and you have a piece of evidence that would be false. Now, that never happened to me. However . . .

JC: Well, maybe the complaint is suggesting that he was framed *for something he did*. In other words, that the detectives, for example, made the case that was valid better by withholding from you exculpatory evidence that they knew you would have had to turn over to the defense.

AMS: Correct.

JC: So when you say that there may have been *Brady* violations, they were by the police. They weren't documents you had sitting in your cabinet that you just didn't turn over to the defense?

AMS: No. I think we turned everything over. That was one thing that I think we did, or tried to, do right.

JC: So, when you made this—I suppose, sui generis—decision to self-report to the Office of Disciplinary Counsel, what do you say to them?

AMS: Well, I said that I held myself to a standard—that I said I feel that I've been engaged in conduct that is prejudicial to the administration of justice. I stated that I felt I did so not as a result of acts of commission, but rather acts of omission. And I enumerated the things I thought I should have done, and said that I would leave it up to them to decide whether or how I should be punished. I made the submission in April or May of this year.

JC: And they haven't responded to it. Did you seek any counsel before you did this?

AMS: I told one person I was going to do it and . . .

JC: Is that Mrs. Stroud?

AMS: No, I didn't tell her about the letter until she read it, because I knew she'd probably get upset. Which she did.

JC: Was the person you told a lawyer?

AMS: Yes, and he said "You're nuts. You didn't do anything wrong." But I felt strongly about it and still do. My position is whatever they decide, I'll abide by it.

JC: You mean you think that your conduct was so serious that if they decide to suspend you from the practice of law or worse, you're ok with that?

AMS: I'm not ok with it, but I'm prepared to accept it.

JC: You'll pardon me for this personal comment. But I saw your *60 Minutes* interview and the speech you gave at the University of Pennsylvania. And now I see you here. The reader will never see from the transcript of this, the somberness—indeed, the moroseness—that you exhibit in talking about this. Even the sadness you showed meeting me in your reception area. Is that because of what happened in the *Ford* case or . . .

AMS: I feel like the result of this case has stained my reputation and basically overrides any successes throughout the years. Until you are confronted with the reality that you participated in an injustice . . . it was on a Friday and over that weekend I thought seriously about resigning from the practice of law. But then I talked to a couple of people and decided to see what the bar says. But it's something that I think about every day. I've told all my clients.

JC: How has your very public mea culpa affected your relationship with the district attorney's office?

AMS: Well, I didn't expect to get invited to the Christmas party or anything like that. But what happened here—it is interesting—was that the D.A. died suddenly and now we have a new D.A. An African-American, James Stewart—who I supported. He and I were in the D.A.'s office together.

That he's an African-American is a good thing. Because we need a healing process. The other deal is the prosecutor, Dale Cox, was talking about you know, "We need to kill more people," and all that. And that got everybody riled up in this election. So I think I have a better relationship with the office now.

JC: So the district attorney who set aside the *Ford* conviction is now dead?

AMS: Yes.

JC: His answer to the crime problem was to impose more death penalties?

AMS: Well that was his first assistant, Dale Cox.[11]

JC: So was it Cox who said, when asked on television whether there was an injustice in the Ford case, that Mr. Ford got justice, but "delayed justice"?

AMS: Sounds like something Cox would say.

JC: On what possible theory could someone say that?

AMS: He also said that we need to kill more people. He said that an individual who had gotten a death sentence should be made to suffer all pain possible before he was executed. That executing an innocent person is a risk you take.

JC: It's interesting given those kind of sentiments, why he would want to set the *Ford* case aside.

---

11. Mr. Cox resigned from the D.A.'s office in December 2015 after Mr. Stewart's election.

AMS: I know. And then the DA balked a little bit, but the motion was filed. If that was all that happened, I would not have written a letter. I had discussed it with many people. I heard that Glenn Ford applied for compensation. I read an editorial in the [Shreveport] *Times* and I saw that the state was opposing it and I just—in one of his movies, they asked Harrison Ford why he intervened in an attempted kidnapping and he said "I just got mad"—and I saw that and I got pissed off. I had never written a letter to the paper before, so I said this is asinine. And that's what generated the letter. And then everything else followed from that. The court denied the compensation. It's on appeal.

The haunting thing in this whole case, and it shows you, I think it's a criminal act. I just . . . it's an egregious criminal act for a government to give somebody who's released from death row, having been on death row for 30 years, a $20 gift certificate for "the inconvenience we've caused you." That's inexcusable. It shows a lack of respect for mankind.

JC: Given the torment that you obviously experience from this, do you get any solace from the fact that although Ford was exonerated from the murder charge, he still had some guilt given his role with the gun and the stolen jewelry?

AMS: No. And the reason is I see Glenn Ford was very poor. He lived on the streets. Something was given to him and he was told that here's a way to make some money, I can see that happening. And not knowing what happened or that an offense had been committed. I don't buy that. I don't think he was involved at all. I think he was a patsy that was probably used by other people. I don't accept the argument that he knew it was a murder weapon. One guy said, well he was a principal to murder. Well if he was a principal to murder why did you let him go? He can still be convicted on a substantive count.

JC: Which gets back to the question of other than the district attorney telling you that he had new evidence, you don't really know that he wasn't guilty of the murder.

AMS: Well, other than my sincere belief that he's not guilty of the murder, I guess. Can I show you, do I have a confession from another party that I can show you? No. I don't know what evidence the state has.

JC: So if you went to Mr. Stewart, who obviously you have more confidence in than the prior D.A., and were sworn to secrecy and asked him to tell you what it was, would that be helpful to you in dealing with your torment?

AMS: It might be—if he knows.

JC: Does it help you get through the night to do that public self-beating that you have done—on *60 Minutes*, or your classes that you guest teach? Does it help you?

[30 seconds elapse] It is a long hiatus before you answer, I see, once again.

AMS: You asked . . . you ask very pointed questions. [20 seconds elapse] It doesn't help in the sense, I don't want to be seen . . . I'm not the victim. I'm not the good guy. I was a participant in a series of events that led to the wrongful conviction of an individual in the United States of America. And this is how it happened. Does that give me a peace of mind? Does that make me feel better? No. Is it my intent to beat myself up? No. It's just to tell people what happened in the case of the *State vs. Glenn Ford* in which I was a participant. What it has done—the best description I can give—is that every morning when I wake up I have a hole in my stomach. A cold emptiness with the north wind blowing straight through it. And that's the direct result of my dealing with the saga of Glenn Ford. There's no happy ending here that I can see.

JC: If the result of this horrible tragedy were somehow a contribution to the abolition of the death penalty in the United States, would that finally bring a smile to your face?

AMS: It would finally bring a smile to my face.

JC: Thank you.

2

When "Actual Innocence" Is Not Enough

Michael Wayne Haley discussed by Eric M. Albritton

And the reason he didn't have counsel was simply because he was indigent. So it's not a matter of race, it's a matter of being poor. In our criminal justice system, being poor is just as bad as being black. Or Hispanic. And I'm not suggesting that being black or Hispanic is bad, but if you look at statistics for capital cases, certainly there's inequality with respect to minorities, but there's also horrible inequality associated with socioeconomic status. Poor people just don't get as good a shake as rich people.

—Eric M. Albritton, February 9, 2016[1]

---

1. This interview took place at Mr. Albritton's offices in Southlake, Texas.

Michael Wayne Haley is not exactly a model citizen. He had been in and out of jail for years prior to 1997, when he stole a calculator from Walmart, drove around to the front of the store, and tried to "return" it for a refund. It was a petty crime, but because he had prior theft convictions, one that would subject him to two years in state jail. However, the state also charged him as a "habitual offender"—Texas's three strikes law—predicated on a finding that Haley had two prior felony convictions that were sequential, as that term was defined by Texas statute. Having been found guilty, Haley was sentenced to 16-and-a-half years, rather than the two he could have received for his crime.

However, at the time of Haley's conviction, the three strikes law should not have applied. His prior convictions were, on their face, not sequential and thus did not meet Texas's statutory requirement for the charge or conviction as a habitual offender. A procedural mistake, no question. Still, a mistake that cost Haley an additional 14 years in his sentence—and a mistake that would have been noticed had anyone actually read Haley's file. There was nothing hidden, nothing secret. Quite simply, at the time of sentencing, the judge didn't realize that the crimes were not sequential as Texas's statute required, nor did Haley's then-attorney and nor, presumably, did the Texas state prosecutor.

With this background, Eric Albritton, the man who ultimately became Haley's lawyer much later after Haley had done so much of this work on his own (pro se), talks about how this mistake—this unquestionable error—took both men to the U.S. Supreme Court and ultimately back to the courts of Texas.

After Haley was convicted and sentenced, still relying on his state appointed trial counsel, he appealed his conviction to the state appellate court. No one argued that the habitual offender law did not apply; apparently still no one actually read the file describing his prior convictions. The court, finding no credible arguments, affirmed. Haley, with no lawyer to represent him, apparently then did his homework, read the habitual offender statute requirements, and argued in a post-conviction writ in state court that he never should have been charged, much less convicted, under the habitual offender statute. He argued that his sentence should have been no more than two years. The state court rejected Haley's claim, primarily because he did not raise the claim at the time of his first appeal—a "procedural default" in the parlance of the law.

With no place else to go in the state court system, Haley—still pro se—turned to the federal courts. And by the time he turned to the federal courts, the state knew—Haley had previously explained to them in the last state appeal—that it was simply wrong when it charged him as a habitual offender. Thus, the state knew that Haley was *actually innocent* of the crime of being a habitual offender.

"Actual innocence" is a loaded term in the U.S. criminal justice system. It essentially allows someone who is "actually innocent" of a crime for which he was convicted to be exonerated. The principle is manifest—there was a miscarriage of justice that should be corrected. And, since the prosecution has an overriding obligation to do justice—to look at the facts of each case and do the right thing by both the people of their state and the defendant—one could conclude that, once it learned that Haley was actually innocent of the crime of being a habitual offender, it should have made arrangements to re-sentence him to two years. Indeed, a prosecutor's job is to seek justice, not merely to convict.

But that is not what happened. Haley went to the Federal District Court filing a habeas corpus proceeding based on the fact that he never should have been charged, much less convicted of, and sentenced as, a habitual offender. He also argued that, in large part because his state-appointed trial counsel (practicing for about a year at the time of trial) missed the prosecution's error in charging that his prior crimes were sequential, he was denied "effective assistance of counsel." Effective assistance of counsel, as interpreted by the courts, is a right guaranteed by the Sixth Amendment to the U.S. Constitution in a criminal trial—"In all criminal prosecutions, the accused shall enjoy the right . . . to have the assistance of counsel for his defense." It is such a fundamental right that the Supreme Court has held that it applies to the state criminal justice systems as well.

The Federal District Court concluded that it never had to address the issue of whether Haley's trial counsel was "ineffective" because counsel failed to challenge the habitual offender charge; it decided that because Haley was "actually innocent" of that charge, Haley should be resentenced. By the time the district court made that determination, Haley had already served three years of what should have been a two-year sentence.

But here is where it gets complicated. Had the district court decided that Haley should be resentenced on the ground of ineffective assistance of counsel, the state likely would have done nothing to continue to fight against Haley. There was no precedent being set, no real legal issue that would have been of concern to it. Haley, we can presume, would have been returned to the state court that originally sentenced him and set free. However, the court decided that Haley was actually innocent and as far as the State of Texas was concerned—at that time represented by its then Attorney General (and now Governor) Greg Abbott and, at the federal appellate level, the then Solicitor General and now U.S. Senator Ted Cruz—a convicted defendant should not be able to argue his petty theft conviction to the federal courts using his "actual innocence" to justify his "procedural default" in having failed to raise the issue earlier when back in state court.

The doctrine, the argument goes, should be used only in capital cases—cases where a defendant is convicted for murder (for example, when DNA evidence shows years later that the defendant never committed the crime). More to the point, because Haley did not argue that the habitual offender statute did not apply to him in his first appeal (where, we note, he was still represented by his trial counsel who never noticed the error to begin with), he had "procedurally defaulted" and thus waived any right to later argue that he was actually innocent.

From the state's point of view, there should be "finality" to court determinations—that without finality and comity (basically deference to the state court findings), every convicted criminal will appeal and claim he was actually innocent. And the appellate courts would be inundated and overwhelmed. What Texas did not take into consideration in this case, however, was that there was an actual mistake here—and the actual mistake was made in the first instance by the State of Texas, and the state knew it!

Now, once the state understood that it had made a mistake, it could have easily made an application to resentence Haley. It could have decided to default in the state appellate proceeding. It could have joined in Haley's motion, acknowledging its mistake. It could have done these things before Haley ever went to the Federal District Court. But it didn't. And at the point that the district court ruled, the state could have said—"Well, we don't like the decision the judge made but, it's a lower federal court and the decision doesn't bind any other judge or court, so let's resentence Haley and do justice and let Haley go." But it didn't do that either.

With apparent complete indifference to Haley himself, the state appealed the district court's decision to the next federal appellate court, the Fifth Circuit Court of Appeals, whose decision—whatever that decision was—would be binding on all federal courts located in Texas, Louisiana, and Mississippi. In other words, the State of Texas made a calculated bet—it would challenge the decision in the hope that the Fifth Circuit court would find that a convicted defendant who had procedurally defaulted could only argue that he should be released or resentenced if he was actually innocent in a capital case.

But the state's gamble backfired, and the Fifth Circuit did exactly what Texas did not want it to do. It concluded—in a decision binding on three states—that Haley had the right to claim that he was actually innocent, and it ordered the lower courts to resentence him accordingly. Even though, as best anyone could tell, Michael Haley was no longer relevant to the State of Texas—the only thing relevant now was a procedural point about when a prisoner can claim that they are "actually innocent" of a crime—the state argued that Haley should remain incarcerated while the state made a second application to the Fifth Circuit (denied) and then first asked the U.S. Supreme Court to hear the case.

At about this time, Eric Albritton had run into a lawyer who told him about Haley's situation—the state's use of his case to try to make a legal point and that Haley remained in prison while the state apparently ignored the undeniable fact that Haley should have been sentenced to no more than two years. Albritton agreed to represent Haley, petitioned the court and Haley was released over the strenuous objection of Texas—nearly six years after he was sentenced and four years longer than the two years he should have served.

But the state was still not finished; it doubled down because it couldn't rest with the Fifth Circuit decision out there—a decision, which some would note, occurred because of the state's own appeal of the district court decision. In fact, one could argue that the Fifth Circuit decision only existed because the state refused to simply admit its mistake back when they were in state court and ask the state court to resentence Haley.

The state asked the U.S. Supreme Court to hear the case—and it did. And in an appellate argument, the judges interrupt the lawyer's presentation; they ask questions about what they want to better understand. And in this case, less than two minutes into the state's presentation—given by then Solicitor General Ted Cruz—Justice Kennedy asks simply and unequivocally: "Is there some rule that you can't confess error in your state? . . . Well, so a man does 15 years so you can vindicate your legal point in some other case? I just don't understand why you don't dismiss this case and move to lower the sentence."

One might conclude, from this questioning, that the U.S. Supreme Court—in a decision binding on all federal courts—decided that a defendant could claim his actual innocence regardless of whether he previously failed to claim it and regardless of whether he was convicted of a capital crime. But, no. Instead, the Court—relying on Cruz's implied concession that the state would not challenge it if Haley argued that he had received ineffective assistance of counsel—decided not to decide the broad and hotly contested legal issue before it. In a decision by six judges (with three dissenting), it chose not to decide the issue Haley argued. It said in effect, "Go back—let Haley claim that he had ineffective assistance of counsel and if he wins on that ground, no one ever has to decide if he was actually innocent." So after all this, Albritton took Haley back down through the court system and the state defaulted—it did not oppose Haley's motions, or put in any response for that matter. Haley was thus resentenced to two years, after he had already served six.

Now, one steeped in the criminal justice system might read this interview and conclude that Haley got his relief—he was ultimately resentenced and that is what he was after. Sure, the courts went through procedural machinations to get him there, and it is unfortunate he served more than the statute allowed, but justice was ultimately done, as they say.

Others, however—particularly those not in "the system"—would read this story with utter disbelief. Haley was innocent of being a habitual offender; no one realized it at trial or on his first appeal (the one where he used the same trial attorney who missed it in the first place); the state knew it once Haley himself told the courts that the state had made an undeniable mistake; the courts knew it; yet, the state did nothing until the case snowballed and it wanted to—apparently needed to—settle a procedural point all the way to the U.S. Supreme Court.

And even though the state continued to challenge Haley's attempt at freedom while the appeals were pending, by the time it got to the Supreme

Court, Haley himself was not the issue. Except that it was he—representing himself, by the way—who argued sufficiently forcefully that a Federal District Court and the Fifth Circuit appellate court would announce the precedent the state so feared—that a defendant's actual innocence could be argued at any time, even if the defendant was found guilty of only a petty crime.

The Supreme Court never decided whether defendants could claim in an untimely federal habeas corpus proceeding that they were actually innocent of a crime in noncapital cases. However, in their written dissents in the *Haley* case, Supreme Court Justices Stevens, Kennedy, and Souter wrote about the grave injustice in Texas's failure to simply acknowledge its mistake and let justice be done.

Justice Kennedy perhaps best described Michael Haley's journey:

Texas officials concede Haley did not violate this [habitual offender] law. . . . Yet, despite the fact that Haley served more than two years in prison for his crime, Texas officials come before our Court opposing Haley's petition for relief. They wish to send Haley back to prison for a crime they agree he did not commit.

The rigors of the penal system are thought to be mitigated to some degree by the discretion of those who enforce the law. . . . Among its benign if too-often ignored objects, the clemency power can correct injustices that the ordinary criminal process seems unable or unwilling to consider. These mechanisms hold out the promise that mercy is not foreign to our system. The law must serve the cause of justice.

These mitigating elements seem to have played no role in Michael Haley's case. Executive discretion and clemency can inspire little confidence if officials sworn to fight injustice choose to ignore it. Perhaps some would say that Haley's innocence is a mere technicality, but that would miss the point. In a society devoted to the rule of law, the difference between violating or not violating a criminal statute cannot be shrugged aside as a minor detail.

It may be that Haley's case provides a convenient mechanism to vindicate an important legal principle. Beyond that, however, Michael Haley has a greater interest in knowing that he will not be re-incarcerated for a crime he did not commit. It is not clear to me why the State did not exercise its power and perform its duty to vindicate that interest in the first place.

The Dialogue

JC: Mr. Albritton, this interview is about the Michael Wayne Haley case. Or maybe it's not.

Maybe it's an interview about the intersection of law and justice. Or an interview about Ted Cruz's view of justice. Or an interview about Texas criminal justice.

Leading me to this case was an essay in *The New York Times* by David Brooks, by New York standards a conservative journalist. He talked about the *Haley* case. And he said: the *Haley* case "is almost the dictionary definition of pharisaism: an overzealous application of the letter of the law in a way that violates the spirit of the law, as well as fairness and mercy."

The public won't read this conversation for about a year. But one week ago today, Senator Cruz won the Iowa caucus, seeking the nomination of the Republican Party to be president. Tonight is the New Hampshire primary. So, by the time the reader sees this, Mr. Cruz will either still be a United States senator, or maybe president of the United States.

From your experience in the *Haley* case, is Mr. Brooks's comment a fair statement of the criminal justice that Mr. Cruz sought to impose?

EMA: In my view Mr. Cruz and his colleagues at the Texas attorney general's office were overzealous—more interested in policy than in justice.

JC: From all accounts—I've read much of the litigation file in the case—Mr. Haley is not a particularly sympathetic victim of "injustice." Fair to say?

EMA: Well, Mr. Haley's background was not terribly appealing, and he certainly had legal problems. However, none of that, in my view, justified the state's refusal to do what was right. "Right" in this case was to recognize that Mr. Haley was not subject to any more than a two-year sentence. So once that realization came to light, they should have released him immediately, as opposed to continue to litigate to try to make some broader point about the importance of "comity" and "finality" concerning state criminal convictions.

JC: Well, you certainly know his criminal background better than I. But reading the record itself, Mr. Haley had six convictions before the three that entered into the mix—the misdemeanor he was convicted of and the two prior predicate crimes in the case you handled in the Supreme Court.

EMA: Mr. Haley had had a couple of misdemeanor theft convictions and a couple of felony convictions. He certainly had a significant criminal history.

But I don't think we can lose sight of what is relevant because of his criminal history. The real question is: Was he treated unjustly? In our system, folks get punished in accordance with statutes. Here, irrespective of whether you found his background to be horrific or distasteful, or however you want to characterize it, unquestionably Michael Haley should not have served more than two years in the penitentiary. And there's no question that he served three times more than that.

And the state knew it! At some point the state knew unequivocally that he simply wasn't supposed to serve more than two years. Still, they insisted all the way to the Fifth Circuit that he should not only have served eight times more than he was statutorily permitted to receive, but that he should continue to serve a sentence that they agreed was not statutorily authorized. I found that simply outrageous.

JC: What did you mean by—that the state wanted him to "continue to serve" the 16-and-one-half year sentence?

EMA: This is actually pretty interesting. By the time the case reached the federal court or even earlier, the state knew that Haley should have served no more than two years. And the state admitted it. Haley won, pro se—representing himself—at the Fifth Circuit, and by that time he had already served more than the two years he should have. So, just as I came into the case, there was a big fight because the state wanted Haley to remain in jail while the Supreme Court proceedings were underway. Obviously, the state didn't even know if the Supreme Court would grant cert, that the Court would even accept Texas's petition to hear the case. But the state fought tooth and nail to keep him in prison in the interim, even though the Fifth Circuit had ruled in Mr. Haley's favor.

JC: Were you in the case by that time? Or was he still fighting that by himself?

EMA: I was already in. I represented him at rehearing at the Fifth Circuit and also regarding the stay the state requested which would have kept Haley in prison.

JC: What was their theory in trying to keep him in jail while the federal appeals were pending?

EMA: Look, if you really want to talk about it, there was no legitimate theory. Why in the world would they want to just keep him in prison? If they had some broader agenda to overturn what they perceived to be bad precedent, they certainly could have done that and let him out of prison. They absolutely, positively, knew at that point that he was in jail for more time than allowable by law.

JC: That's astounding, actually.

EMA: Truly outrageous. But not the only point of outrage. Once the district court had ruled, the state didn't have to appeal. If the state did not appeal, the district court's decision would only be binding on the district court. And even then, maybe only on the judge who decided it. It certainly would not have been a binding precedent for the Fifth Circuit.

So there were lots of decision points, and that's where the real injustice lies. I don't think this is a story about the courts gone wrong. It's a story about the attorney general's office going wrong. They could have just gone back, reopened his state criminal sentence, and resentenced him. That's where the real outrage lies.

JC: Did you learn anything from dealing with either the Texas Solicitor General's office or the Texas attorney general's office, or even from the United States solicitor general's Office that filed an amicus—friend of the court—brief, that suggested that Haley's recidivist background went into the mix in terms of the aggressiveness with which they pursued the case to the Supreme Court?

EMA: That was not my sense. My sense is that the state's position—I wasn't much focused on the United States' position—was not driven by Haley's criminal history.

JC: You're basically saying is it wouldn't have mattered if Mr. Haley had an uneventful criminal background?

EMA: I don't think so. The state did make a big point, as an advocate, that Haley was a "bad guy." And the undercurrent of their argument was along the lines of "Oh well, he's a bad guy so it's not that big of a deal." That was somewhat the tenor of the argument. But I don't think that's what drove the state. I don't think that the State of Texas was trying to treat Michael Haley badly because he had a criminal history. Rather, they were myopically focused on a broader principle—that federal courts ought not interfere in state convictions. What I find outrageous is that policy considerations eclipsed common sense.

JC: You refer to policy considerations. Only a judge or a lawyer— someone actually locked into "the system"—could possibly *appreciate* or understand why a "policy consideration" should eclipse an effort to impart justice. The State of Texas and the solicitor general absolutely knew that the trial judge and trial lawyers had tragically erred in imposing more than a two-year sentence. The solicitor general unequivocally conceded in the Supreme Court that there was a "very strong case" to believe that Mr. Haley had suffered the "ineffective assistance of counsel." Yet he argued that because Haley's was not a capital case, he wasn't entitled to petition the federal courts to get out of jail based on his claimed "actual innocence" because he raised the claim too late. Fair statement?

EMA: It is certainly true that the state, Ted Cruz's office and Ted Cruz all knew that Michael Haley had been in prison more than three times longer than he should have been, and was still in prison. But nevertheless they fought to keep him in. And it had nothing to do with Michael Haley in particular.

The state and Cruz simply lost sight of what lawyers and judges and courts are supposed to do—"Justice!" And Justice Kennedy, during the Supreme Court argument, recognized that. He started questioning Mr. Cruz immediately, and indignantly asking something like, "Is there some rule in Texas that you can't confess error?"

JC: This case is different from the other cases that you read about or see on *60 Minutes* where the state concedes that someone is actually innocent having been exonerated, for example, by DNA evidence. In those cases, the state doesn't know about the defendant's innocence until many years after sentence. In this case, the state knew that Haley's sentence should not have been more than two years way before they had to argue the case in any court.

EMA: Oh, no question. Certainly at the Supreme Court and also at the Court of Appeals. No question that an eighth grader . . . no question that anybody—*anybody*—could have known from the beginning that Michael Haley could not receive more than a two-year sentence. It's apparent on its face. It is totally different from DNA evidence where there is something hidden. This was open and obvious and the state knew for a very, very, very long time that Michael Haley had received a sentence more than eight times more than he should have, and that he had served more than three times what he should have received. They knew that and they did nothing about it. They didn't care.

JC: Did you know the lawyer who represented Haley at the trial level?[2]

EMA: No, I didn't know him.

JC: He graduated from law school in 1996 and he represented Haley in 1997.

EMA: I don't know. He was clearly not competent, no question about that. Whether he'd been a lawyer for a week, or for ten years, he was grossly incompetent.

JC: But if he was only a lawyer for one year, when representing Haley at trial and sentence, it was akin to a surgeon operating on someone one year out of medical school with no supervising surgeon in the room.

EMA: Well, it's complicated to do surgery and maybe if you're a ten-year experienced surgeon, you're better than a one-year experienced surgeon. But that is not a fair analogy here because anyone who could read would have known that Michael Haley's sentence was wrong.

JC: Justice Kennedy went after Cruz literally within one minute of beginning his argument, and Justice Stevens, joining in and asking Cruz "Is there some rule that you can't confess error in your state?" And saying, "So a

---

2. Author's note: We have intentionally not included the name of the trial lawyer. On February 10, 2016, after this interview, I spoke to him. He did not know the case went to the Supreme Court and he denied that Mr. Haley had received inefficient assistance of counsel at trial. He said there was a "backstory" and that there was no injustice, but that he could not describe the backstory because it was protected by the attorney-client privilege. He acknowledged that he had been admitted only one year when he represented Haley, and also said he had been a police officer for five years before that.

man does 15 years so you can vindicate your legal point?" What did it mean to you that six other justices of the Supreme Court didn't join in and just remand the case to the lower courts to resentence Haley to two years?

EMA: Well, I don't know if I really agree with that because there were broader issues involved that they didn't want to decide. So the six justices remanded the case and Haley finally got the relief he wanted—he was resentenced—but on the ground that he had "ineffective assistance of counsel" at the trial level. So I don't believe that the Court adopted the view that it was okay to sentence Haley to 16 years when he was only eligible for two. What the Court did was basically "punt" on the issue of when a defendant can claim "actual innocence" for a noncapital case.

But I don't think you had a majority of the Court sanction the notion that it is actually okay to keep people in prison for 16 years when they're only eligible to receive a two-year sentence.

JC: But did the Supreme Court give Cruz the victory he wanted in terms of limiting the "actual innocence" exception to the prosecution's claim of "procedural default" to capital cases only?

EMA: What they did was they punted and just effectively said we're not going to decide this broader issue in this case. I would be a little surprised if Cruz thinks this was a victory.[3]

Look, should the Court have come out and said that there is an "actual innocence" exception after a default in a noncapital capital context? I certainly think the answer should be "yes." Senator Cruz clearly thought the Court should have said to the contrary; the Court said neither. They instead said "we don't have to decide this in this case" because Haley can win on ineffective assistance. And so they vacated and remanded and Haley won.

JC: But if the non-lawyer general public (or the proverbial Martian having arrived on Earth) were to look at what happened in this case, they'd say "we can't believe this." Meaning, both sides and the court agree that Haley was simply "screwed" by his sentence, yet the courts don't just say,

---

3. Author's note: Cruz is quoted by *The Texas Tribune* as having said he quickly switched strategies when he heard the tenor of the Court's questions: "I would regularly talk to my students about the *Haley* case as a good example of how an advocate can rescue victory from the jaws of defeat." We invite the reader to listen to the argument (see Selected Materials).

"You know what, this is wrong—the State of Texas should confess its error. And if they don't want to, we'll do it for them."

EMA: Well that's a hard question, because it depends on how you define the general public, right? The general public where you live (New York) and the general public where I live (Texas). You started out asking questions about Haley's background and I candidly don't believe it was relevant, but if you're asking about some segment of the population here in Texas, his background would be quite relevant. I mean there would be many people not terribly sympathetic to him and would not find what happened to be an injustice, given that he'd done bad things in the past. So I think there are some folks in the world, at least here and probably some folks in New York too that would sort of subscribe to that view.

JC: And race may play into it in both of our hometowns.

EMA: But Michael Haley's a white guy.

JC: Is that right? Really? I guess that says something about me.

EMA: So I don't think race played into it.

Look, it appears from your questions you're sort of looking at this in two ways, right? Does this undermine confidence in the courts, and does this basically undermine confidence in the State of Texas? On the court question, I'm not really sure that Michael Haley's case undermines the public's confidence in the courts. Because ultimately Michael Haley did prevail, and he prevailed as a result of what the Supreme Court did. Haley won at the district court; Haley won at the Fifth Circuit; and what happened at the Supreme Court was not an outright affirmance of what had been done before, but he still got his relief. So I don't think that this case is instructive on or creates mistrust or lack of confidence or anything like that in the courts. I just don't view this as being an indictment of the court system.

I view this as being more relevant as it relates to the state. I think it does undermine the state. The mistakes were made long before Ted Cruz was involved. When the assistant attorney general (and the supervisors) realized the state could have fixed this, there never had to be a big fight about whether there's an "actual innocence exception" in noncapital cases. So does the fact that the state continued this fight through the district court, the Fifth Circuit, and all the way to the Supreme Court impact our confidence in the state and the prosecutorial arm of the state? Absolutely!

They could have fixed this injustice in a way where they just righted an obvious wrong without getting into any fight over a legal precedent. And they chose not to.

JC: Mr. Haley represented himself pro se in the state court appeals, in the Federal District Court proceeding, and then the Fifth Circuit, correct?

EMA: All the way.

JC: OK. So had you entered the case earlier and seen what had happened—would you have gone to the prosecutor and said "Hey, this is a screw-up. Let's fix it. Release this guy"?

EMA: Absolutely. There was always an alternative route. Part of the problem was Haley did not have counsel. And he had good judges. The magistrate judge was trying to do the right thing. The problem is it could have been done in a much less controversial way. Haley could have just received relief on "ineffective assistance of counsel" at the district court, which would have gotten him past all these procedural hurdles.

So had I been involved early on he could have gotten relief for having received "ineffective assistance of counsel"—which is of course how he ultimately won—without having to fight all the way through the Fifth Circuit and the Supreme Court about actual innocence.

If you really want to talk about where Michael Haley was sort of failed—and failed is too harsh a word—but if Michael Haley had had counsel in state habeas or federal habeas at the district court level, he would have prevailed and been out of jail much sooner.

And the reason he didn't have counsel was simply because he was indigent. So it's not a matter of race, it's a matter of being poor. In our criminal justice system, being poor is just as bad as being black. Or Hispanic. And I'm not suggesting that being black or Hispanic is bad, but if you look at statistics for capital cases, certainly there's inequality with respect to minorities, but there's also horrible inequality associated with socio-economic status. Poor people just don't get as good a shake as rich people.

JC: Let's assume that, as soon as he was sentenced, and he had gotten a lawyer of your caliber to represent him, what would you have done right then?

EMA: Certainly I could have appealed the sentence because it was apparent from the actual trial exhibits that there was insufficient evidence to justify the sentence. It was a lot of years ago and it's pretty technical. In

Haley's case, it was a misdemeanor grade theft, but he was charged with a state felony theft because he had two prior theft convictions.

JC: He stole a computer from Walmart . . .

EMA: A calculator!

JC: A calculator worth less than $1,500 bucks.

EMA: No, no, no, no. Way less than $1,500 bucks. It was a misdemeanor theft. But then once it was made a felony, you can then increase in Texas any felony up to a higher degree if you have two prior sequential felony convictions. That means your first felony has to become fully final before the commission of the second offense that then becomes final. In this case, they were not sequential. So Haley only had one felony offense they could use to increase his sentence. And you had to have two. So he could not have gotten more than two years.

JC: And if you had handled the direct appeal from his conviction, you would have raised that and shown that the evidence was clear.

EMA: All you had to do was look at the judgments from the two prior felony convictions and you could tell that they were not sequential.

JC: Did you spend any time with Haley?

EMA: Oh yes.

JC: Do you have any continuing relationship with him? It's now ten years later.

EMA: When the Supreme Court case was completed, I helped Michael back through the federal and state courts through the resentencing. But he had had subsequent troubles. I don't remember the specifics, but he's had additional problems.

JC: You're being kind. You mean criminal problems?

EMA: I believe so.

JC: It would be natural based on his background and returns to jail. You're not cured of recidivism when you go through the system again.

EMA: Especially after you get mistreated.

JC: The system grinds you down.

EMA: That's right.

JC: Have you had other Texas state prosecutions with similar injustices?

EMA: I have file cabinets full of cases. The criminal justice system in my view—capital or noncapital cases—with all of this post-conviction stuff . . . they erect crazy rules with enormous procedural hurdles and roadblocks, simply for policy reasons, so that federal courts don't interfere with the business of state courts.

It's for "comity" and "finality." Capital cases or noncapital cases. And that was what drove the state in this case. They weren't focused on whether this was just or unjust concerning Michael Haley. Nor on Michael Haley's background. Michael Haley was being ground up in the habeas machine, which is all about making sure that federal courts don't grant relief to state prisoners.

JC: And that ties in to Cruz's philosophy of government?

EMA: There seems to be lots of interest in vilifying Ted Cruz over this, and I'm not saying that's what you're doing. But this case has nothing really to do with Ted Cruz. In my view, these decisions were made long before Ted Cruz was involved with this case. These were decisions made by others at the attorney general's office. The solicitor general's office didn't even get involved until the last of it. I'm not fond of his politics and I certainly would never vote for him, but he's an effective advocate. He's a smart guy.

JC: But he's an effective advocate . . .

EMA: Yes, he is. But in this case the state's position, in my view, was crazy. But I don't think that he was the policy maker setting those crazy positions here.

JC: Fair enough. But the problem that we have—both you and I—is we're part of the system. We buy into the system. We understand why courts or attorneys general would want to enforce "comity" and "finality" and that kind of thing in the way they do it.

But what about when there is an injustice as there is here? And the courts, because they're applying those precedents, are willing to allow such injustices to continue.

EMA: Let me go back. First of all, we don't know to what level, what level of involvement the solicitor general's office had.

JC: I'm not talking about Cruz any more, I'm talking about . . .

EMA: Yes I know, but I just kind of wanted to revisit this Cruz thing. So we don't know what involvement he personally or his office had at the Federal District Court level, the Fifth Circuit level. Although, obviously, we know his involvement at the Supreme Court. To the extent that he and his office were involved in the making of that policy, and he and his office chose to do nothing about it, then certainly his hands are dirty as well. I just don't know the level of involvement that Cruz had.

Could he, at the Supreme Court, have confessed error or agreed to relief in some way that would not have these broad policy implications to establish this precedent? I don't know. I'd have to think about that more. I suspect that by the time we got to the Supreme Court—certainly by the time we got through the Fifth Circuit—that actual innocence applied to noncapital cases was the law in the Fifth Circuit. And if you're of their persuasion—more focused on the broader principles than the individual injustice to Michael Haley—there was probably nothing that he could do at that point.

JC: But the United States Justice Department in the person of the U.S. solicitor general's office, filed an amicus brief supporting Texas solicitor general Cruz's position.

EMA: Absolutely they did. And I don't think that any of that had to do with Haley or his circumstances. Haley was just a small piece of this.

JC: Haley represented himself in the district court. Did he understand all of the problems with the precedent—that the State of Texas would object to what he was creating?

EMA: Michael Haley is a reasonably bright, but an uneducated guy. So I'm sure he did not understand it all. Because, candidly, if he had understood it better, he could have avoided the problem by focusing on ineffective assistance.

JC: How did you get involved with Haley?

EMA: I had a friend who had been an assistant United States attorney who had left the office and was doing criminal defense work. Michael Haley was a trustee at the Smith County Jail. Haley had become somewhat friendly with her and had been keeping her apprised of his case on some level. She called me and said that she knew this kid who had prevailed at the district court level and had actually won on appeal at the Fifth Circuit; that the state was continuing to fight and would I please help him. And I did.

JC: So you're in the Supreme Court. Through Mr. Cruz the state acknowledged that there was a significant claim of ineffective assistance of counsel; and the Supreme Court remanded so the courts could address that issue first. What happened then?

EMA: Let me tell you, I do think, by the way, that that was a bit of a wink and a nod at the Supreme Court. I think the state was fine with what ultimately happened. Look, I don't know if Ted Cruz thought that Michael Haley should ultimately get relief or not. But I wouldn't be terribly surprised if he wouldn't tell you *privately* that what happened is exactly what he hoped would happen, and thought should happen.

JC: So what happened on remand?

EMA: It procedurally went back to the Fifth Circuit that remanded it to the district court. The district court granted the relief and we went back to the state court and he was resentenced to two years. I think Haley was back in custody on another charge by that time.

JC: Did the state take a position back in the district court?

EMA: No. There was never any fight. No one ever argued after the Supreme Court that Haley should spend a day more in jail.

JC: So you think if you and I were having a drink with Mr. Cruz (and his colleagues from the attorney general's office), he would acknowledge that there was ineffective assistance of counsel and that Haley should be released.

EMA: Unquestionably.

JC: Did you ever talk to the original judge, the original A.D.A., or Haley's counsel about this case?

EMA: No. By the time I was involved, there was nothing they could do.

JC: If I were having a drink with you—in vino veritas—what would you tell me about the case that you haven't told me yet?

EMA: Nothing else. Haley did have ineffective assistance of counsel. It's terrible that he got this sentence. In hindsight it would have been much better for the magistrate judge to have decided the case based on ineffective assistance so that "actual innocence" would not have been an issue.

I do agree with the Fifth Circuit (as well as the district court) that "actual innocence" should indeed be available in noncapital cases. It makes perfect sense. It works exactly in line with all the Supreme Court precedents. But I do think it's unfortunate that the lower courts decided it the way they did because if they had decided on ineffective assistance of counsel, it could have saved Haley a bunch of time in the penitentiary. Because I suspect that if the magistrate judge had decided on the ineffective assistance grounds, the state would never have appealed that. Haley would have been out of the penitentiary years earlier.

JC: So let me ask you this—a difficult question. If you (leaving your role as a defense lawyer) were the Texas solicitor general or the attorney general—whoever was calling the shots at the Supreme Court level—would you have confessed error, given that the precedent in the Fifth Circuit created by Mr. Haley said that the "actual innocence" exception to the procedural default rule would apply to future noncapital cases?

EMA: I would have never let it get to that point. I would have fixed this issue much earlier.

JC: But work with me. Let's assume you just came into office and this case was already on the Supreme Court docket. And Justice Kennedy was asking *you* as Texas solicitor general "Why don't you confess error?" What would you have done?

EMA: I would have said expressly that the Fifth Circuit's opinion—again in my role as chief law enforcement official—I would have said that the Fifth Circuit's opinion should not be affirmed, and that it should be vacated and remanded. I would have expressly suggested to the Court that they do what they ultimately did—vacate the decision and remand to let the lower courts consider ineffective assistance of counsel.

JC: But you wouldn't confess error?

EMA: I don't know exactly what that means. I would have expressly acknowledged that Mr. Haley could not lawfully be sentenced to more than two years, and I would have expressly acknowledged that he had received ineffective assistance of counsel below.

JC: Solicitor General Cruz pretty much did that.

EMA: But this is all hard to say, because *I* would never have let it get to that point. It should have just never gotten to this point.

JC: Fair enough.

EMA: And, that's a very unfair question—because I have my own views about the criminal justice system. I have my own beliefs about what is right and wrong. I have my own beliefs about the proper way to interpret that precedent. So it's very hard for me . . . you're asking me to put myself in that position. And if I was in his position and I had a boss that was the elected attorney general of the State of Texas telling me that this is an important principle that we want to maintain and I had been instructed to do that, well then certainly I would do my job.

Would I, Eric Albritton, if unconstrained by external forces, personally want to have confessed error? Absolutely, positively, because I thought my position was right. But I don't have the luxury of making that judgment.

JC: So, *as an attorney,* you understand what he did?

EAM: Intellectually, I sort of understand once the Fifth Circuit ruled the way that it did given the state's agenda. I understand why it would push back to fight against the proposition that you can claim actual innocence in these circumstances. I can understand that. So I give Cruz a bit of a pass on it.

Also, you were asking about Justice Kennedy's comment. You've got to take that in context. I don't really think that Justice Kennedy was saying, "Why aren't you confessing your error at the Supreme Court?" I think one can interpret his question to be "Why did we get here to begin with? Why didn't the state confess error three or four years ago?" I think that's what Justice Kennedy was getting at because that's where the real outrage lies. They knew! It's all over their papers. You know they knew. And the question is, "Why didn't they fix it earlier?" That was crazy. Because, at that earlier point, there were no broader principles. No comity. No finality. No federalism. None of these grand principles at play. They simply chose not to fix it, and that's what's truly outrageous.

JC: Well, Dostoyevsky said, "The degree of civilization in a society can be judged by entering its prisons." And that's something that you and I can certainly both agree on.

EMA: Look, I think that Michael Wayne Haley was treated terribly. I think it was outrageous that he received a 16-plus-year sentence when he was only eligible for two. I think it is outrageous that he had that terrible lawyer. I think it's outrageous that the district attorneys did not figure this out on their own. And if they didn't, then shame on them. I think it's outrageous that the state trial court didn't figure it out. I think it's outrageous that the state court of appeals didn't figure it out.

I think it's great that the Federal District Court got it right, but I think it's unfortunate that they didn't appoint him a lawyer. If they had appointed Haley a lawyer, it would have been handled differently, and he would have spent less time in jail. But I think the district court and the Fifth Circuit were right on the law, and right on in what they were trying to do. I think that the attorney general—including the solicitor general who was appointed by him (and everyone that worked for him on this case)—did the wrong thing.

This is all a very poor reflection on us as a society.

3

A False Confession to Save His Family

Abdallah Higazy

At the end I was convinced they were going to bring me
my brother, and would either get me to confess again
that the device was mine, or they were going to frame
my brother with something. I had no doubt about this.

—Abdallah Higazy, March 22, 2016[1]

When most of us think about the events of 9/11, we think about the lives lost, the devastation, the sadness. We think about Osama bin Laden, Islamic fundamentalists, and President George W. Bush's "War on Terror." But many of us don't think about—maybe we don't *want* to think about—how many people in the United States (and, for that matter, the world) concluded that simply because someone is Muslim, he is suspect,

---

1. This interview took place at a hotel business center in Pennsylvania.

he cannot be trusted, he hates America, he agrees with the fundamentalists, he is a terrorist! In other words, people made (and, distressingly, often still make) assumptions about people's ideology and sympathies merely because of their religion, or because of where they were born.

The dangers of those generalizations came to the fore starkly in the story of Abdallah Higazy. One American man blatantly lied about him and believed it was his "patriotic duty" to do so. It was a lie that, had another American not come forward, likely would have cost Mr. Higazy years, perhaps a lifetime, in prison—in Guantanamo even.

Mark Twain's words ring truer than ever when one talks to Mr. Higazy: "Truth is stranger than fiction, but it is because fiction is obliged to stick to possibilities; truth isn't."

Abdallah Higazy was born in Egypt, the son of a then-diplomat. He spent portions of his elementary, high school, and college years in Virginia and D.C. Talking to him, although you observe his Middle Eastern appearance, you barely hear the hint of an accent. He speaks English fluently, idiomatically, and is as steeped in American culture as anyone born here. When he was 30 years old, he received an opportunity he had no desire to pass up—no one would. He was offered a scholarship through an American agency to attend the Polytechnic Institute of Brooklyn, a distinguished science and engineering school. In exchange, he would be required to work in Cairo for two years after his graduation.

Higazy arrived in New York to begin his academic program on August 27, 2001. Since the program had not yet secured housing, he was placed in the Millennium Hotel, coincidentally (fatefully, really) across the street from the World Trade Center. Higazy's room overlooked those two great towers. He was still living in the hotel on 9/11 and watched, horrified, as the planes hit the towers. Like everyone else in the hotel, he was evacuated and left with his wallet and the clothes on his back.

Three months later, Higazy was contacted by the hotel—"come and get your things." On December 17, 2001, he went to the hotel, accompanied by his American friends and his American then-fiancée, now wife. He was handed a list of items. They had found his Koran, his prayer rug, his clothes, other miscellaneous personal items. But the list included a "radio transceiver." A what? Higazy did not have a radio with him, and he called the hotel employee over and said—"that does not belong to me."

Higazy spent the next several hours answering questions posed by FBI agents who were there "waiting" for him. Was he told he was under arrest? Told he could refuse to answer questions? Or was the paranoia of the day so great that the FBI was not concerned with his "rights"? Higazy repeated unwaveringly that the radio transceiver was not his. But the FBI persisted. Why? Why did anyone think the transceiver was his? What Higazy did not know at the time is that a hotel security employee, one Ronald Ferry, who had inventoried the belongings of the hotel's occupants, told the FBI that this radio transceiver—through which one could communicate with an airplane in flight—was found in Higazy's locked safe next to his Koran.

Higazy did not go home that night. In fact, he did not go home for the next 34 nights. On December 18, 2001, Higazy was assigned a lawyer— Robert S. Dunn. After briefly speaking with Dunn, he was brought to the courtroom of Judge Jed Rakoff in the Southern District of New York. For those not familiar with Judge Rakoff, he is firm—to both sides—and does not tolerate, shall we say, hyperbole, well. When Higazy was brought to court, the assistant U.S. attorney asked that the government be permitted to hold Higazy as a "material witness" so that he could testify before the grand jury that had been impaneled to investigate the 9/11 hijackings. You see, the prosecutors did not actually have evidence to charge Higazy with a crime. And so they came up with the next best thing—detain Higazy as a "material witness," giving the prosecutors time to look for evidence that Higazy committed a crime.

Higazy had no real ties to the U.S., and Judge Rakoff reluctantly allowed the government to hold him in custody for ten days. During those ten days (and it was ten days only because there would be anticipated delay during the Christmas holiday), the government was to call Higazy as a grand jury witness. Higazy repeated that he had never before seen the radio transceiver. He insisted that he be permitted to take a polygraph, a lie detector test. What did Higazy's capable lawyer, Dunn, think about a polygraph knowing that polygraph results are inadmissible in court proceedings? Did Higazy think about the possible repercussions—the possibility that he might "fail"—or was he that sure of his innocence? That polygraph—a crucial event, really—was administered on day nine of Higazy's ten-day hold, during which, we note, he was never presented to the grand jury.

Now, the FBI has a rule—when a polygraph is being taken, no one is permitted in the room except for the agent administering the examination and the person being examined. Higazy and his lawyer had to sign a waiver—Dunn would be just outside the room, leaving FBI Agent Michael Templeton and Higazy alone. But there were limits—Templeton could take the polygraph only; he could not "interview" or question Higazy.

Except that's not the way it works in the real world. Templeton spent hours with Higazy. Before strapping on the polygraph gear, Templeton asked Higazy a series of questions in the guise that he needed them for a "baseline"—where were you born, how old are you, where did you go to school, where do your parents live, siblings, what do they do?

What exactly happened in that polygraph room? Did Templeton talk to Higazy about the case—ignoring that he was only supposed to take the polygraph exam and not "interview" Higazy. Did he try to extract information from Higazy and, if so, what tactics did he use? Did Templeton threaten Higazy? And how did Higazy react? Did he stand firm—repeating that the transceiver was not his?

Ultimately, Higazy folded; he said the transceiver belonged to him. But why? He was in the U.S. legally, and at the Millennium through the auspices of a respected school program. He had never been in trouble with the law—here or in Egypt. What in the world would convince him to tell the FBI that the transceiver was his? Was he worried about his family—the brother living in Ithaca and his parents and siblings in Egypt? Did he believe the FBI would harm them, "investigate" them or, perhaps worse, ask the Egyptian authorities to do those things? Why did Abdallah Higazy confess—and exactly what did he confess? Maybe the device was indeed his!

When they appeared before Judge Rakoff the day after the polygraph, the government announced—Higazy confessed! And Dunn and Higazy never challenged that statement. They both knew it would convince Judge Rakoff to keep Higazy in jail. And Judge Rakoff did just that—holding Higazy in custody was "no longer a close call." And for Higazy, did custody mean he was in general population—a supposed terrorist exposed to violent criminals? Or was he in solitary, alone all day, every day? And which was worse?

On January 11, 2002, while still being held as a "material witness," Higazy was technically "arrested" and charged with making false statements to the FBI. Those statements? That the radio transceiver did not belong to him. Yes, relying on the polygraph session confession, the U.S. attorney charged Higazy with lying to the FBI when agents first met him at the Millennium Hotel and Higazy said the radio did not belong to him.

During this time, Higazy's only visitor—his only friend—was Dunn. Did he believe Higazy was a terrorist? That Higazy had something to do with the 9/11 attacks? And what of the defense Dunn would present? Was it enough that he create "reasonable doubt" in the minds of a jury—a jury is not to convict a defendant if there is reasonable doubt whether a defendant committed the crime charged. Or did Higazy want something else? But—let's face it—did it really make a difference once Higazy confessed?

On January 14, 2002—just three days after Higazy was formally charged and a magistrate judge denied bail keeping him in custody—what some would call an honest to God miracle (there is no other way to put it) happened. A U.S. airline pilot who had also been staying at the Millennium on 9/11 went to the hotel to collect his belongings. And his belongings included that transceiver radio, which he lawfully and legitimately had in his possession.

Higazy knew none of this. No one told him. What, then, did he think when he was taken from his cell two days later and put into "holding" for hours? And what were his thoughts, feelings, reactions when he was told "you can go." Did he actually believe he was free, or was he worried it was some ruse by the government?

And what did Higazy think of the story he learned? Ronald Ferry, a security officer at the Millennium Hotel who had a questionable history (he had resigned from the Newark Police force amid drug charges), or one of his colleagues found the transceiver in the clean-up after 9/11. It was not in Higazy's safe and it was not next to his Koran. But Ferry lied— intentionally—believing he was doing his "patriotic duty" by attributing the device to the guest who had the Koran in his safe; the guest who had an Egyptian name.

The lawyers appeared before Judge Rakoff, who still had the case on his calendar. Now, many judges—perhaps most judges—would simply have apologized to Higazy for his "inconvenience" and let it go at that. But not Judge Rakoff. He demanded to know what investigation had been done and whether the government had lied to him; lied to the court. While the judge ultimately concluded that he was not lied to, his questions raise a fundamental question we may never know the answer to—had the government even questioned Ferry's story that the transceiver was found in Higazy's locked room safe?

Whether because it was now under questioning eye of Judge Rakoff, or because it wanted to prosecute Ferry's crime, the government arrested Ferry, who pleaded guilty before another judge to lying to the FBI. His "patriotic" lie could have placed Higazy in jail for life. Yet he was sentenced to serve six months of weekends in jail. Did Higazy attend Ferry's sentencing? And what did he think of this sentence?

Templeton, for his part, ultimately did not contest Higazy's statements about what actually happened during the polygraph and the government assured Judge Rakoff it would investigate Templeton's actions. If Templeton was in fact investigated, it does not appear that he was reprimanded. Higazy sued Templeton, and the Millennium, and the individuals who lied and threatened him. Ferry acted intentionally, so under the law Millennium was not responsible for his acts. As to Templeton, an appellate court found that there were questions concerning Templeton's polygraph "interview" and the government's use of his findings. After that decision, Higazy settled with the government, which had defended Templeton.

Higazy finished his school program—the program Templeton contended he would never complete—and returned to Egypt, where he and his American wife lived for almost a decade before returning to the U.S. Does Higazy have anger toward the United States for what was done to him? And, even though he understands that Templeton's behavior, and his own resultant false confession, could have landed him in Guantanamo for his lifetime were it not for the airline pilot coming forward, does Higazy accept these as acts of individuals? Or are they the acts of a country? Can Higazy ever really forgive; and does he ever forget?

But here's the real issue. What happened to Abdallah Higazy is far from an isolated incident. And even if he blames only the individuals who harmed him, we must ask: What does the story that follows—the profound injustice described in Higazy's own words—say about polygraphs, false confessions, bullying tactics, and the labelling of someone based on his religion or his country of birth?

The Dialogue

JC: Mr. Higazy, I have thought about the materials I've read about the injustice done to you. I have spoken to a number of people who have nothing to do with the events that you encountered. All of them are Caucasian and American born, having lived in the United States all of their lives. And maybe that's why it's hard for them to understand precisely what happened and why you reacted as you did. I'm not sure I understand it myself.

You're a law-abiding citizen. You came to the United States from Egypt with a passport that belongs to you. You came to study at the Polytechnic Institute under a program that brought foreign citizens here to study. You had absolutely nothing to do with the transceiver device that was alleged to have been found in a safe in your room at the Millennium Hotel.

You came to the Millennium Hotel three months after September 11 to retrieve your belongings, and were confronted with the accusation that the transceiver device was in fact yours. You were arraigned in court. You asked for a lie detector test to establish your innocence. The FBI ultimately agreed. The lawyer appointed by the court to represent you sat directly outside the room when the polygraph was administered. And yet, though you had nothing to do with the transceiver device, the FBI through the United States attorney represented to the judge that you acknowledged— when interviewed by the FBI polygraph examiner while you were alone with him—that it was in fact your device. Is everything I've said so far true?

AH: With the exception of you calling me a law-abiding *citizen* . . .

JC: Yes. Law-abiding "person." But yet you admitted to the FBI—with your lawyer sitting probably 15 feet away, although not in earshot of what was transpiring—to what the United States government properly believed was a very serious issue. A person from the Middle East having a transceiver device in a hotel directly opposite Ground Zero during the colossal attacks.

How did that happen? Why?

AH: For starters, before I had a lawyer, I had absolutely no idea about the device's capabilities. To me, it was just a radio transceiver. As things progressed, I was given information by the FBI about the device. So at that very first time they showed me the device I was asked, "What is this?" My immediate response was that I had no idea. "But, it was found in your hotel room inside your wall safe." I said, "No way, that's impossible."

This was the day I went to retrieve my belongings from the hotel. So on that day I had absolutely no idea what this radio was. When the polygraph examiner, Agent Mike Templeton, sat with me, he gave me all the details about the device. He told me what it can do, its surprising capabilities, that a person can talk to a plane from it. Like I said, though, I had no idea what it could do. So when I got to know the details of it, that really scared me.

JC: Let's back up. You had been in the Egyptian Air Force?

AH: The Egyptian Air Corps. We basically provided support for the Air Force. So amazingly, as some of my friends have told me, had someone wanted to frame a person for having this device, he couldn't have found anyone better. I am a computer engineer with a good amount of electronics experience. And, when I was drafted by the Egyptian military I was an officer in a ground-to-air communications regiment.

JC: So, when you were in the Air Corps did you know anything about a transceiver device?

AH: I was responsible for computers, but never given any formal training.

JC: So you had nothing to do . . .

AH: No. No. No. Absolutely not!

JC: Okay. So when you're being asked about it on the day you came to the Millennium Hotel to retrieve your belongings, you knew nothing about it?

AH: When I walked into the building I had no idea it was there. I found out about it when they gave me a list. I was with the young woman who eventually became my wife. And I remember the gentleman at the Millennium desk giving me a list of the things found in my room.

I remember it with crystal clarity. It was the second item on the list: "Radio transceiver." I looked at her and said this is strange. "I didn't bring anything electronic from Egypt. What is this?" So I went straight to the man and said "Sir, this isn't mine."

JC: The FBI agent?

AH: Oh no—the man who gave me the paper. I had no idea that FBI agents were there. So I told him this isn't mine. He said, "Please go check on everything else." So I said okay. I went through everything. A couple of things were missing—probably stolen.

JC: What did you go to the Millennium to retrieve?

AH: My clothing, mostly.

JC: They also said that there was a Koran. Was that yours?

AH: Any practicing Muslim traveling from place to place would carry one. This is something I love, so I put it in the safe.

JC: Did you also have a prayer rug?

AH: Yes, but not in the safe.

JC: Did you have maps of JFK and Reagan airports in your room?

AH: Yes, the agency that brought me to the United States gave everyone a map so we would not get lost while here, and they acknowledged it to the FBI.

JC: What else. Clothes? Any personal items?

AH: Clothes, and a couple of gifts. It's really funny because on 9/11, I was actually planning to meet someone at the World Trade Center to give him a gift that his mother-in-law gave me in Egypt to give him. It was really strange.

JC: Did you tell that to the FBI?

AH: I don't think I ever got the chance.

JC: Do you know the name of who you were giving the gift to?

AH: At the time, of course. I had his phone number. Immediately after 9/11 I tried to contact him to make sure that he was okay.

JC: It might've been helpful for you to tell the FBI—that you were actually going to visit someone at the World Trade Center to give him a gift on 9/11.

How did the FBI know that you were coming to the Millennium the day you came to retrieve your belongings?

AH: The Millennium Hotel called me and asked me if I'd come to take my stuff.

JC: So you now work with the assumption that the Millennium tipped off the FBI that you were coming on a particular day.

AH: I'm positive.

JC: So after you're shown this list of items on a piece of paper by the Millennium employee, you were interviewed by the FBI. And during that conversation they asked if the transceiver device was yours, correct? And you said "No."

AH: Correct.

JC: Was there any hesitation at that point about whether you had seen it before, whether you knew about it, whether you had found it near the Brooklyn Bridge, whether you had anything to do with it?

AH: Absolutely not. That was all invented by me during the polygraph interview.

JC: Okay. So the FBI told you that that device was found in your safe. Any further conversation about that?

AH: They kept asking me, "What is it?" And I said "I don't know." And then they kept asking again what does it look like. It looked like a police walkie talkie. I had no idea what it was.

JC: Mr. Higazy, as we speak here right now, you seem very calm—of course, 15 years after the fact. What was your state of mind then?

AH: Absolute fear.

Somebody telling you that they found an electronic device in your room when you know that it was never there, that you had never seen it before. And these are FBI agents investigating an attack on American soil that resulted in the murder of 3,000 people. I assure you, I was very afraid. Somebody was doing something to me, and I had no idea what.

JC: At some point—later on—they mentioned your brother. Was it that day?

AH: No. My brother lived in Ithaca at the time. He was preparing for his master's degree in physical therapy.

JC: I take it your brother is also a law-abiding person?

AH: Absolutely.

JC: Were you concerned that they would bring charges or somehow bring him harm?

AH: No. This is the FBI. They do things by the book. That's what I was assuming. I think I watched too many American TV shows.

JC: So how long was this FBI interview when you came to get your things on December 19th?

AH: Three or four hours.

JC: Was there any talk about you getting a lawyer during that conversation?

AH: Not then.

JC: Did you know then that you had a right to a lawyer?

AH: At that point, no. I was given my rights when they took me to the FBI building.

JC: Did you believe during those hours that you were free to leave if you wanted to?

AH: No, that was not said at all. I was "under arrest as a material witness in the 9/11 attacks investigation."

JC: How long after the interview began did you know that you were a "material witness under arrest"?

AH: Before I was processed and fingerprinted. I was taken to meet a police officer and a female FBI agent, and they gave me my rights. Until that point I was like "Okay, this is obviously some kind of mistake," and they asked me the same questions the other three gentlemen asked, and I gave the same exact answers. They told me I had a right to remain silent. I told them I didn't need to remain silent. "Why? I didn't do anything wrong."

After that, I was processed, fingerprinted, mugshot. I remember some of the questions that I was asked. "Are you a member of the Jamia Islamia?" "No."

JC: What is that?

AH: Literally translated, it would be the Islamic group or Muslim group. They were a militant group in Egypt in the '70s and '80s and definitely the '90s. The people responsible for assassinating President Sadat.

JC: You said no to that?

AH: I said "No, absolutely not." I don't remember that they mentioned specific terrorist organizations. I only remember the Jamia Islamia, the Muslim Brotherhood, and Al Qaeda, in which of course I have never been a member or associated in any way.

JC: So then what happened?

AH: They said that they have to find me "lodgings." "Lodgings!" Because when they said lodgings, the first thing that went to my head was maybe a small hotel.

JC: So during that three- or four-hour stretch did anyone know where you were?

AH: Yes. First, my then fiancée who was with me and two friends, all Americans. They stayed for two hours and had to leave. And until then they had no idea what was happening. *I* had no idea what was happening. It was just a long interview. They were outside.

JC: So after you were asked about these terrorist groups, what next?

AH: I asked if I could make a call. They said yes. I called the family I was staying with after the attacks. I told them where I was. And then after the call I asked if I could make another call, and they were kind enough to let me. I called the agency that gave me the scholarship and eventually learned that they laughed very hard when they heard my message. I said I was arrested by the FBI: "I'm truly sorry I have to miss my final exam." They burst out laughing. And after I hung up the phone, the police officer said "You're arrested by the FBI over the investigation of 9/11 and the only thing you're worried about is missing your final exam?" I said yes, because if I was going to get an "F" I would lose the scholarship and really that's all that was on my mind at the time.

I was then processed and taken to the "lodgings" which turned out to be the Metropolitan Correctional Center. My first time ever coming face to face with actual criminals.

JC: Were you in the general population, or in solitary confinement?

AH: I was getting my information from the media. When they mentioned that a lot of those guys had martial arts training, I was asked if I ever took martial arts. I said yes. I took some aikido and some karate and they said "Oh no, you belong in administrative segregation." A fancy word for solitary confinement.

JC: When did you first see a lawyer?

AH: The following day. I couldn't believe it. The attorney, Robert Dunn, God rest his soul. He first asked me if I could afford an attorney and I told him I have $350 in my bank account, and would that be enough. He laughed and said it wasn't enough, and he became my attorney, compensated by the government.

JC: I didn't know Mr. Dunn, and until this moment that he died. But in reading the transcripts of the proceedings before Judge Rakoff, it seems he was a very aggressive proponent of your cause.

AH: Yes he was. He spoke to me about his strategy and actually told me something that made me upset. I hope I'm never viewed like that again. He said, "Look Abdallah, I know you. You're a great guy—but believe it or not, you're the perfect mole." I said, "What do you mean?" He said, "You know our customs. You speak like us. You know how to joke. You actually understand American humor. You follow sports. Football, baseball, basketball. You're the perfect mole." And the only thing that went through my head was: "If this is what my attorney thinks of me, how does everybody else think?"

JC: When you're first being interviewed by Mr. Dunn to prepare for an arraignment, I'll ask this hard question—Did you think Robert Dunn believed you, or that he thought that the transceiver was actually yours, that you had a bad motive in possessing it?

AH: Robert told me this: "Whether you did it or not, whether you were responsible or not, whether this thing is yours or not, it's my responsibility, my solemn sworn oath that I will protect you and have your best interests in front of me. This is what I need to do for you, your best interests, your best interests at heart."

JC: Did you believe him?

AH: I had no choice but to believe him. He was the only person I actually could call a friend. Everybody else was looking around me, like "Why did you do it?" I didn't do anything. While I was being taken from one place to another on the street going from place to place with two FBI agents, they were stopped and told: "Wonderful, you caught one of those terrorists." So I could do nothing else but call Robert Dunn my friend.

JC: Do you see him as your "friend" now?

AH: Absolutely.

JC: Mr. Higazy, I've been known to "beat up" clients sometimes. Did he beat you up? Did he basically say, "Come on, Abdallah, cut the crap"?

AH: Not once. I know we want to focus on the polygraph examination—but immediately after it was over and I started to make stuff up to try to convince [Agent] Templeton, if you can believe it, that the transceiver was mine, Robert saw the paper that Templeton wrote for me to sign and looked at me and said, "You were lying to me?" And I told him "No." He said, "This paper means you were lying to me." I still remember what I told him. I said. "Robert, I swear by Allah the Great, I'm not lying to you. I told you the truth." He said, "Why, then, were you lying to him? Why did you say it was yours?" I simply told him, "Look, it's better this way."

JC: I see you're tearing up. If you're okay to continue, let's back up. At some point you appeared before Judge Rakoff. I take it you learned that Judge Rakoff is a very well-regarded judge?

AH: I'm okay. I really had no idea about the judge. All I knew is that he was the judge responsible for meeting with the material witnesses.

JC: Before you appeared before Judge Rakoff with your lawyer and the prosecutor, did you tell Robert that you wanted to take a lie detector test?

AH: The idea of the lie detector test came when I made my first phone call to my friends. I said, "This is obviously just some mistake." The gentlemen whom I was staying with—ex-military whom I met one week before 9/11—said, "Abdallah, listen. You're telling the truth, right?" I said "Yes." He said, "Then you want to take a lie detector test."

JC: If you raised the idea with Robert Dunn, what did he say?

AH: He recommended against it—he said the courts don't recognize polygraph exams, and I asked why not. He told me because a pathological liar would pass—it can't detect lies by a pathological liar. So I asked why then would the FBI be willing to give me one. He said that in some way it helps them, it guides them, gives them an idea. But that's about it. But I wanted to do it. Actually when Robert mentioned it to Judge Rakoff, the judge said, "Well, apparently the young man looks like he wants to cooperate."

JC: What did you understand that to mean?

AH: That I'm not being "malicious" in any way—not being obstructive, trying to work cooperatively with the FBI.

JC: Mr. Dunn, the United States attorney, and the FBI negotiated the terms of this polygraph examination?

AH: Yes.

JC: So you sit down in the room, and Agent Templeton straps on the polygraph apparatus?

AH: No. That's not what happened. Over about an hour-and-a-half, he tried to convince me that there was no reason or need to take a polygraph—that I was lying and there was no way I would pass the exam. I was alone in the room with him.

JC: How did he try to convince you that there was no need for a polygraph?

AH: He drew a line on a piece of paper. He said, "Here, at one end, we have a man who is innocent and here, at the other end, we have the terrorist. You are somewhere in the middle." And I told him "No, this is where I am. I am innocent. I have no idea what this device is and in no way can I help you." And he told me, "What's your biggest worry?" I said "That I'm going to lose my scholarship." His response was, "You've lost your scholarship already, and because of you no other Egyptian will ever get a scholarship again." And he went on, "You told Agent Christopher Bruno that you didn't want to have the Egyptian consulate represent you." I said, "Look, I'm sure we can finish this right away."

JC: What was his demeanor?

AH: Over time, he started screaming, banging the table. His face turned red. He yelled: "TELL ME THE TRUTH."

JC: Yet you're speaking to me in a very matter of fact manner. Was that how you talked to him?

AH: Oh yes. I'm trying to imitate as much as I could from that day. I tried to be calm. I said, "Don't worry, sir. I intend to fully cooperate." And he said, "And you better cooperate. Because if you don't, the FBI will put your brother, upstate, in constant scrutiny and will make sure Egyptian security makes your family's life a living hell."

JC: How did he know about your brother?

AH: In the beginning they asked if I have relatives. Who was I staying with? I told them I have a brother. "Where is he, what's he doing here, when was the last time he was here, how old is he?" All the details that they could get. And they said they would talk with Egyptian security about my family still in Egypt. My father, my mother, my sister, and my other brother were there.

JC: Was he specific about what would happen to your family?

AH: As other reporters eventually said, their methods are draconian. Alright, so let's say for example, "Mr. Cohen, we are accusing you of this." "I didn't do it." "Really, you didn't do it? Well, here's your family, here's your father, here's your mother, and we're going to do this and that to them if you don't confess."

JC: Were you afraid . . .

AH: Oh, absolutely.

JC: Were you afraid that the FBI would tip off Egyptian security and they would torture your family?

AH: Yes, that's why I told Robert "It's better this way. I'll take the hit whatever they're willing to give me for the device if it will make sure my family is safe."

JC: So, what did you say before Agent Templeton strapped on the polygraph apparatus?

AH: I couldn't speak. In my head I said "I have to pass this exam. My family is in danger."

JC: So you were denying until taking the exam any connection to the transceiver device?

AH: Absolutely, until he unstrapped me. When I felt like I was going to faint.

JC: So he straps you in, and then what questions does he ask?

AH: Robert had explained to me that they start off with basic questions. "Is your name Abdallah Higazy?" "Are you here on a scholarship?" "Did you ever do anything that would bring your family shame?" So after the baseline questions, then he finally did ask *the* question—"Did you have a device with you on 9/11?" And I said "No." There were other questions basically saying "Do you know anyone who's a terrorist?" "No." Those kinds of questions.

Then, here's what happened. I could hear my heart pounding in my ears. The things that they use that somehow measures how you're breathing, a heart monitor, blood pressure monitor. I don't remember if there was anything else. But that thing that was strapped on me made me feel like I was going to explode. So I cried out, "Please stop it, please stop it, please stop it." So he did.

JC: So when he took all of the devices off, you had a calmer conversation with him?

AH: Yes, because here's what went through my head. First, I was in absolute disbelief. How could this happen during a lie detector test and I said, "Did this ever happen to anyone before?" He said that it never happened to anyone telling the truth. That I could hear my heart—but also the fear and the feeling of the blood pressure measurement device.

My blood pressure was just so high. I understand now that it was just my blood pressure.

JC: During this torment you're explaining when you were alone with Templeton, though, you knew that your lawyer was sitting just outside. Why didn't you just say, "I need to talk with Robert"?

AH: I was trying to save my family. Robert's number one goal was *my* protection. What could Robert do to protect them?

JC: What could you do?

AH: If the only thing that would make my family safe was saying that the device was mine, I needed to. So I said, "Sure, the device is mine!"

JC: What did you think would happen if you admitted the device was yours?

AH: I would lose the scholarship. I'd go to prison, but my family would be safe.

JC: You didn't realize that by saying that the device was yours that they would try to connect it to the attacks?

AH: Yes.

JC: You were basically admitting to perhaps participating in the biggest crime in the history of the world?

AH: I wasn't in a mental state to think that far ahead.

JC: But you did tell him different versions of how you came to possess the device. What did you tell him?

AH: I honestly don't remember. I remember saying I found it at the other end of the Brooklyn Bridge, and that I stole it from J&R Music World. I don't remember with precision.

JC: Did you say that you brought it from Egypt?

AH: No.

JC: But you were trying to convince him through these stories that the device was actually yours?

AH: Yes. It didn't matter whether it was on the other side of Brooklyn Bridge or J&R. At first, I thought I convinced Agent Templeton. He wrote up a piece of paper and wanted me to sign it. I said. "Okay, I just want my lawyer to see it." I don't know how I came to remember at that moment that Robert was sitting outside.

JC: Do you remember what the paper said?

AH: I don't remember what story I finally used to convince him.

JC: But the paper he wanted you to sign said the device was yours?

AH: Yes.

JC: So you asked to speak to Robert alone?

AH: I was cold. I was shaking. And he looked at me and said "What is this?" I told him, "Look, I just made it up." And he started reading and he said "You lied to me." And I told him, "No" and I swore to him. Then he said "Then, why are you saying this?" I told him "It's better this way." And he told me "No, no, it's not, it's not better this way." He said a lot of people participated in 9/11 without knowing that they were participating and this is going to persuade them that you were one of them.

JC: Again, hard question: Did you think at that moment that Robert believed that you had nothing to do with the device?

AH: I honestly don't know, but I had to believe that he was the only person I could trust.

JC: We now know that a month or so later a pilot went to pick up his belongings and asked about his radio. The device the government said belonged to you was actually his and you were released.

AH: Yes.

JC: I must say in all candor—and Robert was right, you're very likeable—but if you were being interviewed right now and I didn't know that a legitimate pilot came forward and proved your innocence, I'd probably believe that when you admitted that the device was yours, that it was yours. That's the way the facts lined up, plus I wouldn't know that the security officer at the Millennium had *falsely* accused you. Can you understand that?

AH: Fully. And I swore back at the time if I ever met that pilot's mother, I would kiss her hand.

In Arabic and Muslim culture, kissing someone's hand is one of the biggest ways to express gratitude. And the reason I said I would kiss his mother's hand was what he said. He said his mother heard about the device on TV or radio and told him, "Listen, I think that is your device." He told her, "I don't think so. This man just confessed that it was his and it was found inside a locked safe." I have no doubt that it was because his mother spoke to him that he asked about the device and that is how my innocence was established.

JC: Mr. Higazy, there was a young, very able lawyer at my law firm, whose family came from Afghanistan. Right after 9/11, he told me he was afraid that he would be hassled by the police in the subways because of his appearance. I told him, "Just cooperate with them, call me 24/7 and I'll come there." From time to time back then, he was in fact hassled a bit, or looked at suspiciously by the police who monitored the subway stations then. Did you experience that?

AH: If I did, I tried everything to ignore it, look the other way, be fully cooperative, deal with people with a smile.

JC: Did those you knew from Arab countries experience harassment, or people staring at them?

AH: Women more than the men. A lot of the women are covered, and basically it's a calling card that you are a Muslim woman. This is not one of my proudest moments but after 9/11, the lady responsible for the International Student Services—up until this day I still call her Titi, meaning "auntie"—when I needed to buy a laptop, she sent me with her son. They are Puerto Rican, and I was "cousin Raul." Nobody knew, unless you were close to me, that I was Egyptian.

JC: So, after you admitted to the FBI that the device was yours, you became a criminal defendant charged with lying to the FBI.

AH: It didn't exactly happen right away like that. They still hoped that I would become a valuable witness—that I would come forward and tell them "Yes, here's what happened."

JC: Did you and Robert have any discussions after you became the defendant rather than the "material witness"?

AH: Before going in front of the magistrate, Robert told me that I will be thoroughly investigated by the FBI and so will my friends. I told him that I am worried about something that they might find. He asked me "what?" and I said "it's something that is legal in our country, but illegal in America." He asked "does it have to do with underage marriage?" I said no but that a friend of mine has two wives. Robert looked at me in surprise. He said "That's all you're worried about that the FBI is going to discover?" When I said "yes" he told me that polygamy is a state crime and not a federal crime so that even if it was discovered, the FBI wouldn't care about it.

JC: Did they ask you who your "contact" was regarding the device?

AH: No.

JC: Never asked you names?

AH: Not once.

JC: Did they ask you if you knew any of the 19 hijackers whose names were publicly identified quickly?

AH: If they did, I really didn't know any.

JC: Between the date you were first put in jail and the date the pilot came forward, were you in constant solitary confinement?

AH: I was in solitary confinement 24/7 during the entire period, with the exception of one hour. I was actually supposed to get one hour every day. But I was just in a bigger cell where I could exercise. It happened once in the 30 days.

JC: How often would Robert see you?

AH: Robert tried to see me twice a week. We talked about how he intended to defend me, or his strategy. I honestly didn't like it. Because if he could give a convincing argument that I *might* be "not guilty," it was not 100 percent saying that I was *actually innocent*. There's a big difference between the two, as you know.

JC: You only wanted a defense that showed you were actually innocent? Did you have an idea as to how to establish that?

AH: Yes. But I had absolutely no idea how to show innocence.

JC: So you weren't satisfied with his plan, but you didn't have a better one?

AH: Absolutely correct. His idea was simply this: He would argue that the device was mine, but would require the prosecutor to prove that it was going to be used on 9/11. So he would thereby cast a shadow of doubt. But it's not 100 percent. People would always have a doubt about me. Even after I was released, people would still say, "No, he was just a well-connected Egyptian who got out."

JC: How did you learn that the pilot came forward?

AH: (Long pause, sigh) It was the night of January 17th. I was told that I have to go to court, and I knew that I didn't have court scheduled for that day. So, when they came to get me in my cell, they told me that I *did* have court. I said "No I don't," but they said "Yes."

JC: Did these correction officers know what you were charged with?

AH: Absolutely. I was the "World Trade Center radio man." They knew.

JC: Did they mistreat you?

AH: They couldn't, and it really was enlightening. While I was being transferred from place to place, I was surrounded by six guards and a captain. Shackled. If you can imagine Hannibal Lector shackled, that's exactly how I was shackled. And a seventh with a video camera would record the entire process. I was instructed by Robert to speak with no one, and I took his instructions to heart. I spoke to none of my neighbors. But they spoke to each other, and it was interesting to hear. One guy asked another, "Why are they videotaping?" And the other said, "It's because of the guard with the tattoos. He took one of us, and he beat him up, I think he either broke his arm or did something with one of the sticks. And when his attorney saw it, he immediately told the prosecutor, 'You're going to release my client, and you better thank God that we are not suing you.'"

JC: Going back, so you were told you had court. Then what happened?

AH: I was shaking, and the guard with the tattoos asked me what was wrong. In my head I thought, "What's wrong with *you*, I'm scared for my life." But all I said was "I'm cold." So I'm taken to the U.S. marshal, who put me in a holding cell. I stayed there for three hours, trying to imagine what was going on? Why do I have court today? Is something up?

My head went back and forth with stories. First, I thought, it must be a mistake. Then I thought, why is this taking this long? At the end I was convinced they were going to bring me my brother, and would either get me to confess again that the device was mine, or they were going to frame my brother with something. I had no doubt about this.

Amazingly, the door opened and it was the U.S. marshal and I didn't see my brother. So I thought—okay, it was a mistake. The marshal said "Come on." So I did what I was now used to doing for 30 days—I gave him my hands held outward for him to cuff me. He told me "No, that won't be necessary." Not necessary? And he starts walking, and says, "Follow me." Now, I was always moving with a U.S. marshal behind me, and a marshal in front of me. Now they were entrusting me, the "martial arts master," to walk behind them?

He takes me to a room and turns me over to a gentlemen whom I later found out was *the* U.S. marshal for the district. He said "Please sit down."

I'm thinking, "*Please,* sit down"? He asked me my name, my age, my address, the number of scars I have. And he said "Okay, you can go." I just looked at him, "Go where?" He said, "You can leave." I had no idea what he was talking about.

He looked at the deputy and asked him, "Are we releasing the right guy?" And the deputy said "yes." And then he asked me the same questions again. So, he made a phone call. And then I heard the following: "What? He didn't attend his court today? You mean he has no idea?" And he hung up, and said, "Mr. Higazy, the real owner of the device came and you're free to go." I had no idea who the other person was, why his device was in my room's safe. I still had no idea that someone lied to the FBI and made the story up. I found all that out the next day when Robert and I spoke. He said, basically, check CNN.

JC: Fast forward ahead. Have you stayed in the United States from the time of your release until now?

AH: Not exactly. I stayed until I completed my scholarship. I wanted desperately to say to his face: "Agent Templeton, I got my scholarship!" I left America in 2004. The original condition for the scholarship was to remain in Egypt for two years. Those two years became nine or ten.

JC: It's hard to understand why you would choose to return to the United States after all this.

AH: My wife is American. And every time she would come to the U.S., I wasn't with her. It was actually quite interesting, because when my attorneys were finalizing the settlement of my lawsuit against the government, they wanted me to come here. They sent me a letter, which I presented to the U.S. embassy in Cairo, and at first I was given an okay. Two days later, I got a phone call telling me to come to the embassy. The person there said his boss won't approve it. I asked why and she said, "You speak English like an American, you're married to an American, and you have a masters' degree from the United States. Statistically speaking, if you're going to America, you're not coming back to Egypt."

I started asking people, "If this was the reason for them not wanting me to come to America, what should I do?" They said, "Apply for immigration. Your wife is American." This way, her family would not keep asking why I wasn't with her when she went to the U.S. to visit.

JC: Did you at any time or even now have anger against the United States?

AH: The United States? Never! I lived in Virginia from 1978 to 1982, and I lived again in Virginia from 1987 until 1991. I loved those eight years. I met wonderful people, I made great friends. I probably was naïve, but I believed Ronald Reagan when he called the Soviet Union the Evil Empire. I've said this to many people: Let's say you have befriended a bear and he absolutely loves you. He'll give you a kiss and you'll pet him, and everything's absolutely fine. Then when you're at the front end of the bear, someone comes and stabs the bear in the back with a knife. Now you're his friend. But remember, this is a very, very powerful creature, and you unfortunately are right in front of his face. Well, how do you think the bear's going to react? It'll hit you.

I was at the wrong place at the wrong time, and I look like the people who did this. But add to that, I wasn't worried. I was a law-abiding individual, and I wasn't doing anything wrong. I wasn't scared. The only thing that worried me was someone coming up and saying something about me, and that's exactly what happened.

When Agent Templeton made that threat to go after my family, it may have looked to some people like an empty threat. But absolutely not. My mother told me of a friend of hers whose son was living in the United States. Then he left here and returned to Egypt and everything was absolutely fine. His friend was married to an American. The friend and his wife got into a huge argument. So she accused him of being a member of Al Qaeda. And she reported him to the FBI, and he was arrested. Well, since the guy living in Egypt was his friend, they passed on the information to Egyptian security, and a platoon of armed soldiers were sent to arrest this guy. So no, the threat was very real.

JC: I asked you if you were angry at America. Are you angry at Agent Templeton?

AH: Agent Templeton and Ronald Ferry . . . if I never see them again, it will be too soon. Agent Templeton had no right to threaten my family! Yes, sure, you have your job to do, you are trying to find if this person is lying or not. You have your technology and if you believe in it so much, why the heck did you have to threaten me? Or does a person have to be under so much stress while taking a polygraph or else it isn't valid?

JC: But you're angry at what he proposed to do to your family and not what he proposed to do to you?

AH: I was in America. What's the worst they were going to do? As Judge Rakoff put it, kill me? If it's my time, it's my time.

JC: Have you ever met Judge Rakoff outside his courtroom?

AH: No, and I would love to. Hearing him yell at [Assistant U.S. Attorney] Dan Himmelfarb was, to me, confirmation that there is indeed justice.

JC: Are you angry at Ferry?

AH: Yes! He was trying to be the hero. You see, Ferry was a disgraced cop. He was a junkie, and that's why he worked as a security guard in the Millennium. He was trying to apply what they teach them at the police academy to make himself look good. When you see someone giving someone else something, you say it was drugs. Do we know these were drugs? No, but that's what they teach at the police academy. You try to make sure the claim sticks.

So for me, he found the transceiver in my room. Why not say it was in my safe? It sticks better. And the second he did this, there was really no way for me to get out.

JC: When he was indicted, did you attend the court proceedings against Ferry?

AH: Yes. I was really angry. His sentence was a joke. Weekends in prison.

JC: You probably don't know it, but the judge who sentenced Ferry is viewed as a very harsh sentencer.

AH: And he gave him a very light sentence.

JC: What do you think that's about?

AH: I'll say in the United States generally, not just New York, people would say that not all people of a particular group are responsible for what happens. And you have the other people who say, "Hey, kill 'em all, let God sort it out." Now, I really can't say anything about the judge; I don't know him. At that same time, I remember someone played a joke, and sent talcum powder to his own colleague at work. That person got many years in jail—for a prank. So, I honestly don't know.

JC: What would've happened in Egypt to someone who made a false accusation like the one made against you?

AH: (Sigh). I'm sorry, Mr. Cohen, I'd rather not answer that question.

JC: I think that in declining to answer that question you're saying an awful lot, aren't you?

I see you nodded—you wouldn't even say "yes" to my comment.

AH: Actually, I shrugged. For the record, I shrugged.

JC: You're an amazing man. Thank you.

4

Always Hope, Never Expectation

Kenneth F. Ireland, Jr.

I was groomed by the prison system to not care about what happened to people around me. I was only interested in myself, my own survival. . . . Prison is a hard place. I saw people assaulted in the most horrendous ways, and fall down right in front of me bleeding. I would just step over them, keep moving. None of my business.

—Kenneth F. Ireland, Jr., Milwaukee,
Wisconsin, June 28, 2016[1]

---

1. This interview took place as Mr. Ireland was traveling, at a hotel in Milwaukee, Wisconsin. Mr. Ireland would only agree to be interviewed if the author agreed to donate a portion of the proceeds of this book to the Community Partners in Action (www.cpa-ct. org), which will be done. As you will read in this interview, Mr. Ireland is a free man—a man who was exonerated—in large part because the Innocence Project, unsolicited, took an interest in his case.

As of this interview, Kenneth Ireland is 46 years old. He is driving across the country in his RV with his fiancée and two cats. Had you met him ten years ago, you would have met a completely different man—one with little hope that he would have left prison before his 54th birthday, maybe not even then. How did he get to where he is now? Ireland will be the first to tell you that his journey is not one he would want, for anyone—although, astonishingly, he doesn't even seem to want it for those who framed him.

Kenneth Ireland was just 17 years old when the police first questioned him about a murder in the small, working-class town of Wallingford, Connecticut, a town whose murder rate was one murder every ten years. And this was not just a murder—a 30-year-old mother of four was brutally raped and bludgeoned to death. When questioned, Ireland had no lawyer and no parent with him. The police lied to him about why they wanted to talk to him, and later about the strength of their case against him. Yet Ireland was insistent. They had the wrong man (boy?). He did not know the victim and had nothing to do with her murder.

After that first interview, the police visited Ireland periodically; they assured him that if he would only confess, he would get a lenient sentence. But Ireland repeated—he was not there and knew nothing that could help the police find the murderer. There was another man, Kevin Benefield, who should have been a suspect—indeed, *the* suspect. He knew the victim, and the police interviewed him shortly after the murder. Yet, the police never pursued him, even though his version as to where he was the night of the murder was somewhat different from the version told by his alibi witness—his girlfriend.

The case grew dormant. Ireland, a bit of a wild kid who had bounced around the streets, had had no trouble with the law. He got his GED (he had attended school only until eighth grade) and joined the National Guard. Ireland was ready to put his life on the straight and narrow. But a year after the murder, the media announced the state's offer of a $20,000 reward for anyone who had information leading to the killers. A couple, financially wanting, told the police that Ireland and another man, a friend of Ireland's, told them about the crime. A third witness said Ireland admitted to being the murderer, although she admitted she was drunk and that her memory was unreliable.

Imagine—in a town with almost no murders, the police had no leads and no real suspects one year after a notably vicious crime until these witnesses came forward. More than a year after the murder, Ireland—just 18—was arrested two weeks before he was to ship out to Fort Benning. There was no physical evidence, no fingerprints, nothing other than the testimony of these three people.

Ireland couldn't make bail, so he spent the two years waiting for and during trial at the county lock-up. The judge made rulings during trial that Ireland and his lawyer said impermissibly limited him [Ireland] from a full and complete cross-examination of the state's witnesses (those rulings were ultimately upheld on appeal). At the start of the Thanksgiving holiday weekend, the jury told the judge they were deadlocked, 6–6. The judge, however, insisted they each go home for the holiday and think about the evidence and the trial. Within hours after they returned to court on Monday, Ireland was found guilty by all 12 jurors. The judge sentenced him to 50 years, sternly scolding him because he showed no remorse. Yes, Ireland was punished more severely because he showed no remorse for a crime it was ultimately proved he did not commit.

Ireland was adamant that he was innocent. He appealed his conviction, and also brought a second action (a habeas corpus proceeding) seeking release. He was shot down each time in large part because DNA evidence did not rule him out. The murder was committed in 1986 and the testing and use of DNA was in its nascent stages. Ireland understood that his best defense was that his DNA would be found nowhere on the victim. How, then, did he react when, after his habeas proceeding, the lab report came back: "Not enough sample for testing. Sample consumed during testing."? Did he believe, at that point, that it was over and that hope was gone; that he would not be free before he served all of his 50 years, a term that would have let him leave prison at the age of 69?

Let's look at Ireland's life in prison. County lock-up, it turns out, was mild compared to what would be Ireland's new home. Because Ireland was convicted of a violent rape and murder, and even though he was only 20 years old, he was placed in a maximum security prison where his fellow inmates were, in fact, rapists and murderers. Ireland was locked in a six foot by eight foot cell with another inmate, and a toilet. Jail house fights, beatings, stabbings, and fires (often a mattress; once a person) were commonplace. At one prison, when he went to see doctors and dentists, he did so with a guard holding a Taser at his neck.

How did he handle his new reality? Ireland took advantage of whatever educational programs the system offered, but did he join a gang to be "protected" by those stronger? Or did he make sure he was the protector? Did he fight to prove he could defend himself? Did he employ a vehicle that other prisoners do—that is, "find God," and use such a belief system as a path to ease his torment? Did his family visit, or were they embarrassed; did they leave town now that a very public rapist and murderer was one of their own?

Ireland was angry, but at whom? And who had he become while in prison? Here was a kid—an innocent kid—raised by prisoners in the system. What did it teach him about survival, and what he had to do to survive?

Then, in 2007, the Connecticut Innocence Project heard about his case from a local paralegal. While they were looking into it, Ireland was transferred to a medium security prison in early 2009. At least in his world, things weren't that bad. Did he want to get his hopes up yet again with the Innocence Project or, as before, did he continue to manage his own expectations? At least, in Ireland's mind, there was no more DNA evidence to test, no physical evidence to prove he did not rape and murder, no evidence to show that he was "actually innocent," in the terminology of the law. Was it worth it—mentally, emotionally—to go through the steps of questioning the evidence once again?

And then one day, something clicked. There was one more place where DNA could be found. And Ireland realized it while reading the transcript of his trial, something he had read time and time and time again. But this time he put it together—and his lawyers were able to demonstrate that Benefield, the man the police interviewed back in 1986, committed the crime. Now, the reality is that that didn't mean that Ireland wasn't there, only that Benefield was. To their credit, the prosecution did not try to claim Benefield and Ireland committed the crime together. Even so, did they fight Ireland's attempt to be released, to be exonerated, arguing that the jury's verdict must stand? Did any one of them ever apologize to Ireland, or admit that they just got it wrong 20-plus years earlier? And if they had, would it have made a difference?

In 2009, Ireland was exonerated, let free. He walked out of the courtroom with no wallet, no money, no identification. He had never seen a cell phone, or a fax machine for that matter. He had heard of the Internet, but had no frame of reference to even imagine what could be found "online." How did he react to this new life—one where he could go where he wanted when he pleased? He could not have imagined a life where the guards did not tell him when to wake, eat, shower, and sleep. And what was it like the first time he looked in a mirror? Did he even recognize himself, literally or figuratively?

Ireland sought to remake his life but who were his friends—the boys he hung with as a kid, whom he hadn't seen in two decades? Or were they the prisoners, the murderers he had grown up with? Does he keep in touch with those he served time with? And what does he tell potential employers about those 20 years missing from his résumé?

At one point after Ireland's release, the governor of Connecticut did something fairly remarkable—he put Ireland on the parole board. Ireland became one of the people who would decide whether to let convicts be released prior to the end of their term. Was his approach different from other members of the board? Did prisoners appeal to him in a way that showed they knew his past?

Years after his release, Ireland made a claim to the State of Connecticut for money damages as a result of his wrongful incarceration—for loss of earnings, loss of liberty, and pain and suffering. In essence, for being innocent, yet locked up for 21 years, and in particular the years during which most people finish school, get a job, get married, start a life.

Kenneth Ireland is putting—likely, has put—his life in order. He tells us about his journey, and the perspective he brings that now allows him peace.

The Dialogue[2]

JC: Mr. Ireland, we've never spoken except for a five-minute call when I tried to persuade you to do this interview. You had originally turned me down. I've looked at some documents and a few short interviews of

---

2. Because they have been travelling cross country without a final destination and this interview accordingly took place in Milwaukee, Wisconsin, with Mr. Ireland's fiancée present. One wonders whether the presence, during a probing interview, of a third-party loved one impacts the manner in which questions are asked, or answers are given.

you. And I have seen your testimony before the Connecticut Office of the Claims Commissioner.

I must say, I don't get it. You've gone through a virtually incomparable atrocity. You were imprisoned in maximum security jails for 21 years for something you simply didn't do. While in jail I'm sure you observed other prisoners turn to God or Allah or Jesus to help get through the night— accepting, as it were, that "this is the path that God chose for me, and so this is God's 'test' that I must endure." Or they spent all their time as gym rats in the weight room until their muscles had muscles. Some, pardon me, fucked their brains out to deal with the constant misery. Others simply gave up and became slaves, or even sex slaves, in order to be protected by gangs or stronger prisoners.

When I listen to the recordings of your interviews or testimony, however, you seem to have no affect; your affect seems as flat as a pancake. You show no anger. No passion. You almost smile or even giggle a couple times during your videotaped testimony when asked about the inhumanity of what you had to endure.

How can that be? No anger? Absolutely no passion, about all this?

KFI: I've always seen anger as a wasted emotion when it comes to my situation, believing that the State of Connecticut couldn't care less if I'm angry. The prosecutor who did this to me doesn't care if I'm angry. So the only person I'd be hurting by being angry would be me. To me, it's sort of "get over it and move on."

There's no doubt it was a horrendous time. And it was over an extended period of time that I saw extreme amounts of violence. But, still, I came out the other side, and I was just so incredibly happy and relieved to be out that I didn't have time to dwell on the negativity of what happened. I was just so focused on moving forward and enjoying to the fullest that piece of life that I have left: the past is the past. I sort of compartmentalized the different parts of my life. I had my childhood before prison, my prison time, and my time after prison. And I've always been focused on just getting through the day and lining up the next day. Just enjoying life to its fullest.

Prison was terrible and horrible. And every moment that was beyond my control was horrific. Like when the administration tells you when to shower. When to eat. When to turn off your lights. When to go here, when there. Those were beyond my control. But in the moments that were in my control, I had fun, if you can imagine that. You're in prison. There's nothing you can do about it. But you're playing sports or you're reading a book, or you're studying. So you just have to work with it. Anything that I could do to enlighten my brain—I would take full advantage of that.

JC: But you were framed, right? The police didn't go after the real killer even though they interviewed him. And you had a judge that went off on you at sentence for showing no remorse for a crime you couldn't possibly show remorse for because you didn't do it. You were absolutely innocent! In all those years, you weren't angry at these people?

KFI: Let me make this clear: when I was in prison I was the angriest person imaginable. Extremely angry. I channeled a lot of anger through sports and reading and education. But I got into a lot of fights. I was of the mindset that if the administration wanted to keep me a prisoner, I'd make them pay any way I could. I would break anything I could get my hands on. I'd start fires in the grass, in the trash. I'd break windows. I'd flush gallons of floor wax down the toilet—or scrape paint off the walls. Anything to cost them money. I was an angry person.

JC: Wouldn't that cause reprisals within the institution?

KFI: Yeah. But you pick your fights, right? You pick your moments where you could not be noticed, or get away with things. Or you just take your lumps.

JC: You fought with fellow inmates?

KFI: Yes.

JC: When you were incarcerated in Connecticut what was the demographic of the prison population? You're Caucasian. What was the percentage of Caucasians versus blacks and Hispanics?

KFI: I was definitely in the minority. I was also one of the youngest men in the adult prison system at the time. And not only in for felony murder, but also for sexual assault. So I had all kinds of tick-boxes against me. I basically had to go in fighting and present myself as wildly aggressive. I firmly believe that there's always an easier target. So you don't make yourself the easiest target and you pick your battles. In prison, it's weird—you have to re-up your reputation like every six months or so. You have to get into a fight, or mouth off to a correction officer. Or do something that shows you as a bad ass.

But after, say, six months, people forget and might try and target you again. So you have to keep re-upping. You have to talk aggressive, move aggressive. You have to be confrontational all the time. It's extremely exhausting, but it's a survival mechanism in prison.

JC: And you could do that—engage in that activity in prison and not risk getting killed?

KFI: You choose your battles. The Connecticut prison system, when I went in, was probably one of the more violent ones in the country. It had the influxes of all the gangs. Arrests for drive-by shootings, for assassinations, for drug dealing—whatever the gangs are doing. They all get put into this little microcosm of a prison. So now you have this diverse population put into this one tiny little prison—absolute chaos for the first ten or so years.

The gang violence was so over the top, you couldn't go a day without seeing someone stabbed, or beaten up. Sometimes one inmate would be beaten by many people. People were murdered in prison. The emergency medical helicopter came to the prison almost once a week. The staff was assaulted every day. And the staff just wanted to get home safely, so they basically took a step back to many little infractions that were going on. Except, those little infractions always lead to bigger ones. And gang violence.

So it was a horrible, horrible place until around 1994 when they started "control unit prisons." There, you're in a unit with 96 other guys and you don't move with anyone other than those 96 guys.

JC: We're sitting here and you tell me that since your release, you've managed to move on with your life. You look forward rather than backward. But you tell it like a journalist, not someone who endured it. I've not endured it and yet it's hard for me to listen to it. Yet, you seem to have no problem talking about the past, suggesting something like "Yeah, I had a bad couple of weeks." You're even almost snickering now when I say that.

KFI: Look, it was a bad 21 years. But I'm so happy that I'm out that I look back on it as an "experience." My life really was terrible. But when they released me, it's like something switched in my brain. It went from confrontational and violent and real anger to who I am now. Just everything is—I'm all about the future; I'm all about positivity. I'm all about doing the best I can in life, and having as much fun as I can, because I'm a firm believer that we're only alive for just so long. That large portion of my life is already gone, and it's in the past. So I have this short period of time in front of me, and I'm going to enjoy every minute of it. I will not be affected by my past.

JC: Fair enough. But when you talk about your anger while in "hell" . . . it was hell, right?

KFI: Right.

JC: When you talk about that, you talk about that anger as a pragmatic "mechanism" that you employed to get by. Getting into fights to show a violent side that enabled you to not be harmed. To present yourself as someone to not mess with. That doesn't seem a genuine anger, but rather a methodical anger.

KFI: I had a genuine anger. And that's separate from an anger in feeling sorry for myself. I didn't commit the crime, obviously—and I was pushed down this road, taken to trial, maligned in the press. I was called all kinds of names by the prosecutor and judge. And the media portrayed me as this horrible person. Family members of mine actually left Connecticut because they shared the same last name. It was a large, very public, case in Connecticut. And so along with the anger I felt humiliation. I was feeling sorry for myself. And then, on top of that, I had to portray myself as more violent than I actually was, simply to get by.

You know the main players in the prison as soon as you get there. You don't mess with the gang leaders. And even the smaller gang members—you mess with one of them, you're messing with all of them. So you really have to pick your battles. And so if you need to present yourself as aggressive, you need to do something aggressive. You try to find someone who's offending you in prison that's not "connected" in any way. And, frankly, someone who's not bigger than you. And you have a scrap with him. And word gets around.

Or you have a go at it with one of the correction officers. Word gets around. You have to carry yourself as if to say "Don't mess with me because I will defend myself at all costs." I was in a position where I wouldn't have hesitated to stab someone. I wouldn't have hesitated to kill someone to defend my life. It wouldn't have crossed my mind to *not* do that.

JC: At the Claims Commission, you testified about fires in prison.

KFI: That's back at my early time in the prison—from 1988 to 1994 when the prison was wide open. Fires were an everyday thing. Inmates wouldn't like what would happen at a football game, so they'd start a fire. Burning mattresses, burning blankets. You'd have to stay in your cell and the whole unit would fill up with smoke. The officers would come and put the fire out, but then it was business as usual again.

So fires were every day, like gang violence. It was nothing to leave the chow hall and you'd see a trail of blood down the hallway toward the medical unit. You'd just walk around it. Or there'd be a body lying in the hallway and you'd just step over it and keep on moving: "It's none of my business; I'm moving on." The nature of the beast of being in prison.

At one time I was in segregation and an individual two or three cells down from me was burned alive. Some kind of gang violence. He was lit on fire and burned to death. I couldn't do anything but watch it.

JC: But you knew who the perpetrators were.

KFI: I know who they are now. I didn't at the time. I ran across them in prison after they had been charged and convicted of the crime. I'm actually friends with them, if you can believe it.

This brings up another point I've always made. Soon after I was released from prison, I called up someone I knew and said, "Do you want to hang out, maybe get a beer or something." And the response was something like "I'm busy, maybe you should go hang out with one of your other friends." And it occurred to me that all of my friends are in prison. All my life-long friends are in prison. I grew up—*I was raised*—in prison, from age 18 to 39. So everybody I've known, for the majority of my life, was from prison. There's men in prison that I genuinely call my friends. They might be horrible people. They may have done horrible crimes. But on a personal day-to-day level, they became friends.

In prison, when you're serving a long stretch, you tend to hang around with people that are also doing long stretches. If I'm doing 50 years I'm not really going to pal around with someone doing five years, because they're going to be gone in the blink of an eye.

JC: Five years being the "blink of an eye" to someone doing 50.

KFI: Absolutely. And people doing large amounts of time, are almost always there for murder. A bizarre moment in my life when I realized how surreal this was.

JC: So when you were doing the 50, assume you observed someone totally innocent engaged in an altercation. And another guy—you knew them both—tried to burn him alive. Would you have ratted?

KFI: Nope. Anything that happened in the prison that didn't involve me was none of my business.

JC: What if the "perp" called your mother a horrible name, like whore, and the victim had tried to defend your mother's honor?

KFI: Tough question. If I had a problem with someone who may have insulted my mother then in my mind the issue is strictly between him and I. If someone would've jumped in to aid me and it was none of his business, then if he gets victimized by the aggressor it would've been somebody else's problem.

JC: How about now on the outside world?

KFI: Whole different story.

JC: You're in a normal life.

KFI: I'm in a normal everyday environment situation. If I saw some horrific crime taking place I wouldn't even hesitate to either intervene or get some kind of emergency response to . . .

I was groomed by the prison system to not care about what happened to people around me. I was only interested in myself, my own survival. And this is the prison mentality—bred into you being raised in prison. Prison is a hard place. I saw people assaulted in the most horrendous ways, and fall down right in front of me bleeding. I would just step over them, keep moving. None of my business.

JC: And all this even though you were a complete innocent in prison?

KRI: Doesn't matter! I was there for more than half of my life before I was released. From age 18 to 39—a couple weeks shy of 40—basically the prime of your life. That's where you build your career, your family. You're making that nest egg for retirement. But I was raised in prison, basically by prisoners and prison staff. Everything I knew was violence.

And if any staff would have asked me, I would have told them "Get away from me. I have nothing to say to you. I don't know anything." You have the survival part—where I can't say anything because that would jeopardize my own life. Because there's no such thing as saying something in prison to a staff member and it not getting back to the gangs. Staff members aren't a hundred percent reliable, right? You have some who are there for the right reason—doing their jobs. But there's always the percentage doing nefarious things, involved with nefarious people. Prison is a business—let's not get that wrong. And in every business, there's a certain degree of corruption.

JC: When you were released, you took all of your papers from the case and transcripts and burned them, page by page, in the backyard, right?

KFI: I went down to Virginia to visit my mother. But I took the case file and we just . . . one night we had like a barrel fire and some family members and I sat there and, page by page, burned them.

JC: Why?

KFI: I think it was a symbolic thing—sort of therapeutic. Not only for myself but for my family members. My mother carried this case file around with her, when she moved to New Jersey and Virginia and North Carolina. It was part of her property that she would move from location to location. So it was therapeutic for myself, for her, for my other family members, to sit there and just burn it.

JC: I picked up a book last night having absolutely nothing to do with any of this—it's called *In Praise of Forgetfulness*. The title caught me. Have you tried in any way to forget, maybe to suppress in your own mind, those 21 years?

KFI: I don't try to. Sometimes I'm not mindful of it, and sometimes I am. When you're doing such a long period of time, days, weeks, years blur together. I measure my time sort of in five-year periods, because every five years I'd end up getting moved to a different prison. I started at Sommers maximum security prison, say from 1990–1994, because I was in county jail for two years. I went from there to MacDougall with the control units, when they were trying to break the gangs up. And I was there for five years. Then I was moved to Virginia for overcrowding for five years. Then I came back to MacDougall. Then I went to the medium security because I had done so much of my time. So in my mind it's not day-for-day or year-for-year.

JC: But you were in a "super max" at one point—where, I think you described, guards held a Taser to your neck when you were being examined by the prison dentist. What was that like?[3]

---

3. Author's note: This question and answer were given via email after the interview.

KFI: That was such a terrible time. Due to overcrowding in the Connecticut system, a large number of prisoners were transferred with no notice to a mountaintop super max in the deepest parts of southwestern Virginia. The staff would fire live ammo shotgun rounds inside the unit for the slightest provocations. And, as stated, whenever you had contact with civilian staff, including medical personnel, a corrections officer and backup would hold you in an arm bar hold and the other would hold a Taser to either your neck or your wrist.

JC: I can't imagine what that was like. I've read that when you were finally released you took a long look in the mirror and you saw an "old man."

KFI: The day I was released from prison, we were at a restaurant and the whole back wall was a mirror. In prison you get these plastic mirrors. It's just plastic—no glass, for obvious reasons—with a silver coating on it. Brushing your teeth, combing your hair, washing your face, shaving . . . it's all done in this little, six-by-four-inch plastic mirror. Never a true image. And that's the only way I could see myself beginning when I was 18 years old. So when I was released, somehow in my mind I was still this 18-year-old kid. Yes, I knew I had some grey hair and I knew I had wrinkles and stuff; but it didn't really register because in my mind I was still this 18-year-old kid. And so we got to this restaurant the day I was released.

JC: I guess you hadn't been in a restaurant in 21 years either.

KFI: Right. And I was with the Connecticut Innocence Project people and my family—about 20 of us. The back wall was a mirror but I didn't realize it. I was on sensory overload with all the colors and objects and things I had never seen, or things I hadn't seen in so long. So I walked by the mirror and I happened to see a person that wasn't with our party. And I wondered, "Who is this old guy?" And it sort of clicked: "Oh, crap that's me." I was shocked by how much older I looked in this crisp, sharp technicolor image. It took me aback.

JC: A clergyman would gladly create a sermon out of that—that you're released from hell and, now, in the cool light of the sun and you see something about yourself that you never saw before. Did you see something about yourself different from the young kid first arrested 21 years earlier?

KFI: Well, I recognized—literally the moment they took the handcuffs off me in the courtroom—that it was different. And this is how I've always described it. Something in my brain switched from this defensive mode of being in prison, the confrontational mode, to "I don't ever want to have to fight again." I'm in a situation now where I'm free. I can walk away and avoid confrontations. If somebody says something to me I don't like . . . I don't have to confront it.

Now, if somebody says something offensive to me, who cares? "That's your opinion. You're entitled to it." I don't have to fight you—you and your boys aren't going to come after me with a sharpened piece of steel. So being released, it was just a natural transformation into probably the character that I truly have always been underneath but was so buried underneath this defensive, angry, aggressive person.

JC: When did you really believe you were free? When those handcuffs came off?

KFI: It was odd because when I was in the courtroom, my lawyer said her piece. The prosecutor said his piece. And the judge said "We're going to let him go." They didn't exonerate me that day. They just released me on my promise to appear and then two weeks later I had to go back for the actual exoneration.

So when he said, take the handcuffs off him, it's such a rare occasion that somebody is exonerated or released like that that the sheriff said, "I can't just let him go. I have to bring him back, we have to process him out of the prison, we have to do paper work, photographs." The judge said, "No, he's free to go." And the sheriff says, "I have to at least call my boss." And the judge says "No, he's free to go!"

And my attorney said quietly to the sheriff, "We'll sit down and wait, go make your phone call. It's all been arranged." And the judge sees me still sitting there, and my attorney explains that we don't want the sheriff to get in trouble, that he can call his office. And the judge says "Well if he gets in trouble I'll exonerate him too."

So we all had a laugh and they took the handcuffs off me and I walked out the door. I was at the top of the stairs of the courthouse and it was surreal—I keep saying that word—the overwhelming information coming into my brain. I can go down these stairs and nobody can stop me, or can I, is what I am really thinking. I'm so used to being told where to go and how to go. You look at the photographs of me at that release. I'm talking to people, but the entire time I'm looking around. I'm not looking at anyone. I'm sort of just dazed.

JC: You talked about how when you were released, all of your anger and aggression sort of faded away. What if, right now, I punched you in the face and called Jennifer a horrible name, what would you do?

KFI: You'd be in a whole lot of trouble. If somebody put their hands on me or I felt like I was physically threatened, or her life was physically threatened, I'd revert back to . . .

JC: That guy?

KFI: I'd revert to what I know: kill or be killed.

JC: I saw part of the video of you being interrogated by the police when you were a young kid, just 16 or 17. You were understandably naïve at that age. These detectives were basically accusing you of murder, although they tried to dance around it.

KFI: You have the disappointment of how a situation like that is handled, because that's the routine technique for police interrogations. The police can legally lie to a suspect to obtain information. So it's irresponsible. I was a kid. I had no guardians with me, nor given the option to. I was offered the option to have an attorney, although I told them I didn't want one: "I'm here to cooperate because I've done nothing." So they interrogated me for maybe eight hours. And it wasn't until they became belligerent toward me and started laying their cards on the table actually accusing me of the murder—that's when I said I'll exercise my right to an attorney. They ended the interview and called my parents who came and got me.

Since I've been released I've been talking at many colleges and law firms just going in and telling my story. Especially the law schools. I am trying to enlighten the kids that they shouldn't get that tunnel vision that the police had or that the prosecutor had with me.

JC: During your claims testimony, your lawyer asked you whether any of the detectives ever apologized to you. You answered with only one word: "No." Did you ever think at any point after you were released to call the detective or write him and say: "Look what the fuck you did to me. Don't you have the decency to apologize?"

KFI: No. Never occurred to me. As far as the detective was concerned, there were bad detective practices that took place in my case and that take place throughout the country. The technique they use manipulates people, especially young people. They try to elicit false confessions, which they didn't get from me. I don't think they were trying to frame me or anything. I think the detectives actually thought I was guilty. So I just think it was poor training. The entire police force of Wallingford didn't do a terrible job. They had an evidence team that did an amazing job collecting evidence. They videotaped everything.

JC: So why didn't they bring the charge against Kevin Benefield? As far as you know, did they take DNA from him?

KFI: Yes, and they used that DNA to convict him many, many years later.

JC: You mean they did the collection, they just didn't match it?

KFI: You have an evidence team that collects evidence, but then you have the detectives that have to follow up on that evidence. And the detectives didn't do a thorough job in following up. Then, because it was unsolved for a year I guess, the then-governor of Connecticut set a reward. At the time, 1987 or 1988, it was substantial—I think $20,000 or $40,000. So two individuals came forward and falsely implicated me and my friends. They're the nefarious ones. They're the ones that created this whole problem to where the police switched gears from what they were investigating.

JC: You haven't confronted them?

KFI: What am I going to say to them, really?

JC: A waste of time?

KFI: Right. What would I say: I'm pissed off at you? You did a horrible thing? You ruined my life? What would they possibly do? They'd either say, "We don't care," or "We're so sorry," and start crying. Either way it doesn't help me. I don't need an apology—I'm not looking for any redemption from them.

JC: Who were the relatives who left Connecticut to avoid association with you?[4]

KFI: No one relative came forward and boldly said that they were leaving the state because I ruined the family name. Yet one-by-one all of the

---

4. Author's note: This question and answer were given via email after the interview.

relatives that shared a last name with me moved out of state before my trial was done.

JC: When you were imprisoned over the 21 years, did you tell other inmates that you were innocent?

KFI: Every single one.

JC: What did they say? "Who's kidding who? The jails are full of innocent people."

KFI: Right. But there are prisoners who will tell you straight out: "Oh, I'm absolutely guilty. I did it." My crime would come up occasionally—that I was in for a sexual assault. And they'd say "You're in for a sexual assault, we don't want to have anything to do with you." And I'd say, "Well listen, I didn't do it, if that means anything to you. If not, screw you, keep moving."

JC: But they'd basically conclude that you're full of baloney, right?

KFI: Right. And people in prison—they're typically not honest people. People in prison are there for a reason. You have your innocent people in there, but it's a microscopic percentage of prisoners. There is one person . . . I've known him and his co-defendant my entire time in prison, from the day I came in to the day I left and I still go visit when I'm in the area. I'm convinced as much as I can be convinced (being a doubter), that they are innocent. And they're going through the process that I went through with the Connecticut Innocence Project. However, their case isn't a cut and dry DNA case like mine.

JC: Let's talk about the DNA. You were basically convicted before law enforcement had the ability to track DNA the way that it does now. But DNA was still an issue.

KFI: When the crime happened, DNA was the stuff of science fiction. I'm sure top scientists knew what it was but it hadn't trickled down to the local police forces. It was this fairy-tale stuff that people talked about. By the time I'd gotten to trial about two years after I was arrested, people knew a little bit more about it and the police had sent out the evidence to be tested for DNA. But it was in the early ages of DNA when it was the very basic tests. And it came back, and it said "not enough sample for accurate testing." And so the state tied in evidence that showed that the person they were looking for was a non-secretor, which I am, but so is, like 20 or 30 percent of the world's population. And they had no physical evidence, but they used that—the non-secretor—as physical evidence. And that's what they used to convince the jury. They had no actual physical evidence.

Then in 1994, I had a habeas petition in. And we are talking about the difference in testing from 1990 to 1994, which was huge. My lawyer was able to get a swab from the evidence kit and it was inconclusive. "Not enough sample for testing. Sample consumed during testing." So I was just devastated. Then, in roughly early 2007, the Connecticut Innocence Project sent me a letter saying that they had heard about my case. The Project in Connecticut is associated with the public defenders' office, and they had heard about my case and they wanted to review it. I said, "Absolutely, I've got nothing else to lose. I'll help in any way I can."

JC: What could you have done?

KFI: So part of examining my case was seeing what could be found for testing for DNA. I was reading my trial transcript again. They were talking to a medical examiner, probably the guy who did the autopsy. My attorney was asking him how do they go about examining evidence, blood evidence, because everything was blood type back then. And he said that they take the smears from the rape kit and they put it on a piece of glass and they put another piece of glass, a slide, and they look at it under a microscope. I had read that, I don't know how many times I had read that. But somehow it clicked in my mind. This time I read it and I said "Where is that glass slide?" It was nowhere in any of the evidence logs and it wasn't put into evidence at trial.

So I furiously wrote a letter to my attorney. She called the state medical examiner and said "Do you have this 20-year-old or 22-year-old slide?" And he had it in his evidence locker. So she was like: "Don't move. Don't do anything with it. The police are on the way." She called the Wallingford police department and the detective over there, very cooperative with us, went and got the slide, brought it to the new Connecticut lab where they do the stuff now and they tested it and they got a hit on Benefield. And it basically exonerated me and my two friends, who they also said committed the crime, even though I was the only one who was prosecuted. One guy drowned in a boating accident. They never prosecuted the other guy.

JC: I'm not trying to undercut your exoneration and, yes, it did decimate their case. But it doesn't really exonerate you in the sense that it doesn't say that you weren't there. It says somebody else was there, right?

KFI: Yes, the state could have come forward and said, well it was four people there. But their entire case was based on the two people testifying and implicating me and the other two people. That was their case because they had no physical evidence on me at all.

JC: Sounds to me like you "got through the night" by basically managing your expectations over the 21 years.

KFI: When I was first arrested my brother-in-law gave me some advice that has stuck with me my entire life. He said "Hope for the best but expect the worst." I'm sure that's a popular saying, but that was the first time I had heard it. And it stuck with me. You can't expect the best when you're in prison. I was investigated, arrested, I went through trial, I was convicted, went through my appeal, went through a habeas . . . had I been expecting the best all those times, my morale would have been destroyed, right?

JC: You'd have been deflated.

KFI: Right. So you take a defensive position. And it's probably a defense mechanism, like nothing good ever happens to me. My life absolutely sucks and I'm gonna be shot down at every point I come to so I don't ever expect to get out of prison. I'm going fight the case the entire time and do everything I can legally, but I don't expect anything out of it, because why would I? The law is stacked against people. The prosecutor holds all the power. You get prosecutors with egos; you get judges with egos; they won't admit their mistakes. I was lucky enough to be in a situation where we confronted them with indisputable evidence. And they had to admit their mistake. But I don't think they would ever admit their mistake had they not been confronted with indisputable evidence.

JC: So if someone was just convicted and he came to you as his counselor, as it were, what would be your advice?

KFI: I would give the advice I give my friend now—fight it every step of the way. Do everything you can legally to fight this, but don't go to bed at night thinking you're going to get out tomorrow. That's just going to drive you mad.

JC: So the current governor in Connecticut, Dannel Malloy, pulls a "righteous" move. He puts you on the parole board after your release. Now, the mechanism of the parole board is to basically demand remorse from people who want release. How long did you sit on the parole board before you resigned (to travel around the country)?

KFI: Fifteen months, hundreds of cases in that time.

JC: Of the hundreds, how many tried to show remorse?

KFI: Most of them. But there were cases where guys would say "I didn't do it, I'm innocent."

JC: And you thought they were lying, right?

KFI: No. I knew everything about their case, but I didn't know enough about whether they're telling the truth or not. I had read their case files, the police reports, their trial transcripts, their post-conviction stuff. But when they sit in front of me and say "I didn't do it," I'd say, "Listen, whether you did it or not, that's been done in the court, that's something you're fighting in court. This is a parole board, all right? You're telling me you're innocent but that's a whole different arena. I have to go by what the court handed down; you're convicted of this. Now my job, as per the appointment by the governor, is to determine if you've conducted yourself in a manner in prison that warrants an earlier release, and you've shown enough remorse for your crime."

And we always take the statements of the victims into account. They're a huge portion of it. If the victims don't show up or show no interest, then I can work with someone on the not showing remorse part of it, if they conducted themselves in a manner showing that they're ready for release . . .

JC: But isn't the readiness for release partly based on whether the prisoner is remorseful, whether he fully recognizes and appreciates what he did?

KFI: That's part of it, but there's also a sense of change. Have you changed in your time in prison? Can you convince me that you're beyond what sent you to prison, that you want to be a participating member of society and not come back to prison. The governor in Connecticut is all about second chances, a second chance society. He's about paroles, pardons, give people a chance. So we took that cue. That's what was expected of us.

So we were trying to get people out. And if you came forward and did all the right things, and you had the right setup outside, the support outside, you had community support, social activities outside, you had done everything you could inside to better yourself, you took advantage of the programming, whether it's drug programming, sex-treatment programming, whatever the programming was, if you took advantage of that, and you did your little educational piece if you needed it and you had your exit plan solid, we're trying to get you out. We wanted to give you that chance. But, we also took into account criminal history.

I've read somewhere that murderers have the lowest recidivism rate. People can argue it's because they don't get out, right? But usually from my experience, murders happen, it's a crime of passion.

JC: It's a one-shot deal.

KFI: You've lost control and you've done something horrible. The chances of that happening again or you not learning from that are probably slim. So I believe the recidivism rate for violent murder is a lot lower. Unless they're serial killers or gang bangers or something like that.

JC: So when you sat on the three-person parole board panels obviously you're the only person who has been convicted and falsely convicted. Were the others deferential to you in terms of your personal experience?

KFI: Everybody was their own person. And if they weren't gonna budge, they weren't gonna budge. And that's what we loved about it. If you made up your mind we don't want you to be swayed, because that's not fair.

JC: Your own case was not a death row case?

KFI: It could have been.

JC: I have spoken to one man, John Thompson of Louisiana, who had been on death row, but was completely innocent. He was exonerated, after decades in prison. I listened to him and even though he is out of jail, he is angry. Really angry. What do you think about that anger? A waste of time?

KFI: People have to deal with it their own way. For myself, I just don't have time for anger, I really don't.

JC: So if you had those 21 years of prime time back, what would you have done with those 21 years?

KFI: People always ask me what kind of person would I be had I not been in prison. I can't answer that. I was so young. I was gearing up to go to the National Guard and to get the college scholarship. I had a troubled youth. I was a street kid. I was always in trouble when I was a kid. So I had turned the corner. I didn't have a clear enough picture as a child to really map it out. So I have no idea where I could have been. I could have gone two ways. I could have been a rocket scientist or I could have been in and out of prison my whole life. I wasn't afforded that opportunity.

JC: What is it you want to do now?

KFI: I just want to enjoy life. I don't want stress. I don't want schedules. I don't want expectations of me. I just want to be left alone. And go and see all the things I've only read about.

JC: What "bad stuff" did you take out of the institution? For example, I read that for a period of time you would sleep in a closet.

KFI: Yes, that was for a short period of time when I was first released. I had gotten an apartment and I sort of kept myself barricaded in the apartment at night. I don't know why—maybe an irrational fear. When you're in prison, you're in a cell. And the correctional officers would just come into your cell any time they want and just tear your cell up and take you away in handcuffs and you'd say "What the hell are you doing?" And they'd put you on a bus and send you to another state. That happened to me once. They just rushed my cell in the middle of the night, handcuffed me, and dragged me off to Virginia, dropping me in one of the worst prisons you could ever imagine. And I had no say in it.

So you have this fear carried over. And I'm still extremely guarded. I don't talk to strangers. I don't trust people. So I'm a very guarded person and make sure the doors are locked tight. I make sure the windows are always locked—especially at night, when you're vulnerable. I'm always in that protective mode.

JC: Any other idiosyncrasies?

KFI: When I get into stressful situations I really get kind of defensive. I don't like stress at all because it puts me into that . . . "I've gotta fight it" kind of a thing. I was seeing a counselor when I got out. She said I had "oppositional defiant disorder." You tell me I can't do something, and I'll be damned if I'm not gonna do it.

JC: What was the transition like—leaving jail and coming into a world that had really changed from when you went in?

KFI: It was a completely different world. No one had computers or cell phones. Fax machines had come into and out of style before I even got out. I still have never seen a fax machine. I had to learn how to use debit cards; I had to learn how to do online stuff. I had never seen the Internet.

In terms of assimilating into the world, I kind of jumped into it feet first. I got a job almost immediately. I took my experiences from prison and I used them to get a job. I found an alternative school in Bloomfield, Connecticut. It was all expelled kids going to this alternative school. So I went to them with this experience in life. I brought to the kids the tools I learned in prison, how to deal with these stressful situations. Because a lot of these kids are from poor, broken homes. So there's conflict resolution I could bring to them. How to disentangle yourself from these conflicts. How to separate your ego from confrontations and use that to your advantage. Don't let someone have control over your emotions. If I let you make me angry, I give you control over my emotions. I refuse to do that.

JC: You've obviously done well following your exoneration and release. But if you had just maxed out after 21 years rather than being exonerated, do you think your attitude would have been different in terms of your assimilation into society?

KFI: I don't think it would have been different. I distinctly remember that I didn't care about the money and I didn't care about saving my name. I didn't care about exoneration. I just wanted out—that's all I wanted. I said to the Innocence Project, basically, "Just get me out the door." So if I had maxed out, it's just about getting out that door. Getting away from the nightmare. Exoneration was secondary.

JC: But when you meet people in the world, even when you met Jennifer, the fact that you're exonerated is different than being maxed out.

KFI: It's a perception thing, right? You weren't exonerated, you maxed out in your sentence, you're a criminal, you're an ex-con. I'm exonerated, I have no criminal record.

JC: So the exoneration over being maxed out does improve your status on the outside?

KFI: Absolutely. It's a perception thing and had I maxed out on the bid or had I been guilty in some way then I'd get out the other side as an ex-con. I wouldn't be able to get a job. I know guys getting out of prison now. They had done major bids and they're having a hard time getting jobs because of their felony convictions.

JC: But if you were running Stop 'n Shop and some prisoner maxed out after serving a murder sentence, would you hire him?

KFI: I don't know. I've never been in that position. I don't know. It's a tough call to make. You can't do a background check to see how he conducted himself in prison, or before he went to prison. It's not like a parole hearing, giving someone a job. It's a difficult subject. In Connecticut the State Board of Pardons and Parole has been working to review cases of offenders for a "Certificate of Employability." A certificate that assures employers that the applicant has demonstrated to the Board of Pardons and Parole a readiness to reenter the workforce and lead a productive life free of crime.

JC: Interesting. On another subject, the State of Connecticut awarded you $6 million as a result of your exoneration. There are people who will read this and say, "Well the guy got $6 million, it's not such a big deal." What do you say to that?

KFI: Ask them if they would trade 21 years of their life for $6 million. For me, not a day! It was just that horrible.

JC: Does it help you at all to have received it, other than financially?

KFI: It affords me the ability to do the things I want to do now. It affords me a comfortable life, but that's separate from what I went through.

JC: You clearly have an uplifting manner about having been exonerated and now being out on the street and living your life as you wanted to before. If you didn't receive the $6 million would your attitude be the same?

KFI: Absolutely. My attitude was what it is now from the day I was released. I didn't get the claim money until five years later. The money part is totally separate thing than being released from prison. The money doesn't make up in any way, not even close to make up for the time in prison.

JC: Obviously what occurred to you is a great injustice, correct?

KFI: Yes, correct.

JC: This may sound to be an odd question, but what do you think is the greatest injustice to a person in history?

KFI: A single person? I don't know what the greatest injustice is. There were much worse injustices than what I've gone through.

JC: Like what?

KFI: Slavery, obviously. The Holocaust, obviously.

JC: My question is about injustices to single individuals.

KFI: Look, single individuals were slaves, and single individuals were part of the Holocaust. War crimes, there's any number of things. I used to tell people in prison who would complain: "You're in the richest state in the country, and you're in the richest country in the world and you're well fed, you have three big meals, you're in air conditioning and you happen to be in prison. Your liberty's been taken away from you and it sucks, but you could be so much worse off, my friend. You could be in prison in a third-world country. For being in prison you're not doing so bad." On the flip side of that, we were in Connecticut, which has the largest prison population per capita in the United States, and the United States has the largest prison population per capita in the world. So you're basically in the most overcrowded prison in the world.

We were in prison but once they got rid of the violence and made control units, violence in Connecticut prisons is rare now. It's a relatively safe environment now compared to when I first went in. So being in prison sucks, but you can be so much worse off in life. In terms of a worse injustice than what I suffered, or a worse injustice that can be done to a man, I don't have an answer.

JC: You gave an answer. You're an unusual man. Thank you.

5

White Haired and Spirited— A Victim of the Red Scare

Miriam Moskowitz

I didn't know anybody who wanted to overthrow the government. I knew we wanted change. I felt that that change would not come about necessarily by slaughtering people.

—Miriam Moskowitz, December 14, 2014[1]

In order to understand Miriam Moskowitz—98 years old at the time of this interview—and the events of her life, we need to place ourselves in the social and political landscape of the 1940s and '50s. World War II was raging and the U.S. was actively involved in the war. Franklin Roosevelt—the beloved FDR—died during his fourth term in office and Harry Truman was now

---

1. This interview took place at Ms. Moskowitz's home in Washington Township, New Jersey.

the president. The Manhattan Project was in full force—yes, the U.S. and certain allies were on the verge of creating an atomic bomb, a bomb that would ultimately be used to kill some 130,000 people and bring an end to the Asia-Pacific war and thus a final end to World War II. The U.S. was left with the Truman Doctrine, the Cold War, and what has colloquially been called "McCarthyism," the term used to describe Senator Joseph McCarthy's merciless pursuit and conviction of communist sympathizers.

To Moskowitz—born in 1916—and to many of her generation, the U.S. was headed in the wrong direction. Moskowitz, like many others, joined the Communist party. But what did that really mean in the 1940s? Was it an effort to bring about change; to show support for the left and vote in a new administration that would encourage unions and programs like the Works Progress Administration? In other words, did they want to overthrow the government or did they want a democratically elected administration that would work for the people and provide jobs for those who needed them?

There were those who, perhaps, believed that the way to achieve change was to fortify the Soviet Union. You see, the Soviet Union was an ally during WW II, yet the U.S. and Britain did not share the findings and advances of the Manhattan Project. And some believed Russia should have that information. There were those Americans who committed treason—spied on the U.S. and/or sold or gave information about the bomb to the Soviets. And then there were those who delivered documents that—whether intentionally or not—were harmless or otherwise in the public domain.

But let's turn to Moskowitz and those in her life. Born to a Jewish, middle class family in New Jersey, she attended City College. In 1944, she became the employee and eventually the lover of the married Abraham Brothman, an engineer who, through a network of Soviet spies, provided blueprints that he undoubtedly knew would land in the hands of the Soviets. It appears, in retrospect anyway, as if the blueprints he handed over were his personal property (and not those of the U.S. government) and were largely useless. But Brothman—himself never a "card-carrying" member of the Communist party—passed his blueprints on to those who eventually confessed that they were Soviet spies: Elizabeth Bentley and Harry Gold. He and Moskowitz—who *had* joined the "Party" at Brothman's urging—were now closely watched by the FBI.

When one was under the watchful eye of the FBI in the 1940s, one was in the sights of McCarthy, the House Un-American Activities Committee (HUAC), and Irving Saypol and his young acolyte, the now infamous Roy Cohn. Saypol was the U.S. attorney for the Southern District of New York and was, at least in his mind, tasked with routing out communism. Indeed, it was Saypol and Cohn who prosecuted the government's cases against Brothman, Moskowitz, Alger Hiss, and—perhaps most famously—Julius and Ethel Rosenberg.

Again, let's look at context. The Red Scare (actually, the second Red Scare—the first having taken place after the Bolshevik Revolution of 1917) was at its height. The country feared communism and all that it stood for. The Truman Doctrine—announced in 1947—solidified the U.S. goal to stop Soviet expansion in its tracks. And Saypol and Cohn knew—indeed, they were positive—that Ethel and Julius Rosenberg gave U.S. secrets to the Russians.

But Saypol and Cohn also knew that their case against the Rosenbergs rested in part on the testimony of two admitted Soviet spies—Bentley and Gold. So they decided that, before they prosecuted the Rosenbergs, they would see how Bentley and Gold fared under cross-examination. They would do it by prosecuting not only Brothman, but Moskowitz as well. In other words, they would get to test their star witnesses *and* they would test how the jury and the public in general reacted to their prosecution of a woman.

Brothman was charged with conspiracy to obstruct justice and endeavoring to persuade a witness—Gold—to give false testimony before a federal grand jury. Nonetheless, the government had a problem with Moskowitz—there was no evidence that she had passed documents or secrets to anyone and no evidence that she tampered with any witnesses. She was not charged with espionage or treason or "subversive" activities; her crime—she was indeed convicted—reduced to its simplest terms was to be present when Brothman and Gold, the one witness who testified against her, conspired to lie to the grand jury about their Soviet-related activities.

Moskowitz, for her part, refused to testify. It was too dangerous—she was facing two years in prison based on the pending charge. And what if, while she was on the stand, she was asked to "name names"? Would she do it? She likely correctly believed years would be tacked on to her sentence for contempt when she refused the judge's direction that she answer. Such was the tenor of the day.

Moskowitz was ultimately convicted largely if not exclusively based on Gold's testimony. Moskowitz served two years in prison and paid a $10,000 fine, which she paid over the course of two decades given her meager earnings. And the government had its cast in place for the trial leading to the conviction and death (some would argue assassination) of Julius and Ethel Rosenberg. Saypol and Cohn prosecuted; Judge Irving Kaufman presided; and Bentley and Gold testified.

When Moskowitz left prison, would the stigma of her communist association continue? What was her relationship with her family? Would FBI agents see fit to visit her work place and make sure her bosses knew about her communist activities and incarceration? Would she be stalked or at least followed until "the world changed" and the FBI no longer had time for her? And what was her relationship with Brothman? Did she ever marry—him or anyone else?

After a series of jobs, Moskowitz became a math teacher and tutor in New Jersey, not far from where she grew up. She played the viola in string quartets and enjoys chamber music to this day. Yet, she tried to hide her past whenever possible, and remained in fear that some student, co-worker, parent, or neighbor would find out about her life—although it is unclear which would have been worse, that she was an ex-convict or a communist. Even so, Moskowitz would not be silenced and she continued to support "leftist" causes, writing for newsletters and marching for civil rights and against the Vietnam War. Indeed, she participated in demonstrations to "Ban the Bomb."

Many would think that, more than 60 years after she was released from prison, Moskowitz would leave well enough alone. She has lived her life in relative peace and, at least to her knowledge, the FBI was no longer pursuing her. But then, in 2008, with Kaufman now dead, certain historical, research, and educational institutions would ask that the court release various then-sealed records. Judge Alvin K. Hellerstein of the Southern District of New York would order that the grand jury testimony and prior FBI statements given by Harry Gold and other documents be released as they were of "substantial historical importance."

In a grand jury, the prosecutor presents evidence and examines witnesses in front of those citizens chosen to sit on the jury. No judge is present. The defendant and defendant's counsel are not present. What takes place in the grand jury—the testimony, the evidence—is secret. And the grand jury decides whether a crime will be charged. Now, under certain circumstances today given liberalized statutes and Supreme Court decisions reached in the 1960s, years after Moskowitz's conviction, grand jury testimony and a witness's prior statements must be released to the defendant's counsel. If they were not released, the conviction would likely be reversed. Those rules, of course, did not exist in 1950 and, as a result, Moskowitz and her lawyer had no access to Gold's testimony and his prior—sometimes inconsistent—interview memoranda, until they were released by Judge Hellerstein in 2008.

It turns out that, in interviews with the FBI, Gold told agents that he "recalls telling Brothman practically nothing in Moskowitz's presence" and that Gold and Brothman spoke only when "Moskowitz had gone out for coffee or something." Indeed, Gold admitted to the FBI he "never discussed his espionage activity in [Moskowitz's] presence if he could avoid it, as he distrusted her because of her violent temper." Far different from his trial testimony that Moskowitz was not only present during these conversations, but that she helped persuade Brothman to stick to the original, untruthful story he gave to the grand jury.

Miriam Moskowitz has always maintained her innocence and wanted nothing more than to clear her name. Never married and largely alone in her tenth decade, she was renewed in her vigor to use the newly released records that, she believed, would exonerate her. Lawyers agreed to take her case on a pro bono basis, and decided to ask Judge Hellerstein to issue a writ of error coram nobis—an arcane and ancient common law remedy generally to "correct errors of fact" and used to "achieve justice" even after appeals have expired and perhaps long after all other remedies have been exhausted. Moskowitz based her motion on Gold's previously unavailable grand jury testimony and witness statements—that is, his statements contradicted his trial testimony and, had her trial attorney had a copy of these files, he would have been able to use them to cross-examine Gold and prove that the story told at trial was false, or at least substantially inconsistent with his prior statements, made under oath.

But the government opposed her attempt to clear her name. It argued that Gold's grand jury testimony—which was spread over days and extensive—was not irreconcilable with what he said at trial. Judge Hellerstein agreed. He acknowledged that Gold's grand jury testimony may indeed have been useful to Moskowitz's lawyer at trial, but ruled that the fact that it was not produced (particularly given the law at the time) was not so fundamental as to require him to grant the extraordinary relief of a writ of error coram nobis.

So where is Ms. Moskowitz today? As of this interview, she is a robust 98 years old and astonishingly lives on her own. She wrote a book before her petition was filed about her extraordinary—and in many ways, quite ordinary—life: *Phantom Spies, Phantom Justice: How I Survived McCarthyism and My Prosecution That Was the Rehearsal for the Rosenberg Trial.* She remains passionate and is not afraid to speak her mind about her life (which is, really, our history) or the issues of the day.

There was so much to ask Ms. Moskowitz. Upon reflection, what does she think about the government's actions toward her and others before and during the Cold War? Did she really support Stalin and his regime? How was her time spent in prison? What did she think about the Manhattan Project? What does she think about the Rosenbergs' verdict of death, having talked often with Ethel in prison?

Does she believe Judge Hellerstein refused to grant her writ for reasons greater than the case of Miriam Moskowitz? Is she still involved in politics and concerned about the direction of the country? And how does she feel about Abe Brothman—her then-married lover who persuaded her to join the Communist party in the first place?

To hear Miriam Moskowitz talk about these issues is to witness our country's—sometimes troubled—history, and to learn how strong-willed people who have suffered can hold their heads high.

* * *

Post Script: On August 23, 2016, I attended by invitation a small celebration of Ms. Moskowitz's 100th birthday, held in her backyard. Somewhat slowed physically (she needed help standing from her chair), she was still alert, completely with it, and gregarious, as always. She told me she had pending before the Obama White House a pardon application—never stop trying. She explained to me privately that the FBI had visited her and her neighbors recently as part of the vetting process. They acted differently towards her, as she described it, than 65 years earlier: "They were gentlemen and courteous." She seemed to wonder how much the change was because she was now 100 and how much was the times. As part of their interview, they asked her what activities she was engaging in recent years. As they took their notes, she simply told them: "I'm 100!" President Obama is no longer in the White House and did not pardon Ms. Moskowitz. Always upbeat, she plans a party to celebrate her 101st birthday this summer.

The Dialogue

JC: Ms. Moskowitz, I read somewhere that you wanted to exonerate yourself. And you wished your parents were alive to see you exonerated. Is that right?

MM: Yes.

JC: From what did you want to exonerate yourself?

MM: I wanted to exonerate myself from the common perception that I was a spy. That I was associated with spies. It was so farfetched, and it made everybody's life miserable. Not just mine. But my parents, all the people who had loaned money to my father for bail for me. Each one of them was investigated by the FBI, and subjected to uncomfortable surveillance and investigation. They were simply ordinary citizens.

My uncles were very Orthodox Jews who spent more time in the synagogue than they ever spent listening to talk that was anti-American. And the friends who loaned money to my father were co-worshipers in the synagogue that he had helped to found. They were just ordinary Jews. They weren't in any way associated with any left-wing organization, and here they were all being investigated.

I lived in a small town. The houses were separated by very little land. Every house was on top of each other. But everybody knew everybody's business. There was this "spy" living in their midst. I had to do something. I couldn't let it go. Either I had to do something or I had to move out of town. And my parents had to sell their house at whatever price they could get and move also. We had to disappear. I didn't want to disappear. I wasn't guilty.

I knew it would take a long time. But I wanted everybody in town and everybody else who knew me to know that this was not true.

JC: Your going to jail was obviously a horrible thing. Ultimately you were released. At some point society changed. There was no communist fear any longer. McCarthy and McCarthyism were gone.

MM: There was. Always is. Still is. But it did change. What changed was that those very brave students, the black students in the South who were sitting in. Martin Luther King was marching. Because there was such a rumble in the South for equal rights—a principled rumble—the FBI was busy. They were surveilling everyone who was marching. Everyone who was demonstrating.

Right on top of that were the explosions on the campuses across the country. Students who didn't want to go to war in Vietnam. It kept the FBI totally busy. The FBI no longer had time for me. They would have continued, I'm sure. But there was a limit to their budget as to how many agents they could dispatch for "the communists." So they had no more time for me.

JC: You say in your book *"Phantom Spies, Phantom Justice"* that you lied to the FBI when they interviewed you. You said that you were not a communist, when in fact you were. What did that mean: to be communist?

MM: It means you get together with a bunch of young like-minded people all for doing things differently. And you are reinforced. You're not an outlier. You're part of a group of people who think like you do, and they let you belong. You're not something strange.

I had a group of friends at home in Bayonne. I never spoke about how I felt about things because I knew they would be deeply uncomfortable. I loved them dearly. They were not used to a "left" perspective. They were absolutely sure that the government did right and was working for them.

When I was with this group [the "communists"], it was as though I was home. I had graduated from City College just previous to that period. I don't know if you know what the campus was like up at City College. A group of young men here, another group here, and a hundred yards away another group, all talking politics and arguing. It was not communism versus democracy. It was the Communist party versus the Socialist Labor party, or the Socialist party. I can never figure out what the difference was. But these students were alive. They were aware and it enabled me to know more about it, because I had come from such a protected environment. I was so illiterate about politics that when I listened to them the whole world opened up. From that, I went to join the Communist party.

JC: So what does it mean that you "joined" the Communist party? Did you get a card? Did you pay dues? Was there a secret handshake?

MM: You walked into a storefront. The Communist party had a storefront in Chelsea, I think it did all over the city. It was open. It was not underground. I walked in, and there was a man sitting at the desk, and I said "I'd like to join." And he looked at me very strangely. Nobody did that. And he filled out a card and said "Two dollars please." I handed over the two bucks. Now I was a member.

JC: Did you get some kind of an identifying card?

MM: Yes, I got a card identifying me as a member of the Chelsea branch of the Communist party.

JC: Do you still have that card?

MM: No. I sure wish I did. It was really unsafe to keep anything around.

JC: I don't want you to "name names," but . . .

MM: I never will.

JC: Did somebody introduce you—was there a person who told you to go to the Chelsea office?

MM: Yes. If you asked me to "name names," I couldn't. There was a jumble. I didn't know one person from another. I knew there was a lot of accusatory speechmaking. And I knew there were some heads that would nod in agreement. There was a Cold War raging when I did this. But I felt that my perspective on peace was being shared.

JC: What year was this? Do you remember who was the president of the United States when you first went to the office in Chelsea?

MM: It was Truman.

JC: How old were you then, do you remember?

MM: I'd have been mid-twenties.

JC: Were you a person who admired FDR?

MM: Oh yes. I wept when he died.

JC: And Truman?

MM: I hated him.

JC: Why did you hate him?

MM: Because he up-ended everything that FDR did. In fact I have a letter—I still have it—signed by Henry Wallace [FDR's vice-president before Truman, and member of the Progressive party]. I was hoping he would win [the presidency in 1948] and I wrote him a passionate letter telling him that. I received a response and I still have it.

Truman was the absolute opposite of anything that I thought Henry Wallace represented. And so, I hated him, especially when he launched his Truman Doctrine. That was a real stinger. I felt that this man with that doctrine really opened up the whole Cold War. The Truman Doctrine legitimized it. It up-ended every democratic principle that had been uttered by FDR.

JC: Were you bothered by the fact that he dropped the bomb on Hiroshima?

MM: Yes. I felt very sad that that happened, and I had arguments years later. I'm sitting in a room playing quartets. I play the viola and I've got a cellist and two violinists and we're playing and somebody mentions they knew Truman and I uttered some negative comment and the cellist stopped playing. He said if it hadn't been for Truman he would not be alive. He had been serving in the South Pacific. And he felt that that bomb brought an end to the Second World War and he was saved.

JC: So was it your dislike of Truman's policies that led you to join the Communist party?

MM: Partly yes, absolutely.

JC: What did you want to do in joining the party, besides the social aspect of not being alone, what did you hope to accomplish?

MM: I hoped simply to strengthen the left by belonging someplace. I had to identify. The Communist party was the nearest thing I could identify with. There was no liberal party or other group that I could identify with. Identifying meant strengthening the left—the opposition to Truman.

JC: A lot of people think that people who are associated with the Communist party in those days supported the potential overthrow or violent overthrow of the United States government.

MM: That was the common perception.

JC: Tell me about that perception as it applied to you.

MM: Everybody thought that the heritage of the USSR from 1905—the aborted revolution then—would somehow creep across the country and get itself immersed in Washington. And the people, led by trade unions, would overthrow the establishment in Washington and would declare a people's country, a people's rule. And everybody would then work for a living wage and everybody would be equally entitled to benefits and the solutions to our economic problems would forever be solved. It was, of course over-exaggerated. It was not going to be that way at all. We were going to have to educate our voting public to a point where they understand what their vote means for any particular person.

However, there was an important change in the Communist party in the mid-forties. Earl Browder had been head of the Communist party and he promoted the idea that the party was now becoming an established part of the American scene. So he proposed changing the name of the American Communist party to the American Communist Political Association, which meant they weren't going to talk anymore about overthrowing the government. We were going to talk about voting in a new administration. We were going to talk about voting—as in the people's right to belong to a union. We were going to talk about voting in everything.

JC: You talk about "overthrowing the government." Were you ever associated with a group that wanted to overthrow the government?

MM: No. I didn't know anybody who wanted to overthrow the government. I knew we wanted change. I felt that that change would not come about necessarily by slaughtering people.

JC: But you thought that if you could bring back another FDR that could accomplish it, correct? You wouldn't need an overthrow. He had been doing what you would want in a president.

MM: That's right. Absolutely. I was weaned on Roosevelt. I thoroughly absorbed the fact that you could get a Taft-Hartley bill by voting, by either presidential decree or by voting it in. I was weaned on the WPA, which was if you had unemployed people you found jobs for them somehow. For musicians, for instance. There were groups of musicians who traveled around the country performing symphonic concerts for people who had never heard music of the kind they played.

JC: If you could turn back the clock 60 or 70 years, and you were at these meetings where people were unhappy with the government; maybe they were unhappy with Truman; maybe they were unhappy with the cold war. Do think that back then you thought—whether you said it in words or said it to yourself while you were lying in bed at night—that if we have to overthrow the government, that's what we should do. Did you ever think like that?

MM: No. I don't think so.

JC: Did the people . . .

MM: All of them were middle class like me. All of them had fairly decent jobs. Nobody in that group ever went hungry. I don't think they would have identified that way.

JC: Obviously at the time, Stalin was the leader of Russia. You would agree that he was a pretty horrible guy, correct? Did you think, "Why would we want to form a government modelled on what Stalin, a horrible dictator, was doing"?

MM: No, we didn't. Stalin's true personality did not come out yet. We recognized that he was rather harsh. But the trials of the 1930s we thought were just drummed up by the capitalist press. We didn't believe it. The fact that they were ultimately so anti-Semitic didn't hit us. They were manufactured stories! They weren't true! So we had no problems thinking about Stalin.

JC: Obviously you've lived with this for many years. Do you ever think back to those days in the '40s when you were associated with the party and the Chelsea office, that there was some naïveté on your part or the people you associated with in the Communist party?

MM: All of us.

JC: You were naïve?

MM: All of us.

JC: Naïve about what?

MM: All of us in the rank and file. I think the leadership was more sophisticated. But the rank and file, we believed in what we were involved in. We did not believe that such a person as they presented Stalin could be real. That was a story that was manufactured and fed to us by the capitalist press. He couldn't have been. He couldn't have done those things. He was on our side, or we were on his side.

JC: I've read most of the trial transcript of your case and your book. You of course deny in your book and have always denied that you were involved in an "obstruction of justice" with Brothman and Harry Gold.

MM: No I didn't deny on behalf of Brothman.

JC: So he's now dead. You were very close to Brothman, weren't you?

MM: Yes.

JC: Were in love with him?

MM: Yes.

JC: Did he encourage your involvement in the Communist party?

MM: Yes. I joined because I thought it would please him. Because he spoke a very left line. He never belonged himself. He was so self-protective. He never actually belonged.

JC: What do you mean he didn't belong? You belonged to the party and he didn't belong?

MM: That's right. I didn't know it at that time. I thought he did. It was not until I began to reevaluate him and I realized the structure of lies that he promoted. He never told a lie so much as that he let you think things that were not true.

JC: Looking back on the whole thing, and obviously you've studied the transcripts, the FBI's memos and the like. Do you believe he was involved in a conspiracy to obstruct justice?

MM: No.

JC: Really?

MM: No, I don't. What he was involved in was protecting himself.

JC: I think you're telling me something more than that. You're telling me that he protected himself, and he placed you out front.

MM: Yes. But I didn't realize it.

JC: What does that say about him? You're giving him the benefit of the doubt. I'm not trying to take that doubt away right now, but it sounds to me like you were extremely naïve about him.

MM: Brothman was an extremely self-centered person. He came first. And nobody else came. He was so self-involved that it was an effort for him to think of anybody else who might be in trouble. Unless it affected him. For instance, I met a man a couple of months ago who had been friendly with him after he was released from prison, when he was working for some engineering firm in Paramus, near here. And he said that he told him that his father refused to help him when he, Abe, had made his father a beneficiary of one of the patents he took out. That meant that if anyone applied for a license to use the patent or bought the patent, which involved the manufacture of certain chemicals, his father would benefit. That's so untrue;

but it's typical of the kind of stories Abe told. He made Harry Gold a beneficiary of that patent because he couldn't afford to pay the guy's salary anymore and he needed him in the lab. He never took care of his father. And his father was penniless. He could have helped him if he wanted to.

JC: So if you see Abe Brothman—my word—as a manipulator, why are you so still willing to say you don't think he was involved at all in a conspiracy?

MM: Because I don't think he was. I think he talked a good line, but I don't believe he was involved.

JC: Did you realize, at any point, that if you basically agreed to cooperate and testify against him, the government would leave you alone—they wouldn't prosecute you?

MM: Yes. I think my attorney mentioned that.

JC: Your attorney was Willie Kleinman.

MM: Yes.

JC: But he was also Abe's lawyer.

MM: Yes, we had the same. We should have had separate trials.

JC: You surely should have had separate lawyers. But how did you come to be Willie Kleinman's client? Was it Abe?

MM: No it was [William] Messing's idea. Messing who was the attorney we consulted early on, who had been a member of the lawyers' guild.

JC: If you had been given the opportunity to testify against Abe, and therefore not be prosecuted yourself, would you have done that at the time? If you had it to do over again would you do that?

MM: No.

JC: Why? You wouldn't want to be a rat?

MM: It's not only that. The whole case was just a phony issue. If I had testified against Brothman I would have substantiated that this was an actually believable situation, when it wasn't. It was rigged. It wasn't a case. And because of the climate at that time, prosecutors would do anything and [United States Attorney Irving] Saypol did. He made a case out of nothing.

JC: Did you ever sit down alone with Saypol and [his assistant] Roy Cohn?

MM: No. Never.

JC: Did they ever ask to meet with you?

MM: I don't know. They would have asked through Messing or Kleinman. They never told me that a request had been made.

JC: Would you have done that?

MM: No.

JC: But you could have told an account that would have exonerated yourself and Brothman. Why didn't you offer that?

MM: Because it would not have exonerated Brothman. It might have exonerated me at his expense. And I wasn't going to do anything like that.

JC: So, fair to say, you were still in love with Brothman when the case was proceeding?

MM: Yes.

JC: I take it that ultimately you were no longer in love with him. When was that?

MM: I was in prison. I was alone. I was besieged by memories of what had happened. Not anything that went back further than two years. And I kept rewinding this script. And I kept saying, "Why didn't Abe tell me this? Why did Abe tell me this, which was not true?" And I began to realize that I had been so blind and had been so trusting that I believed everything he said. And it wasn't true. He misrepresented. I can't call him a liar, although I do in my mind. He just let you think something was true, when the opposite was so.

I got out of prison with this new frame of mind and I went home. A short time later he got out and he came to see me and he embraced me. And I'm nervous, because I have these doubts that are flooding through me. Now, you have to picture—I'm in his arms and I feel uncomfortable and I don't know what to think but I do know that there are situations that have to be resolved. And he says in my ear, as he's embracing me, "I had a terrible time in prison. The guys did thus and so." And I realized he's not asking me how I made out. He's not asking me "How are you?" He never said "How are you?" He never said "How was it in Alderson?" He said "I had a terrible time in prison." And he was looking for sympathy and comfort from me, but not offering me that.

JC: How was it in Alderson? I read about you talking about how it was at the Women's House of Detention in New York. Tell me how that was.

MM: Survivable. You mind your own business, you do your job. You don't join in any cliques.

JC: How did you spend your time?

MM: I worked at the storehouse. After that I found women whose company I could be with without provocation. And I wrote letters and I made notes to myself about things I wanted to remember.

JC: Were you treated as somebody wanting the overthrow of the United States government?

MM: Yes, in the beginning. But on the part of the wardens, that began to soften quickly, because I think they realized that I wasn't going to make any problems for them. I put one foot in front of another and went on with my time.

JC: Were you treated as somewhat of a celebrity?

MM: No.

JC: Not at all?

MM: I don't think so. If I was, that would have been the cause of resentment on the part of some of the inmates.

JC: I read in your book that you continued to have fond feelings for Ethel Rosenberg.

MM: Yes.

JC: I see even in the corner of your living room a poster supporting Julius and Ethel Rosenberg.

MM: I have to get rid of that. A few years ago, I was a featured speaker at a Hadassah meeting or something some place near Princeton. A woman came up to me after the meeting and said she had been a student in France during the early '60s after the Rosenbergs were tried and executed, and there was an active group in Paris. She was a member of it; all the young people were, apparently, and they advocated for mercy for the Rosenbergs. They viewed the Rosenberg case as the American "Dreyfus case." They went into shock when the Rosenbergs were executed. And they issued that poster, and this woman who was telling me that she was a member of that group—this nice middle-class staid Hadassah lady was a member of that group. She said she kept the poster all these years in the attic where it dried out. But whatever condition it was in, she wanted me to have it. I had it framed. So when I get time after this hullabaloo, which I hope will die down, I'm going to offer it to one of the museums in New York City. And if they don't take it, I will sell it to a poster company who will place it some place. It accuses

Eisenhower of assassinating them. It's an electrifying poster. And it captures exactly what happened.

JC: Do you agree with that sentiment, that Eisenhower "assassinated" them?

MM: No. He refused to sign a petition for mercy, so the execution went on.

JC: So put aside [Judge] Kaufman's sentence of death for the Rosenbergs. And put aside Ethel Rosenberg for a moment. Do you think that *Julius* Rosenberg was a spy against the United States?

MM: Spy is a harsh word. I believe he sold information.

JC: You believe he engaged in espionage?

MM: Yes. But you have to qualify that word. He did not steal secrets of the atom bomb. That would have been impossible, to steal any one secret that would have made the atom bomb. That's utter nonsense. The United States had laboratories all over the country, each one working on different aspects. In Tennessee they were working on the separation of uranium. On the west coast they were inventing a man-made element. You have to think of this, a man-made element: plutonium. In Chicago, Professor Urey was working on something else.

The results of those experiments and tests were funneled into Los Alamos and that's where the atom bomb was ultimately assembled. It took the results of experimentation and tests from all over and synthesized it all. David Greenglass was a sergeant in the army and assigned to Los Alamos. This was a guy who barely made it through high school. Now, he's a sergeant where they're putting together the results of all these experiments. He doesn't know A from B when it comes to chemistry or engineering. He sends Julius information about the layout, what the buildings are doing, the names of some of the scientists who are stationed there, what he had for breakfast. And he sends all that information through his wife who visits him in Los Alamos. Sends that information to Julius. His wife writes out all the information because it's all a jumble and she writes it out and gives it to Julius. Julius takes this information and passes it on. He also passes on industrial information that friends are giving him. He does this on a volunteer basis. The USSR or its agents had never asked him to do it.

JC: How do you know all this?

MM: I have a book. Walter and Miriam Schneir wrote a book. It was published about five years ago, in which he synthesized all of these questions. I'll give you the book. I have no use for it.

JC: I'm going to ask you a question. Please think about the question before you answer it and see if you can answer it—yes or no. Do you think that Julius Rosenberg did something—forget about the punishment—for which he should have been prosecuted?

MM: Absolutely.

JC: What is that?

MM: He should not have done it, and he deserved jail time.

JC: But you are bothered more so by Judge Kaufman's treatment of him in terms of the sentence.

MM: I was bothered by the accusation that he sold the secrets of the atom bomb. That drives me crazy.

JC: I see that. So Roy Cohn says in a book, and you say in your book, that the prosecution of Miriam Moskowitz and Abe Brothman was a run-up to the prosecution of the Rosenbergs.

MM: It was a warm-up.

JC: It was a warm-up. What was the benefit of prosecuting *you* as you saw it. What did they see in you?

MM: They were setting the stage for the Rosenberg trial.

JC: I understand prosecuting Brothman. What was the benefit in prosecuting you?

MM: I was a woman and they needed a Mata Hari. A modern one.

JC: And you were she, in their eyes?

MM: Yes, because I had an unworthy relationship with a married man. So what kind of woman can that be?

JC: You're so obviously a terrible woman. So where were you located— were you still in jail when the Rosenbergs were electrocuted?

MM: I was jailed July 29, 1950. Ethel was jailed a couple of weeks later. But she was kept on a different floor. So we never met except when we went to court when the van would pick us up, and she would be in the van and I would be in the van and we would sort of nod to each other but we couldn't talk.

JC: So were you still in jail when she was electrocuted?

MM: I was in prison when she was electrocuted. After she was convicted she was moved down to my floor because they had a better surveillance of the cells—they wanted to prevent her from hanging herself or something. So we became friends. We would have coffee every afternoon together and talk. It was nice for me to have somebody to talk to.

JC: When you would talk to her, would you talk about "communist" stuff?

MM: No. She would do the talking mostly. About her boys, about the social workers' report; difficulties about her mother who would come to see her and berate her for what she was doing to David, and never concerned about what she was herself undergoing.

JC: Did you look up to her as a woman who was involved in the communist movement?

MM: No. We didn't talk about that.

JC: But did you look up to her in your own mind?

MM: I admired her for her fortitude during the trial. I admired her because I felt several times like I was going to dissolve and my situation was not nearly as harsh.

JC: My dear Ms. Moskowitz, you are evading my question. My question is—"Did you look up to and admire her as a communist in terms of her view of the political situation in the United States at the time?"

MM: I don't think I thought about that at the time. But I would have admired her for standing up—she didn't dissolve.

JC: Do you still admire her now?

MM: Oh, absolutely.

JC: Aside from Julius Rosenberg having done things for which, you acknowledge, he should have been punished, did you admire him for his views about communism?

MM: No. I always thought he was . . . well, I don't want to say it. I didn't admire him for his intellect. I guess I admired him for feeling that he was helping bring about. In his mind he thought he would help to bring about a better society. But I didn't admire him.

JC: Who in the American Communist movement in the United States did you admire the most?

MM: Earl Browder. As a matter of fact, years later I met a man at a summer camp for musicians, who played the flute. And his last name was Browder. And we were in a group that was playing. And I said, "Your name is rather famous." I didn't specify how or why. And he smiled and said "I'm his son."

JC: Did you ever communicate, before his death, with Judge Kaufman? Did you ever write to him or . . .

MM: Kaufman? No way. You had to be in that court to see how totally involved he was with his own career and how unreachable he was.

JC: How did you perceive that? I've been in judge's courtrooms and they haven't necessarily been friendly to the cause I was espousing on a particular day. What did you see in the courtroom when you were on trial or at sentence, that led you to believe . . .

MM: He let Saypol manufacture a case out of nothing. Harry Gold had a bunch of blueprints that he had saved, he had never returned to Brothman. They were meaningless. They were designs of kettles and heat exchanges and stuff like that. They had no application to any secrets that Brothman was giving to the Soviet Union. He was trying to sell them on his services. And when Saypol got these blueprints he waived them in front of the jury like they were secrets. Now people aren't used to looking at blueprints. Blueprints must be secret. They must be related to the atom bomb. So when Saypol waved these meaningless blueprints in front of the jury, Kaufman did not ask him pertinent questions about the meaning of what he was doing. Also, whatever was in those supposed secrets, Brothman had written up in technical magazines, which were published nationally in this country. Our lawyer subpoenaed the magazines and wanted them to be entered as evidence that everything that was on those blueprints had been discussed technically in these magazines. Kaufman permitted the blueprints to be waved in front of the jury, but did not permit the articles explaining them.

JC: Did your lawyer seem to feel any fear or reluctance to represent two communists like yourselves?

MM: No. I should be grateful, and I am in retrospect. I probably didn't convey it to him. But I was grateful.

JC: He was a great lawyer, that man. Let me ask you this: You say in your book and I'll ask you to tell me about it, about you not attending Judge Kaufman's funeral but going to Judge Kaufman's funeral, correct?

MM: I went to the funeral, yes I certainly did.

JC: Tell me about that.

MM: I don't know why I went. I often thought about it. I heard that he had died. I heard that he was going to buried out of the Park Avenue

Synagogue. I said I have to go. When I got there I said "What am I doing here?" It was a cold blustery morning. I was so uncomfortable physically and I would not go inside because if I did so I would have been taken for a mourner. So I stood outside asking myself, "What on earth am I doing here? I'm not registering any protest. There's no protest movement here." I just thought about it and then when the side doors of the synagogue opened and the casket rolled out I walked over to it and I stood next to it and it was a moment of real nasty horror. The ushers accompanying the casket had moved off the curb looking for the hearse that was coming up the block and the block was clogged with traffic so the hearse was very slow. So I stood there and I thought. And I talked to him.

JC: What did you say?

MM: I said words to the effect like "You miserable creature, you. You hooked up with other miserable creatures to let them present a case against me that wasn't true and you sentenced the Rosenbergs to death when you really had no evidence that they deserved the death penalty." I had read in *The New York Times* that two of his three sons had died and I connected immediately with those deaths. "Now I'm not invoking God in this but I'm saying if you believed that you had punished the Rosenbergs for something, did you also believe that this was divine retribution when two of your sons died. It was an even exchange? One son for Ethel and one son for Julius." And I said to him "You're a miserable person. You knew you were faking a case against us." Maybe I thought these things.

JC: Is it fair to say you would have wanted him to burn in the fires of hell?

MM: If there are such things.

JC: I noted when I read your book, and I noted it when you said it now—that you seem more bothered by what he did to the Rosenbergs than what he did to you.

MM: Oh, sure.

JC: Why is that? You're basically saying that he caused you this torment over the course of your life that you're still trying to get exonerated in 2014, but you're more bothered by the Rosenbergs?

MM: How can anyone compare a two-year sentence with loving parents waiting for me and no responsibilities to children? How can you compare that situation to walking down the path to the electric chair?

JC: You're truly an amazing woman. It becomes clearer as I talk to you. What I don't understand is this. We've been talking for about an hour now. And you're totally comfortable talking about this. You're totally comfortable with what you did, you have no hesitation about talking about these details of your life. You want to get exonerated, but I must ask you, has your life in any way been harmed since, say, 1960 as a result of all of this? And I'm not meaning to understate the horror that was done to you. But for the last 55 years, how has your life been harmed?

MM: First of all, a couple of weeks after I got out of prison I went to the B. Manischewitz company that was in the next town.

And I got a job. I listed my qualifications. I was a college graduate, I had worked for a company named B. Brothman Associates as an executive secretary. I was hired on the spot. They asked me what salary I wanted. Now I was out of commission for two years so I didn't know what salaries were. So I asked for a ridiculously low salary and I was hired immediately. And they put me in charge of public relations. I didn't know what public relations was from the man in the moon. In the two years I was out of circulation the world had changed. So I first had to ask around among friends, what is this business called public relations? And I finally found out you write publicity releases. OK, that's why they hired me because my application indicated that I was fairly literate. But I didn't know what to write about. Because they weren't feeding me information.

Over the next few years I functioned as an assistant to the sales manager, so that went pretty smoothly until the FBI visited the personnel department at which time—now this I did not discover right away, I discovered it years later when I was reading the FBI files to write that book—they told the personnel manager that I was a spy, a convicted criminal, and a communist. That got relayed to the man I reported to, who was the chairman of the board, B. Manischewitz. He didn't communicate it right away, he was very puzzled, I guess. It was spring and everyone had to submit their vacation schedule. I submitted mine, and as a routine he called me in to discuss the vacation schedule. He looked down and said "Yeah, August 15th to 20th looks okay." And then he said very quietly "But your job may not be here when you return." I resigned. I could have let them fire me and collect unemployment insurance. I couldn't get by five minutes more there. I just, next day, resigned.

JC: What did you do after that?

MM: Then I looked for a job and found some rinky-dink thing in Manhattan and it was hateful. I was there two weeks and resigned. The worst part of all this ordeal from the very beginning was hiding it from my parents to spare them. I didn't want them to aggravate about my situation. So I didn't tell them why I resigned from Manischewitz Company. My father said you're making a very serious mistake. I couldn't say "But Daddy I have to, they're going to fire me if I don't." I just let it go. I let him think I was being foolish. When I quit the job in New York two weeks later, he said, "Why are you doing this?"

I found another job about ten miles away from where I lived and this was better. It was a packaging firm. It printed packaging labels and boxes. But it was not the kind of firm that Manischewitz was. It wasn't stable. Two brothers who ran it were not talking to each other and competitors were bidding for it. In the meantime the same thing happened. The FBI went to them. I had to get out. They didn't ask me to leave. They said they would have a board meeting and decide what to do, which was most generous. And they called me to the board meeting a month later. The lawyer had read the record. He said to me as an aside "You made a very serious mistake to not take the stand." Why does he tell me this? I can't undo it.

JC: Why didn't you take the stand?

MM: Because in the first place, my father was sitting in the audience and Saypol would have instantly asked "Did you have relations with Brothman?" I would have gotten over that. And then he would have said "Are you now or have you ever been a member of the Communist party?" I would have had to say yes. His next question . . .

JC: You could have said no.

MM: No, I wouldn't have. I was a member.

JC: Truth was too important to you to lie about that?

MM: He could have made a case about lying. I would never take that chance. Then he'd ask me to name some of the people I had met in the Communist party. And I would have refused to do that. Kaufman would have said "Miss Moskowitz, I order you to answer the prosecutor's question." And I would again refuse. And he would have cited me for contempt of court. Saypol would have continued asking questions that I wouldn't answer. The judge would have continued citing me for contempt of court.

I was already facing two years. There was no way I was going to take the stand.

JC: I'm not asking you to "name names," but if I asked you to name names today and you remembered them, would you answer it now, on December 14, 2014?

MM: No.

JC: Why? You wouldn't be exposing them.

MM: As a principle.

JC: It's a principle? I'm not asking you to tell it to the FBI, I'm asking you to tell it to me. You wouldn't do it with me?

MM: In the first place, I don't remember.

JC: Put aside whether you remember or not. I could probably refresh your recollection and you'd probably remember some. But you wouldn't do it?

MM: I wouldn't do it.

JC: That's interesting, don't you think? They wouldn't suffer any consequences today, but you still wouldn't do it.

MM: No.

JC: Why do you think there were so many people who were celebrities in Hollywood who obviously were well-to-do, they lived well, they were at the top of their game, why were so many of them interested in communism in those days?

MM: Because in the war that was prosecuted previously, the Second World War, the Soviet Union had borne the brunt of the fight. They were the ones who lost, the people themselves, not just the army, the country was overrun by marauding Germans who set fire to everything they could. They laid waste to the country as far as they penetrated. Stalingrad and Leningrad were notable battles. They've gone down in history. Their losses, their casualties far outnumbered the total number of casualties of all of the other allies put together. Those people suffered terribly. I think that fact reached humanistic thinkers in Hollywood and elsewhere. It certainly touched me. Eisenhower himself, I have it in my book, noted that Leningrad was a siege that went down in history for its savagery.

JC: You told us about losing your job at Manischewitz then what you referred to as a rinky-dink job and a third job. When did it stop? When were you able to live your life free of the harassment?

MM: Those blessed students who started "sitting in" in the South demanding an end to segregation—they just saved me.

JC: So you're saying the civil rights movement made the communist issue as it related to you passé?

MM: Absolutely.

JC: By when—the time Martin Luther King died in 1968?

MM: No. That event, plus the student rebellion against the Vietnam War made my life whole again. I was able, because the FBI no longer had time for me. They went on to harass the students and the demonstrators who demonstrated against segregation.

JC: So that sort of ended, just picking a date, when King died in 1968? Since then, which is more than 45 years, have you had any repercussions?

MM: No.

JC: No repercussions since then?

MM: No, but I was always apprehensive that there would be. I was always on edge that someone would discover my past, fire me, or shun me. The rabbi in the local temple I had belonged to shunned me. He made the Rosenbergs a topic of his sermon on one Rosh Hashanah morning. I was staggered because he so misrepresented the whole story. Not just that they stole the atom bomb, but he manufactured one.

JC: Did the rabbi know you were sitting in the congregation that day?

MM: Yes. I went up to him after the service. He turned away from me.

JC: When was that?

MM: It must have been eight years ago.

JC: That recently?

MM: Eight, ten years ago.

JC: Judge Hellerstein in his opinion a few weeks ago, denying your coram nobis petition, said that you no longer can allege a legal justification—a continuing prejudice in your life—for why he should grant the motion. In other words, you're no longer suffering something. Are you suffering something now?

MM: I'm always apprehensive socially. I'm apprehensive living in this community that my neighbor across and my neighbor next door will discover who I am. By now they know who I am.

JC: You've sort of made it public, right?

MM: Right, but I've always been afraid that a brick would come sailing through my window. Always on tenterhooks.

JC: Judge Hellerstein doesn't sit in the exact courthouse where Judge Kaufman sat when you were tried but they are of the same court. Do you see him as sort of a continuation of what happened to you?

MM: No I see him as a new breed. He's more interested in the law than in protecting the victim. That's simple. The law should not be abused. I agree. But you should look into the background more carefully, and he did not.

JC: I should tell you this: I don't know if it will make you happy or not. Judge Hellerstein is a dear friend of mine. He was a law partner of mine and let me add this: He's about as fine a man as I've ever met in my life. And you could not have gotten a better chance of winning your motion than with a judge like him. I see you hitting your head.

MM: But I will tell you this: he did not read the record of the trial.

JC: So tell me about that.

MM: He did not see how Judge Kaufman steered it. How he led Harry Gold to say certain things. He did not read the background of my relationship with Harry Gold. He did not know Harry Gold saw me in one light and when I rejected that he turned and saw me in another light. He did not know, he did not relate the case to the McCarthy era. And what he was most afraid of—if Judge Hellerstein had encouraged in any way my suit, he would have opened a hornets' nest. Because if he decided that I was convicted wrongfully, that opens up the whole question of the Rosenberg case.

JC: I think there's another issue involved too. If he opens it up there is a very high bar legal standard for a coram nobis application, then he opens up thousands of convictions since 1950.

MM: I'm not concerned about thousands of convictions, I'm concerned about the Rosenberg case. They were not executed, they were assassinated as that poster says. They were killed without justification and that has to come to the fore at some time. People have to know that American justice is imperfect. Hellerstein solidified that.

JC: Do you think American justice has changed now?

MM: No, I don't think so. I think entrenched interests keep it the way it's always been. I think the Supreme Court, the *Citizens United* case is such a warped point of law. No, it hasn't changed.

JC: How about the current president of the United States, President Obama?

MM: I think he does the best he can. I don't think he's going to go down as a great president, but I don't think that's his fault. I think that's a fault of a recalcitrant Congress. He's being victimized.

JC: This will be my last question, today at least. Put aside labels. Put aside your membership in the Communist Party. Do you see yourself today as a communist?

MM: No. I don't know that there's such an organization.

JC: But your views about society? Are they the same as they were in the 1940s?

MM: Yes, I think we need a better system of representative government. I think the distribution of the national wealth with 99 percent doing without and one percent having it all, I think that's wrong, I think that's immoral. I think that has to change. By any means possible.

JC: I lied to you I said that was my last question. My last question is this: If you were younger now, and you didn't have the conviction and all that in your past, would you consider running for Congress?

JC: Would I consider running?

MM: Me?

JC: Yes, why not?

MM: No, I have no constituency. You can't decide all by yourself you're going to run unless you have people telling you. And you can't run unless you have the background in activities, which sort of propels you toward that activity. I don't have any connection today with left-wingers, although I talk my mouth off when anybody wants to listen.

JC: You certainly have the fire in the belly, don't you?

MM: Absolutely. I'm really regretful that I'm 98 years old because I don't have a lot of time to talk any more. I don't have any people to talk to. My niece, my nephew, equally darling. I don't have friends, they all died off. Other relatives, they know I feel strongly about the way this country has become, and it's so much worse today.

6

Falsely Accused by Those with a Public Platform

Steven Pagones

I was very upset with the way the law was manipulated. And again I was a part of the system. I was a prosecutor. I believed in the system. I believed that you investigate and then you prosecute. Not that you prosecute and then you investigate.

—Steven Pagones, December 29, 2014[1]

Steven Pagones—the name sounds familiar. You can't quite place it, and then it hits you. He was accused of raping Tawana Brawley back in the 1980s. Rev. Al Sharpton was involved. You remember, somehow, that Pagones didn't do it, that Brawley's claims (really, Sharpton's claims) were a hoax. But what happened again?

---

1. This interview took place at Mr. Pagones's offices in Beacon, New York.

Let's go back to 1987. Steven Pagones was a newly admitted lawyer and he had his first job—rather than go into private practice, he decided to serve the public and was an assistant district attorney in Dutchess County, New York. As an A.D.A., he worked for the person charged with enforcing the laws within the jurisdiction, and he was responsible for prosecuting those who violated the law. And "law" is what the Pagones family did—his father was a judge, his brother and cousin are judges.

Yet, less than a year after Pagones began work, he was accused of participating in a racially motivated kidnapping and gang rape of a 15-year old black girl. What possible circumstances could have led this man—engaged to be married, working in the town he grew up in, and living a perfectly ordinary middle-class life—to be accused of such heinous crimes? The story is so unbelievable it has to be true.

November 1987: Tawana Brawley, a black 15-year-old, was found behind her apartment complex in Wappinger Falls, New York. She was wrapped in a garbage bag with "KKK" and "Nigger" smeared in feces across her body. She claimed to have been kidnapped and sexually assaulted by three men, one a "white cop," words which she scribbled on a pad while in the hospital. Her stepfather insisted that the "white cops" would do nothing to help Brawley and law enforcement immediately insisted that a black police officer from a neighboring town interview her.

A few days after Brawley was found, Pagones's good friend, Harry Crist, Jr.—himself a policeman—committed suicide. Crist left a suicide note; he was distraught over a failed romance and work problems, and it seemed clear that his suicide had nothing to do with "guilt" over Brawley. But Crist was a "white cop" and he had killed himself. He was a convenient pawn—and so, he was now named by Brawley's handlers as Brawley's attacker. And just who were these handlers? C. Vernon Mason, Alton H. Maddox, Jr., and none other than the then-youthful Reverend Al Sharpton, fresh off having successfully pushed for a special prosecutor for the racially motivated Howard Beach killings.

There was one problem—Pagones knew Crist did not attack Brawley. Not only because Crist was his friend and because he believed Crist would never do such a thing. No, Crist and Pagones were together for most of the time period during which it was alleged that Crist attacked

Brawley. And Pagones, as soon as the claim was made against Crist, told this to his boss, the district attorney charged with investigating the Brawley kidnapping.

So how did Pagones go from being a witness to an accused? Pagones's picture appeared in the newspaper as Crist's alibi witness. And then, Brawley's handlers—by this time, Brawley was no longer speaking to anyone in law enforcement—publicly accused Pagones of participating with Crist in the kidnapping and rape. And that was all it took to cause Pagones to begin a travel through hell.

Yes, even though Brawley—the alleged victim—herself never once identified Pagones or uttered his name publicly, Pagones was now branded and the press ate it up. Bigotry, racial hatred, attacks on a teenager; "KKK" and "Nigger" smeared on her; white law enforcement being investigated by white law enforcement; Mason, Maddox, and Sharpton screaming about the oppressed minority and the then African-American icon, Bill Cosby, offering a reward for those who came forward with the "truth"— the story had it all. Brawley wasn't talking, but her advisors were and here are just some of the headlines of the day: "State Probes Klan Attack," "Ku Klux Klan Abduct, Sexually Abuse Girl, 15," "Race-Sex Attack Enrages a Town," "Black Leaders Plan to Protest Violence," "Bias Cases Fuel Anger of Blacks," and "Attack Puts Quiet Hudson Area in Civil-Rights Fight." The story went national.

And to fuel the already burning fire, as law enforcement dug into the story of what was being portrayed as a racially motivated attack, there were, shall we say, huge inconsistencies in the account Brawley's advisors put forth. By January 1988, in response to the hue and cry of politicians, the press, pundits, and the public, Governor Mario Cuomo, after the district attorney felt the need to disqualify himself because he would effectively be investigating his own assistant (Steve Pagones), appointed a special prosecutor—Attorney General Robert Abrams—to investigate.[2]

A grand jury was empaneled and, over the course of eight months, it heard more than 6,000 pages of testimony from more than 180 witnesses. Its mandate was broad—to investigate whether a crime was committed

---

2. Robert Abrams and the author have been law partners since 1994.

and, if so, by whom; whether any law enforcement official attempted to conceal anything relating to the crime; and whether sufficient evidence existed to indict anyone for the crime. But the grand jury also had another role. Because Pagones was a public servant under investigation, he had the right to demand that the grand jury issue a public report of its findings, rather than the standard protocol, which would have the grand jury's findings remain confidential unless an indictment was brought.

But what was Pagones going through during these eight months of hearings, and the months before that? Was he able to work? Was he threatened? Was his family? And what did the press report? Did he have any supporters or was he hung out to dry, as they say? Did Pagones talk to the press? Did he tell anyone where he was during the time Brawley claimed she had been kidnapped and attacked? And what of Brawley's handlers? Certainly they could not have remained silent during this time. But did they testify before the grand jury to prove Brawley's case?

And then there is Brawley, herself. Did she give testimony, which the A.G. declared would have been "of inestimable value" to the investigation? The answer is a simple "no"; she was first invited, and then subpoenaed, yet, she did not appear. Did her handlers advise her to remain silent? Why is it that she failed to appear?

Pagones, for his part, did testify. And the grand jury cleared his name. In a detailed 90-page report, which came 11 painstaking months after the claimed rape, the grand jury concluded that there was no evidence whatsoever that Brawley had been kidnapped, raped, or attacked and certainly no evidence that Pagones (or Crist for that matter) engaged in any wrongdoing of any kind. And the attorney general did not leave it at that. He referred disciplinary charges against Maddox and Mason, both lawyers, outlining ways in which the A.G. believed they violated rules governing the conduct of lawyers. In a letter to the disciplinary committee, the attorney general listed 19 specific public statements made by Maddox and Mason that were found to have been false. And A.G. Abrams voiced his "strong view" that Maddox, Mason, and Sharpton "had engaged in an utterly reckless, dishonest, and destructive course of conduct."

So Pagones was not only publicly vindicated by the grand jury report, but Maddox, Mason, and Sharpton were found to have acted recklessly and dishonestly. In fact, Maddox was and remains indefinitely suspended from the practice of law since 1990 for failing to appear to answer questions about his conduct in the Brawley case and Mason, on the radar, was disbarred in 1995 for his wholesale neglect of clients. So why isn't this the end of the story?

Pagones, not satisfied, decided to sue Brawley, Maddox, Mason, and Sharpton for infliction of emotional distress and defamation. Why? Did the money he could have received in a judgment matter that much? Why didn't he leave well enough alone now that his name was cleared? Could it have been in response to Sharpton's taunts: "If Pagones is innocent, he should sue me." Or was it something else?

Brawley, for her part, refused to appear in the lawsuit (although she incurred the ire of the judge presiding over the civil case when she appeared at a rally in Brooklyn rather than his courtroom). Ten years after they stridently accused Pagones of kidnapping and raping Brawley, Maddox, Mason, and Sharpton—with no objection from Pagones—were once again given the right to prove those claims. As the judge put it, they had 25 days to cross-examine Pagones "about every possible relevant aspect of the case."

Yet, Brawley's handlers did nothing to prove that Pagones played any role in what was by now generally believed to be have been a hoax. What was disclosed instead—remarkably and, some would think, beyond belief—is that Sharpton, when examined on the witness stand, acknowledged (although he certainly wouldn't describe it as an "acknowledgment") that he never spoke with Brawley about the kidnapping and rape. He testified: "In terms of details, I would not engage in sex talk with a 15-year-old girl."

Given this admission, did Sharpton, even today, apologize to Pagones? Did Maddox, or Mason? What has Tawana Brawley—now an adult—said about the purported attack? Has she admitted it was a hoax? And where is Steven Pagones? Has the fact that his name was cleared, that two of his accusers can't practice law any longer, that he obtained a money judgment against them for distress and defamation really made a difference? And would apologies or even admissions matter to Pagones at this late date—a defiant Sharpton, after all has been said and done, having said in a television interview a short year before this interview that he did the right thing in asking for a public exposition of Brawley's claims?

The Dialogue

JC: Mr. Pagones, this book is about cases where justice may have failed.

You were accused by Tawana Brawley, her lawyers, and Al Sharpton of a horrible crime—participating in a sexual assault on a 15-year-old girl. The matter was fully examined by a grand jury and the attorney general of New York State. You actually requested that the attorney general make a public disclosure of his very thorough findings. He did. The attorney general and the grand jury concluded that the allegations by Tawana Brawley and the others were a hoax. The complete findings were publicly disclosed. You later sued and won a judgment against all of them. Furthermore, the two lawyers, Vernon Mason and Alton Maddox, can no longer practice law. So basically, the justice system worked. Justice prevailed. Wouldn't you say?

SP: No. I had to go through what I went through. And a couple of things I want to correct you about—things, which, to me, are very important. Tawana Brawley, as far as I know to this day, has never publicly accused me of sexually attacking her. She has remained silent about it. So I sued her for emotional distress. But she never swore out a complaint. She has never publicly accused me. It's always been Mason, Maddox, and Sharpton. So, the fact that I had to go through such turmoil and distress emotionally, physically, financially, to basically prove my innocence when there was no official allegation against me by Brawley—the supposed victim—really left me questioning whether I wanted to remain in the legal system. I really felt betrayed by it.

Mason stopped practicing because he was disbarred. I think he stole money from 60-something clients. And of course Maddox was suspended—never actually disbarred. I think he's still suspended. I don't know if he was protecting Tawana Brawley or hiding her. It had something to do with that.

But, I think that the justice system failed. And it failed because it put me in a position where I had to push ahead to prove my innocence, as opposed to someone else pushing ahead to try to prove that I was guilty.

JC: But what could the justice system have done beyond what it did? You were uniquely able to persuade the attorney general to issue a report—almost unheard of in New York State—that basically cleared you (and Harry Crist, posthumously), of any wrongdoing whatsoever. What could the justice system have done better to accomplish you not needing to prove your innocence?

SP: I think the system as a whole could have grown a backbone. Everyone was so afraid of being called "racist," and afraid of Sharpton protesting outside, raising a stink. So that everyone basically ran for cover and did whatever they could do to try to placate him. The system should have said: "Enough. Either you provide information, or we're just dropping it. We're done."

If I call up the state police right now, saying I want to report a robbery, but I'm not going to tell you where it occurred, who did it, or what the facts are, you know what they'd do? They'd hang up on me. They'd say, "See ya." And yet the authorities didn't do that in the Brawley case. They moved forward with an investigation despite the fact that the Brawley team provided them with nothing.

JC: Were you unhappy that there was in fact an investigation, conducted first by your boss, District Attorney Grady, who later disqualified himself, and then later by the attorney general. Would you have preferred no investigation of the allegations?

SP: No, I was placed in a position where there had to be an investigation—that was the only way that that chapter in my life could be closed.

JC: That's why I'm asking. If there was an investigation, and it came out favorably to you, what else could the justice system have done?

SP: If you knew what was going on behind the scenes; the threats that I was getting from law enforcement agencies. You have to remember, this alleged event took place over a four- or five-day period, around Thanksgiving. Nobody knew where I was during that time frame. So therefore, when it came time for Sharpton and Mason and Maddox to publicize specific details of the crime, they couldn't. They would have had to fabricate them around my schedule. And they didn't know where I had been.

Now the investigating bodies, federal, local, and state, all wanted to know where I had been. My concern was that the minute I disclosed that, it would be leaked. And if there were any gaps in my schedule, Mason, Maddox, and Sharpton would say "That's when it happened. And Pagones can't account for where he was during that time period."

So while this investigation was taking place, I was being threatened. Basically, "Either you tell us where you were and submit to a polygraph exam, or else we're going to launch a major investigation on everything you've done since tenth grade." Now here I am, I'm a prosecutor. I know that when people take polygraphs, sometimes they come up inconclusive. That doesn't mean they're guilty. It means "it's inconclusive." My concern was, God forbid, the media found out that I was asked to take a polygraph and I refused—I'd look guilty. Or, God forbid, I said okay and took the polygraph, and it came back inconclusive: that would be the end of it. So while this investigation was going on, my life was just turned upside down.

JC: Which law enforcement agencies threatened you?

SP: It was the federal investigators and state investigators. On the state side, I don't know if they were with the A.G.'s office, or just regular state police.

JC: You say they "threatened" you. Did they call you up, or come to visit you?

SP: They came to visit me. Nothing was done over the phone. They would come to my house. They would come to my office.

JC: Are you saying that the law enforcement agencies who were threatening you were doing so because of the cross-racial nature of the attack being alleged by or on behalf of Miss Brawley?

SP: I think that, basically, they wanted to get to the bottom of this so that they didn't have to worry about any protests, or Sharpton alleging that the system was racist. But they did so at my expense.

I think that people were hesitant and in some instances afraid to stand up to Sharpton and all that he represented at that point in time. Which again was nothing more than a group of people who were willing to come out, protest, and raise hell on behalf of something that was a complete hoax.

JC: Since you raise the issue of a polygraph, were you actually asked by law enforcement to take a polygraph?

SP: Absolutely.

JC: Did you?

SP: No.

JC: Because of your concern that lie detectors are not always a truth-telling mechanism?

SP: That was the primary reason. Also, I didn't feel the need to. Part of my concern was that before taking a polygraph I would be pre-interviewed and have to disclose where I was during that time frame. I wasn't going to do that—that was the only thing I had to protect me from Sharpton coming out and making false allegations.

To this day, I truly believe that if Tawana Brawley came forward and accused me, I would have been indicted and they would have allowed a trial jury to hear the case and acquit me. If Tawana came forward and testified, then the system would have run its course. So they could say: "We did everything we could do. There's no evidence to back it up. We had a public trial. Pagones had nothing to do with this."

JC: Have you ever met Tawana Brawley?

SP: Never. Never.

JC: During this period of time, who asked you to take a lie detector test?

SP: I had investigators and agents come to my place. It was either the A.G.'s office or the state police, and agents of the FBI.

JC: So you're saying that after Governor Mario Cuomo appointed Attorney General Robert Abrams to conduct the investigation, the attorney general's office asked you to take a polygraph?

SP: Yes.

JC: Were you represented by an attorney at the time?

SP: Yes.

JC: Not wanting to invade your confidential talks with your attorney, but did you consider taking a private polygraph examination without giving advance notice to law enforcement?

SP: No. We just never talked about it. And I'll tell you something—so much time has gone by, I don't want to trash people, relationships have mended and it's in the past but, at one point, the D.A., Bill Grady himself, wanted me to take a polygraph. And he discussed it with his senior staff. They told him, "If you make Pagones take a polygraph, we're quitting." Because it was just, the nature of it, on its face—"It almost seems like you're questioning whether or not he did it."

JC: So you're saying that your colleagues, Grady's senior staffers, threatened to resign if he insisted that you take a polygraph? I guess it was your sense that they believed that you were innocent?

SP: Absolutely.

JC: Did you have a sense that Grady didn't believe that too?

SP: No, no, no. But I do think he was bowing to the external pressure, and he wanted to be able to say: "Hey, Pagones took a polygraph and he's telling the truth. There's nothing to substantiate these allegations against him."

JC: But you do recognize that he was in an awkward position, don't you? That he would be called upon to basically side with the credibility of one of his own assistants. So he wanted for you to take the polygraph to say "Hey, my assistant has vindicated himself having passed the polygraph."

SP: I think that's what he should have done without the polygraph. Because, you must remember, there was nothing. There were no allegations. Mason, Maddox, and Sharpton refused to let Brawley cooperate. They refused to provide any information other than saying that "Pagones and Harry Crist raped and kidnapped and smeared feces all over Tawana Brawley." There was nothing there. So even I, as a young prosecutor—I couldn't believe that all of this was going on and there were no facts being provided. Nothing.

JC: In what town was the district attorney located?

SP: Poughkeepsie. 20 minutes from Beacon, where we are now.

JC: So if you were to walk down the street here in Beacon, or in Poughkeepsie, what's the breakdown of blacks versus whites?

SP: I'd say maybe 30 or 40 percent black.

JC: So during that time frame, before the grand jury issued its report clearing you, when you would walk down the street, were people looking at you as if to say, "That's Steven Pagones; he's the guy who raped Tawana Brawley?"

SP: Back then? People were looking at me. People were screaming things out at me. I needed body guards when I was at work. I wasn't allowed to open up packages. I was getting death threats in the mail. I was getting death threats on my home phone.

Because instead of anybody coming forward and saying "There's nothing here for us to pursue," law enforcement turned it around and said "We're investigating." And what were they investigating? They were investigating Steve Pagones. So in a sense it lends credibility to the allegations. And the thing that I heard the most was, "Well, he must have been involved somehow. Otherwise his name wouldn't be involved like this, and he wouldn't be the target of the investigation. So there must be something there."

JC: It seems, in some ironic way, that you almost caused suspicion to circle around you by having told D.A. Grady that you were actually with Harry Crist during that four-day period in issue. Aren't I right?

SP: Yes, in a way. What happens is that Harry Crist commits suicide, having nothing to do with Brawley. I read his suicide note. I was there while he was lying dead in his bed. It was basically problems with his girl-friend, problems with his job. After he commits suicide, his photograph appears in the obituaries along with a brief history that he was a part-time police officer. Lo and behold after that happens, they accuse him. And I knew . . .

JC: You're saying they accused Harry Crist because he was a convenient guy . . .

SP: Yes, and talk about fitting perfectly. He has a badge, he has an old state police car that he picked up at an auction or something. He commits suicide. And I knew that Harry had nothing to do with it because I was with Harry for a very significant period of time during those four days. So I said to my boss, Bill Grady, "He didn't do it. He was with me." And this was nothing more than a situation where there's an opportunity for Sharpton and his gang to accuse Harry, and it's not correct.

JC: You said you read Harry Crist's suicide note. How did that happen?

SP: I got there when his body was found. What ended up happening was, talk about coincidences, I was in the D.A.'s office. I was calling an investigator about a forgery case I was working on and the investigator told me he couldn't talk to me. He had to respond to a suicide. I think he said the suicide of a police officer. I asked who it was, and he said Harry Crist. So I left the office and drove down to where Harry lived. When I got there he was still there, untouched.

JC: So when you tell your boss "Harry was with me, this is ridiculous." What does he say?

SP: Nothing at first. I don't really remember his reaction. But I know it wasn't, "If they're saying Harry did it and Pagones was with Harry, then Pagones did it too." I know that wasn't the case.

JC: How do you know that wasn't the case? In other words, he must have said to himself: "Uh oh. This is more complicated. My own assistant is basically the alibi for the deceased Crist." How do you know he didn't have a worse view of it?

SP: First of all, because I was allowed to continue my duties. Secondly, and maybe most important, they knew me. Everybody there, I mean my family goes way back. My father was a judge, my cousin's a judge, my brother's a judge. My father and my family were involved in politics. I have a good name. A rape and a kidnapping? Come on. Just not plausible.

JC: So do you have some problems in the D.A.'s office then? The district attorney may have to disqualify himself; you're getting death threats; people are staring at you on the streets, probably more so if they're black; and obviously the press is reporting your name negatively. Whether you're innocent or not, they're connecting you with a rape allegation, even though Tawana Brawley herself doesn't directly accuse you. Did you think there was something else you should be doing to try to help clear your name?

SP: I went out and hired Jerry Hayes as my attorney. At that point, Abrams had started his grand jury, and I think we told them that I'd be willing to testify. But I insisted on being the last person to testify.

And we didn't want it to be disclosed that I would testify until it was time to do so. I wanted to be sure that everyone else testified about whatever it was they claimed to know before I testified about my whereabouts and activities during that four-day period.

JC: So basically you wanted them locked in so that they couldn't change their story and make different allegations.

SP: Exactly.

JC: A smart strategy.

SP: I also remember that what we were saying—even though we knew it wouldn't happen—that I would testify but I wanted Tawana Brawley or Sharpton to testify. I wanted one of them to come in to the grand jury and testify, and then I would willingly testify. But, of course, we knew that wouldn't happen.

JC: Why did you want Sharpton to testify?

SP: Sharpton was the one basically saying everything. He was the one claiming that he had information to prove that I raped Tawana Brawley. He was the one alleging that I was involved in organized crime. And that I had murdered Harry Crist. It just went on and on. It snowballed.

This is the other thing. So I'm working on a case in the D.A.'s office during this time, which involved a state liquor authority investigator and two restaurant owners with Italian names. The issue was whether or not this state investigator was guilty of what started out as assault, but it was really nothing more than harassment. Anyway, I worked out a deal where I just got everything adjourned in contemplation of dismissal or dismissed. The two owners call—I think CBS reporter Mike Taibbi—and accuse me of organized crime connections.

So now they run a story about me being organized crime. As if that's not bad enough, I get visited by (I think) M.A. Farber and Craig Wolff from *The New York Times*, and maybe one other person. They come in to my office at the D.A.'s office and threaten me, because at that point they had run a story saying "Pagones couldn't have done this." So they come in, furious. They're saying "We just saw a story about you being involved with organized crime, and we did our own investigation and believe that you're involved in organized crime." They threaten me that I better confess all my organized crime ties. Unbelievable.

JC: In preparing for this interview, I've read a fair amount of coverage of this by *The New York Times*. Generally speaking—tell me if I'm wrong—the coverage about you was very favorable.

SP: It was indeed very favorable. But here's what happens. Remember, early on, everyone is trying to prove that this couldn't happen, and they're trying to basically retrace my steps to create an alibi for me. And again, I'm not disclosing where I was. *The New York Times* tries to get me to tell them where I was. I won't do that. What ends up happening is they run a huge story. I think part of it was on the front page. And there were a couple of insets, and the gist of the story is that Pagones is a good guy; there's no way he did this. After that, Taibbi runs his story about the organized crime allegations, and now these guys think that they have egg on their face. Basically they say, "We ran this story on your behalf, and now we find out you may be involved in organized crime."

JC: So they thought that you had basically sucker-punched them. You had convinced them that you were an innocent, and then another news outlets present you as a bad guy.

SP: Right. I'm in organized crime. That's how it was, but the public didn't see that. So you say the investigation was needed and it was a good thing. And my answer to you is "Yeah, it was a good thing ultimately, but it was hell getting from point A to point Z."

JC: Reverting to my original question—whether the system worked or not—suppose this scenario: Sharpton, Maddox, and Mason and Brawley are making these allegations against you. Instead of what he did, the governor instead says "I see on its face that these allegations are ridiculous, and I'm NOT going to appoint a special prosecutor." And assume the D.A. concludes his investigation, finding nothing. He says, "I'm closing this matter out." How would that help you? You'd still have Sharpton, Mason, Maddox, Brawley making allegations against you, and then claiming a cover-up because no one really conducted a thorough investigation.

SP: I still have that. Sharpton doesn't yell the way he used to yell before. But he still won't admit that I had nothing to do with the Brawley case. Mason is the only one who, afterwards, came up to me and apologized. I've never heard him say another thing about the Brawley case.

JC: He apologized to you?

SP: Yes. After the verdict came in.

JC: He ultimately had that "Come to Jesus" moment and became somewhat of a do-gooder?

SP: Mason, yes. Maddox, to this day, every month, reports about this or that and it ultimately leads to Tawana Brawley and Pagones. "Pagones is a rapist. He got away with this." To this day. What do I do about that?

JC: You show the world the thorough and conclusive grand jury report that specifically found that you did nothing!

SP: Yes. But these guys play. In fact, one of the grand jurors, a black man, claimed that the grand jury didn't really do its job. That it basically went in there, knew what it wanted to accomplish, and accomplished it. That was on the news.

JC: Do you remember how many blacks there were on the jury?

SP: No.

JC: A significant number?

SP: I don't think so.

JC: So today, Sharpton is less vociferous about it, Maddox still is, Mason isn't any more. Brawley doesn't really talk about it. She's out of state. She's moved on. She's a middle-aged woman now. Do you still get feedback suggesting that you got away with a horrible crime? Do you see that on the streets of Beacon or Poughkeepsie?

SP: No. Occasionally I'll hear something. You know what it is? When Sharpton is in the news and the media wants to attack Sharpton, one of their mechanisms is to use me. A lot of times they'll call me for feedback, or to get a statement from me which I really just don't do any more. I don't return calls. I'm done. I don't want to relive it anymore.

But there are still people who believe I did it. They're smaller in number, but they're out there. They believe that something happened, and that I was somehow involved. And the reality is that I'll never be able to change that.

JC: You mentioned earlier that you didn't want to disclose your "alibi" because you were afraid it would be leaked. I don't mean alibi in a bad sense . . .

SP: I'm glad you corrected that. Yes, when I went in to the grand jury that last day, I laid everything out. I said "this is where I was." I had photographs. I had witnesses who came forward to testify. It was during Thanksgiving week. We had a farm back then up in the Catskills and it was me and like 50 other people. And that's where I was for the bulk of that time. And I had witnesses to testify, "Yeah he was with us." Unless you were to argue that I was with my family and then at some point I left my family, went over to where Tawana was and then back to the Catskills, it was ridiculous.

JC: If Tawana Brawley came forward today and appeared on a retrospective—on *60 Minutes*—and admitted the whole thing was a hoax, the whole thing made out of whole cloth maybe because she was afraid of her stepfather, Ralph King, and she needed an explanation for him why she didn't come home on time. And you were to believe that her expression of remorse was real. What would that do for you?

SP: That would make me feel very good. And, to this day that's one of the things that I've said. Although I'm not really sure how I feel at the moment. But I've always said that "All you have to do, Tawana, is come forward and admit that we had nothing to do with whatever happened to you. That it was a hoax." And I would give serious thought to just forgiving the entire judgment against her.

And remember something: during my trial, I made that same offer publicly to Tawana Brawley, through the media. I said "Tawana, come to court and testify. I don't care what you say. I don't care if you take that stand and point at me and say 'Steve Pagones raped me over and over.' I don't care. If you come to court and testify, I will waive any judgment that I get against you. No matter what you say." Because at that point in time I knew if she took the stand we could impeach her credibility.

JC: This is an odd question to ask you given what her accusations have done to your life: do you see her as a victim in this?

SP: Yes. Absolutely then. No longer though. Initially I think that she was scared and I think that she was victimized by her parents. She was victimized by Mason, Maddox, and Sharpton and she was just a young girl who didn't have the right people, the right support staff, to help her. And I think she got caught up in this lie and she didn't know what to do.

However, now, she's a grown woman. At any point in time she could have come forward and said, "Enough. I want to tell the truth. I want to set the record straight." And I don't even care if she says that it was a hoax. But I think it's important for her to say that Steve Pagones, Harry Crist, and Scott Patterson and all these others—they had nothing to do with whatever happened to me.

JC: What was Patterson accused of?

SP: He was accused of the same crime.

JC: So why is the only the name Steve Pagones—the poster child—along with Harry Crist, although he's dead, for the wrongdoing? You don't hear much about Patterson. You hear about Pagones.

SP: Because Steve Pagones decided to fight. If I didn't fight and if I didn't bring my defamation lawsuit, it would be like I was guilty. Like I had something to hide.

JC: But did people have that view of Patterson?

SP: Patterson's name wasn't mentioned as much as mine. You've got to remember, my name sold newspapers. I was in the prosecutor's office. I was an assistant prosecutor to Grady. Grady had to get out and bring it to Abrams because Grady knew that Pagones was involved. It sold a lot of papers. And, although Patterson's name was mentioned as a state trooper, it was not the same.

JC: It seems, in reading the grand jury report, you couldn't have done much better than what the grand jury had to say.

SP: Correct.

JC: Why didn't you let it go? Why did you bring a lawsuit? You weren't suing these folks to get money, were you?

SP: No.

JC: So why did you bring the lawsuit? That was just going to repeat the thing, put it back in the public eye, a big deal because Sharpton was a defendant. Why didn't you just let it go?

SP: Because Sharpton kept saying, "If Steve Pagones is really innocent, then he should sue me. If he's really innocent, he'll sue me." And I had people saying, "Are you going to sue? You can't let him get away with this." And I thought, you know, they're right.

JC: Which people were saying that—your family?

SP: People on the street. Media. Sharpton dared me to sue him. And he promised, over and over again, that if I sued him, he would testify and basically lay everything out. But he wanted to do it in a public setting. He didn't want to do it in front of the grand jury because that was a closed setting. He said he would do it in an open setting where the public and the media were there. I had to sue.

JC: You look like a very intelligent guy and sound like a very intelligent guy, but it sounds like you were extremely naïve. Sharpton says he promises that he's going to testify if you sue. Why would you believe him?

SP: He did testify.

JC: Did he say anything substantive?

SP: No. But I think I proved my point in going after him, giving him an opportunity, bringing everything public, and trying to hold these guys accountable. I was furious at the reality that there was no accountability. To be honest, before this case I had heard decent things about Mason, but not Sharpton and Maddox. I knew what they were about and I was sickened at the thought that that was it—that the grand jury came out and that's it. They go on to the next victim.

JC: Was Sharpton asked either by his lawyer, Michael Hardy, or your lawyer, William Stanton, whether—in making the allegation that you participated in a rape of Tawana Brawley—he was actually told that by Tawana Brawley?

SP: Yes. And at one point in time he said, I think during the trial, "No, no I never spoke to Tawana Brawley directly. I'm not going to speak to a young girl about her being raped." Which was completely inconsistent with other information he gave to the media which he said: "I spoke to Tawana. I have spoken to her numerous times." It was completely inconsistent.

JC: Were Mason and Maddox asked whether they spoke to Tawana Brawley and that the allegations made against you came from her?

SP: I don't remember. I'm sure they were asked.

JC: What would it do for you if Sharpton went on *60 Minutes* and basically were to admit, "I was wrong. I had no basis to make those allegations against Steve Pagones?"

SP: That would mean the world to me, because that's all I've been trying to do—to set the record straight.

JC: Do you still think about it every day?

SP: Not every day, but a lot. You've got to remember, any time I see Sharpton I can't help but think about it. Any time I hear Sharpton making allegations or talking about the importance of the truth, or in some instances the importance of apologizing for wrongdoing, I think to myself "You bastard, what about you? How is it that you continue to do your race baiting and your harassing and your recklessness? How is it that nothing happens to you?"

JC: Accepting the grand jury report as true, and I have no reason to disagree with its findings, do you think that Sharpton, Mason, and Maddox, actually believed it when making their allegations that you and Crist participated in a sexual assault on Tawana Brawley?

SP: Absolutely not.

JC: Why would they accuse specific individuals like yourself, Crist, and Patterson, when they could have just said that it was three white men, one of whom was wearing a law enforcement outfit? Why didn't they just leave it vague—if they did that they wouldn't risk you coming forward, saying "What the hell are you talking about, I was out of town. Or I was here. Or I was with my wife, or my girlfriend." Why would they make specific claims about specific people?

SP: I'm speculating, and going on hearsay—things that I've heard that Sharpton has said. Maddox was the first one who accused me publicly in a press conference. And from what I understand, neither Mason or Sharpton knew that Maddox was going to mention my name. But once he mentioned my name, they just felt the need to run with it. They couldn't look at him and say "What are you talking about?" They had to go on and continue and follow whatever it was that Maddox was saying about me. It was a situation where they just kept digging themselves deeper and deeper.

JC: You mentioned, before we began the interview, that you're unhappy with the legal system over this episode in your life, and that's why you decided not to practice law anymore. Correct?

SP: Not necessarily that I'm unhappy with the law. I was very upset with the way the law was manipulated. And again I was a part of the system. I was a prosecutor. I believed in the system. I believed that you investigate and then you prosecute. Not that you prosecute and then you investigate. I really felt in a lot of respects that I was hung out to dry. So after all was said and done, I just lost my taste for the practice of law.

JC: So you've gone into private investigation now?

SP: I've been doing investigations, security, and executive protection since 1990.

JC: Aside from the fact that it changed your career path and obviously you've gone through torment over the last 25 years—less so in recent years—how else has this experience impacted your life?

SP: For one, it taught me the importance of really looking into allegations before you pursue them. I don't believe everything that I see, or everything that I read. I know that a lot of times wrongful accusations are made. I know that often allegations are made without being investigated. Statements are made without looking into the source. So now, as an investigator, I look at things differently. I realize how important it is to follow up with every lead and to keep an open mind until you're done with the investigation.

JC: I asked my question poorly. How has this experience adversely affected your life?

SP: I no longer practice law. I *live* with the Tawana Brawley case. And numerous times I'm put in a position where people want to talk about it and they bring it up. This is something that my children, now in college, live with, and there are instances where the case is mentioned and people may not realize right away who they are. This is something that they've had to live with. And there are still times when I worry about my safety. When Sharpton's in the news, I'm on high alert. Because when Sharpton's in the news, I know that the Tawana Brawley case lurks in the background somewhere. I always worry about that one percent of people who maybe think that I got away with something, and they're going to make a name for themselves by righting the wrong. Either they will go after my children or go after me or whatever the case may be.

JC: What have you told your kids about this, what life guidance have you given your kids?

SP: I have three girls. My oldest graduated college. I have two kids in college. And I have a son who is ten. And that is also one of the reasons that I brought my lawsuit—because I knew that, at some point, my kids were going to come face to face with this. And I wanted them to know that I stood up for what was right and I tried to hold people accountable.

I was afraid, by the way, that if I didn't bring this lawsuit, Sharpton would always say, "If Pagones was innocent, he would have sued me." So when it came time to talk to my daughters, I didn't give them the raw details, but I basically told them that I was accused of doing some very bad things to a little black girl, and the state came out and conducted an investigation. And when the state was done, I basically went after Mason, Maddox, and Sharpton and I sued them to hold them accountable for the damage they did. I did that because no person should be allowed to hurt another person's reputation like that. No person should be allowed to have that free reign without accountability and responsibility. And that's how I left it. I knew once I told them that, that they would do their own research. Which they did. The computer, right? And aside from the computer, I have bookshelves with thousands of newspaper articles. They've read it. And you know what? They're very proud that I stood up to those guys and tried to hold them accountable.

JC: This may sound crazy, but do you find yourself not wanting to be alone—in the sense that you sort of always want to have a person with you, so in case someone makes a false accusation against you . . .

SP: No, however, I will say this, and this is not a bad thing. But for example, if I'm going to have a female client in the office, I will make sure that I have someone else in the office. Very rarely will I go to a female client's house alone. So I do worry about that. It's not to the degree of being paranoid, but again, especially me, all I need is for a female to make an allegation and I will be viewed differently than another individual because of the Brawley allegations. Could you imagine if I go to Mrs. Jones's house and Mrs. Jones makes an allegation about me and somehow it gets out into the media? Sharpton would have a field day with that. The media would have a field day with that.

JC: So it does impact the way you live your life, even your professional life.

SP: It makes me more aware of the importance of being careful in instances like that, yes. Again I'm not paranoid. I think, though, that I'm aware of circumstances. I'm very aware of the damage that a single allegation can do. And I'm very aware of the fact that my situation is different than another person's.

JC: What's God-awful about this is that you've been exonerated. Nobody gets exonerated by a grand jury as have you. It's almost unheard of—the New York attorney general exonerated you. And nonetheless, you say it impacts your life in subtle ways every day. And this is 25 years later.

SP: Yes. How could it not? That case was huge. And unfortunately for me, Sharpton remains in the news. He remains very high profile, very volatile, very antagonistic. Because Sharpton is there, the Tawana Brawley case is there. And, frankly, that is often how they try to attack Sharpton, by mentioning Tawana Brawley.

JC: How does it affect you that Sharpton is invited to the White House frequently? That the president of the United States or the governor will come to the National Action Network. That Sharpton has a television show where he comments on public events. That he is the probably the leading African-American spokesman in America—succeeding Jesse Jackson—in terms of civil rights issues, like the Garner police killing in Ferguson, the Brown police killing in Staten Island, or the like. How does that affect you?

SP: I think it's despicable. And it says a lot about society. Basically the media and these politicians have allowed Sharpton to rehabilitate himself without actually rehabilitating himself. They've allowed him to gain credibility. They put him in a position of prominence, and he's never had to come clean with the Brawley case.

And I'm not looking for an apology. Everybody says Pagones is looking for an apology. I don't want him to apologize. It's not going to happen. I just want him to admit that now he knows he was wrong about us. About Pagones, about Crist, about Patterson. That's all I want.

JC: One of the people who pushed Attorney General Abrams to investigate the Brawley allegations was Bill Cosby. He was probably at the time the most liked, the most respected figure in the black community in the United States, maybe the world. Now, in the last two months, we read about these many women coming forward, alleging that he date-raped them. What does that mean to you? Did he ever make an accusation against you directly?

SP: No, he came forward and basically supported Tawana Brawley. I think he made a statement, and put up some money. I think his statement was, "Let's treat Tawana Brawley like she's our daughter." Or something like that. Whatever the words were they were meant to lend credibility to Tawana Brawley. And I look at what he's going through now and I think to myself: "Karma, you know? It's a bitch."

Could you imagine if some high-profile person now stood up and said, "Let us treat all these women like they're our wives and our sisters and our daughters." I don't think he'd like it much. It's just funny—more directly, ironic—how things work out.

JC: Obviously you've given a lot of thought to this over the last 25 years, in terms of how you dealt with this issue in 1987 and 1988, and thereafter in the lawsuit. Is there something that you would have done differently if you had an opportunity to do it all over, in terms of how you responded?

SP: No. And I really mean that. There were things that I'm glad I didn't do. There were a lot of times when I really just wanted to lash out at Mason, Maddox, Sharpton, and the media. But I'm glad I didn't, because I didn't want to stoop down to their level. But no, I don't think I would have done anything differently. The reality is that I don't think I could have done anything differently.

I was basically blowing in the wind and operating within whatever parameters the system set up for me. They had a grand jury investigation. "Would you like to come in and testify? If you come in and testify we will consider your request about creating a public document clearing your name. If you don't testify, we're not going to be able to do it." I was limited as to what I could do. I could control certain things, like, for example, was I going to release my schedule or was I going to cooperate with a polygraph. I think in those instances, I made the right choice. And I would make the same choices.

JC: If you were the attorney general of New York, investigating this kind of allegation against John Doe and Richard Roe, what would you have done differently than what was done?

SP: I think I would have said, "Put up or shut up." These guys, Maddox, Mason, and Sharpton, basically held the system hostage, and were allowed to do so. I think that what the A.G. should have done is said "We're closing this. At any point in time if you want to come forward with evidence we will take that evidence and we will launch a huge investigation. But until then, there's nothing to investigate." And there was really nothing to investigate.

JC: Would you have subpoenaed Mason, Maddox, and Sharpton to testify before the grand jury?

SP: I don't know because, let's face it, there's no way that they would come, and all that would do is put an attorney general in a position to say, "Where do I go after them? And if so, what kind of circus is that going to cause?" So would I want to do that? Sure. Should that have been done? Absolutely. Would I actually do it? Probably not. Certain things are just not worth it.

Clearly Maddox, Mason, and Sharpton weren't interested in telling the truth. Clearly they weren't interested in representing Tawana Brawley's concerns and needs. They were all about furthering their own agenda.

7

The Lone Holdout

Adam Sirois

If I look at Jose Ramos and I think about all of the
evidence that the defense presented about him . . .
why does that not line up more closely with him?
Why isn't he the guilty one rather than some bodega
clerk who, without any criminal history, would have
had to suddenly just go psycho and kill a child and
then commit the most amazing job of getting rid of the
evidence. . . . If Jose Ramos had been the defendant, I
think he would have been found guilty unanimously.

—Adam Sirois, January 5, 2016[1]

1. This interview took place at the author's offices in New York City. After this interview which followed the hung jury, Pedro Hernandez was retried for the murder of Etan Patz. Notably, Sirois continued to publish articles about how he perceived the prosecution's case up until the commencement of the second trial (see Selected Materials). Curiously, Sirois and other jurors from the first trial somewhat regularly attended the second trial—Sirois seated on one side of the courtroom, and a number of jurors who had voted to convict on the other. Sirois also explained that he was a consultant to Hernandez's defense attorney in the period at least preceding the second trial. How to interpret Sirois's considerable interaction with the *Hernandez* case post-trial is for the reader to decide. On February 14, 2017, as this book was being finalized, the second jury convicted Hernandez. Had it acquitted, Sirois would have been the

It is, without rival, every parent's worst nightmare.

In 1979, Julie and Stan Patz allowed their six-year-old son, Etan, a measure of independence. He would be allowed to walk the two blocks to his school bus stop by himself. Only he never made it. And as of this writing—36 years later—no one *really* knows what happened.

The New York County District Attorney believes, at least since 2012, that Pedro Hernandez kidnapped and murdered Etan and, only last year, tried him for those crimes. You see, in 2012, Hernandez—who has an IQ of 70 and schizotypal personality disorder—confessed to choking Etan and disposing of his not-yet-dead body by placing him in a trash bag and box and taking him two blocks away where garbage would be picked up. But the confession, which was videotaped, was made after six hours of a not-videotaped "interview" by the police—Hernandez had no lawyer at the time, and never asked for one. The corroborating evidence (a defendant in New York cannot be convicted based solely on his own admissions) was weak. It consisted in large part of statements Hernandez allegedly made to friends 30 years earlier. No body was ever recovered, no clothes or school bag were found and there was no DNA.

The Hernandez trial was held in 2015. While Hernandez did not testify, represented at trial by experienced counsel appointed by the court—he did mount a defense. He argued that his confessions (he ultimately confessed three times) were invalid; that he was susceptible to the police's suggestions given his IQ and mental health diagnosis. The defense also argued that Hernandez was the wrong guy—Jose Ramos, a convicted pedophile who had actually known Etan, admitted that he had been with a boy he was "90 percent sure" was Etan on the day of his disappearance, but that he let the boy go.

The trial lasted four months. After 18 days of deliberation, the jury was deadlocked. One juror, just one—Adam Sirois—voted finally that Hernandez should not be convicted. There was a mistrial and Hernandez is to be retried in 2016.

---

reason Hernandez avoided conviction. Now, however, it turns out that he is the outlier against 23 other jurors who believe Hernandez killed Etan Patz. The reader will have to decide if Sirois's vote caused an injustice by requiring a costly and time-consuming second trial. Or was it instead an unsuccessful attempt to avoid an injustice? Or, finally, was it something else?

What was Sirois thinking? Did he think Ramos should have been on trial for Etan's murder? Did the other jurors vote to convict because they believed Hernandez's confession and the corroborating witnesses or because they simply wanted to give the Patz family—and perhaps the City of New York itself—the closure it finally deserved?

To appreciate the import of Sirois's refusal to vote to convict Hernandez, we turn to some of the most fundamental principles of criminal justice. First and foremost, defendants are presumed innocent. In other words, it is the prosecution that must prove the defendant committed the crime. The burden is, of course, solely on the prosecution and the defendant never has to prove he is innocent. And the prosecution must prove a defendant's guilt "beyond a reasonable doubt" to an impartial jury and *all* 12 members of the jury must find that burden met.

With this backdrop, we return 36 years and begin looking at the events as they unfolded—some which the jury heard; some which were kept from the jury because the judge presiding over the Hernandez case so ruled. Etan Patz—six years old—left home to meet his school bus. When his parents realized he never got there, law enforcement mobilized—initially 30 officers and five detectives were assigned to find him; eventually 300 officers were looking for him and a tip line was created with law enforcement fielding up to 500 calls per day. Neighborhood buildings were searched and, although people were questioned, Hernandez—a then-18-year-old stock boy at a bodega somewhere between Patz's home and the bus stop—was never interviewed.

Etan was the first "milk carton" kid—his face literally everywhere. Parents in cities throughout the country no longer allowed their children that kind of freedom, that kind of independence, to walk two blocks alone. Etan became a rallying cry—and was the first of a series of high-profile missing-children cases that made national headlines. Indeed, four years to the day of his disappearance, President Ronald Reagan proclaimed National Missing Children's Day.

Yet no arrest was made. The police didn't have sufficient evidence to charge anyone. Indeed, not until at least ten years after Etan disappeared did the police focus in on a viable suspect—but it was not Pedro Hernandez. No, Jose Ramos was a friend of Patz's babysitter. He was also a pedophile, and by 1987 was sentenced to 25 years for sexually abusing a boy. During his time in prison, Ramos told investigators he was with Etan on the day he vanished. Indeed, it was reported that Ramos at one point told a cell mate—"Etan is dead and there will never be a body." Yet Ramos was never charged.

The police continued investigating Etan's disappearance. No one would let it go. In 2000–2001, they searched the building where Ramos lived at the time of Etan's disappearance. They also searched the workroom of another person who had been in the neighborhood on the day Etan disappeared—Othneil Miller. The police found nothing and no arrest was made. Hernandez—who had never been in trouble with the police until his 2012 confession—was not even on the radar.

Ultimately, a federal prosecutor who had been involved in the case supported Etan's father's petition to have Etan officially and finally declared dead. Still, to this day Etan's body has never been found. Etan's father then did something rarely, if ever, done. In 2001, he commenced a civil action against Ramos—the convicted child molester never charged with any crime concerning Etan—arguing that Ramos kidnapped and killed his son. Patz obtained a judgment against Ramos, on default, and was awarded $2 million, a sum which, of course, could never be collected.

The mystery surrounding Etan Patz's disappearance continued. In 2010, Cyrus Vance, Jr., district attorney of New York County, decided to reopen the investigation, and did so in a very public way. In 2012, the police spent five days excavating a SoHo basement, anticipating that they would find proof that Etan was buried in the walls. But Ramos never used that basement; Hernandez never used that basement—no, the police were looking for clues that Miller murdered Etan.

Once again, the police found nothing. But the newspaper coverage of the excavation prompted a call to a missing persons hotline—Pedro Hernandez, the stock boy who was 18 years old in 1979 had, in that year, spoken to his charismatic church group and told them that "he had done a bad thing and killed a child in New York."

A dozen police officers went to Hernandez's home in New Jersey at 7:30 on a Saturday morning. Hernandez went to the police station and spoke to the police voluntarily; he never asked for a lawyer, but kept asking when he could go home. The police did not read Hernandez his rights until at least seven hours after they began questioning him. And it was not until that time—not until Hernandez was ready to confess—that the police turned on the videotape.

Hernandez confessed. And he confessed again later that day at 2:00 in the morning (after being questioned for another five hours); and again two years later when interviewed by mental health professionals. He escorted the police to the place where he said he left the trash with Etan's body. And five people came forward to say Hernandez told them—in 1981 or thereabouts—that he had killed a child. The five people? An embittered ex-wife, a childhood friend, and three members of the prayer group who spoke in tongues as part of their religious practice.

In 2015, Pedro Hernandez was tried for the 1979 murder of Etan Patz. The confessions were played for the jury—Hernandez was cold, almost conversational in telling how he choked Etan, but did not kill him; that he threw Etan, still alive, in the trash. Law enforcement testified—some for the prosecution and some for the defense. Those who heard Hernandez say he had once killed a child were called. And there were experts—did Hernandez confess to expiate his guilt, because he had indeed attacked Etan, or did he confess because his IQ and mental health status made him susceptible to the police's suggestion that he killed Etan? Indeed, did the police—during the seven hours Hernandez was questioned prior to his confession—influence Hernandez in any way? Hernandez, for his part, did not testify. Nor did Ramos—but the law enforcement official who had interviewed Ramos 30 years earlier did testify, and a chilling tape of him talking about Patz in 1982 was played for the jury.

And what happened in the jury room? Did they come to the trial with preconceptions? What were they thinking, discussing while they listened to the confessions and looked at evidence? Was the jury disturbed that Hernandez did not testify; that he never recanted his confession? The jurors made spreadsheets of what they could agree about and argued (however politely) over the inferences that could be drawn from that evidence. And when they first realized they were deadlocked—that not everyone would vote for conviction, or acquittal—the judge did what judges do. He sent them back to the jury room to try once again to reach a unanimous verdict. But when the deliberation lasted 18 days—the longest in at least a decade in that courthouse—the judge finally said "enough" and declared a mistrial.

At the end of the day, Adam Sirois, a health care consultant who has degrees from Johns Hopkins University and George Washington University and who has worked in global health both domestically and internationally, was the lone holdout. But did he have the support of other jurors during the deliberations or was he alone throughout? Sirois spent the last two weeks of their deliberations trying to convince others to vote not guilty. Why would he do that? Was he trying to get others on board—others to vote to acquit—to send the prosecution a message: "Your case against Pedro Hernandez is wrong"? Or was he—as two of the other jurors have suggested—seeking media exposure for himself, having nothing to do with Hernandez's guilt or innocence.

Was Jose Ramos the real murderer? Indeed, had he been on trial, would he have been convicted?

Finally—perhaps the most troubling question of all—did the other jurors vote to convict because they believed Hernandez was indeed the murderer, or because they simply wanted to convict *someone*? Was it easier to believe the story told by the prosecution because they felt it was time that *someone* pay for Etan's death?

Was justice done?

The Dialogue

JC: In the classic film, *12 Angry Men*, Juror No. 8 (Henry Fonda) felt that he had reasonable doubt about the defendant's guilt. Unable to persuade his fellow jurors, he told them that he would abstain from the next vote and let the others vote in secret. If their vote was unanimous, he would put aside his doubts and vote to convict. What do you think of that?

AS: The movie was nothing like our reality in the *Hernandez* case. Obviously, Fonda manages to convince everyone in a few hours. That didn't even come close to what we experienced in our deliberations. We didn't even take a vote until day four.

JC: But what do you think about the idea of saying, "If you are unanimous, although I have my doubts, I will vote with you"?

AS: I think my actions speak for themselves. I strongly disagree with it.

JC: Why? What were you thinking at the time this happened?

AS: What I was thinking at the time was that, for me, "reasonable doubt" is a very, very high threshold that the prosecution needs to get over, and I felt that nothing corroborated the stories of five witnesses who ended up being the only evidence in the case worth listening to. Nothing, for me, pulled it together and gave me something close to an "aha moment," like, "You know, I now see the dots that the prosecution has tried to connect." Nothing even close to connecting them.

JC: Did you think that the other jurors didn't think that reasonable doubt had a high threshold?

AS: I don't think they truly understood what it meant. I honestly don't.

JC: What did it mean to you that you think it didn't mean to them?

AS: Interestingly, we were all very wary not to cheat and study things at night. We tried to base everything off what the judge told us. So he gave us his definition of reasonable doubt during the read backs. And, for me, it meant that as a reasonable person I can't have the doubts that I had, not even one.

We agreed on many facts. It was the inferences from those facts that differed greatly among us. I feel like a lot of them were leaning towards guilt. They even wrote when we took votes, until the last vote—three or four people would write "60 percent guilty" or "80 percent guilty." We were told at the outset not to ascribe percentages to things like that in determining guilt or non-guilt. I understood people wanting to use numbers. But, for me, it wasn't like a 51 percent. A lot of my fellow jurors were like, "Well we're halfway there, so he's guilty." And I couldn't stomach that concept.

JC: Did you think your fellow jurors were too interested in giving closure to the family that had suffered so much over the years?

AS: I think some were. There were a lot of thoughtful jurors. Not everyone was. We put a lot of work into it. A lot of people were very quiet the entire time. But about six of us really engaged in argument. Me on one side most of the time, until one of the other jurors started talking on my side the last week—although he changed his mind at the last minute.

JC: So when you thought there were indeed jurors who may have been too influenced by sympathy or wanting to give closure to the Patz family, how did they articulate that, if they did?

AS: It was funny. They wanted to give closure to the Patz family, and to New York City as a whole; but they were focused on the Patz family. And also in a very bizarre way, several wanted to give closure to the Hernandez family—arguing things like, "Let's get this over with so they won't have to keep driving here from New Jersey to spend money and spend time at court."

No one was really pushing. Only one juror mentioned several times that she had things to do and needed to get going with her life. We were very dedicated. Even she was. She at least put time in to hear people's arguments. But about six of us did most of the talking; and of those six, at least half really wanted closure. That was a big thing for them—like, "Let's give them peace."

JC: Were the jurors who opposed your position vocal?

AS: One. Overall, it got heated sometimes, but not personal. It wasn't like "You're stupid" or "You're an idiot." Nothing like that. Which was great, I thought. But there was one juror—we spoke the most. She and I argued across the table a lot. And I just felt her arguments, and a lot of the other arguments, were more based on just doing everything to make the story that the prosecution put forward make sense. And sort of like anything that I put forward as a hypothetical, or as a "What if," or as "Now let's think about this possibility" was simply looked upon disdainfully. They didn't want to even try to entertain any other option.

JC: Was this the juror who referred to you after the trial as having "a small heart and a big ego"?

AS: No. She was the forewoman. She actually was almost silent the entire time. She said maybe four things during the entire 18 days.

JC: Where would she come up with the idea—the woman who said you had a small heart and a big ego? Was there something that you articulated during the course of deliberations that would lead her in that direction?

AS: No. I did read that in the press of course. Any time we sent a vote to the judge—that it was a hung jury—the first vote we sent out formally was 8–4, then I forget, I'd have to look it up to remember all the exact voting numbers that we had. But as she would sign the letter to send out to the judge with the fact that we didn't reach a verdict, she would say under her breath like, "I can't believe I'm signing this." Just things like that. And she was in charge of who got to speak because we tried to have rules on speaking. You had to raise your hand and get in line and stuff. And she would—I'd be raising my hand sitting right next to her and she'd just look past me and put down other people's names. I had to be sort of like, "Could you put my name down to speak?" So it was tough; I had to push.

JC: Did either she or any other juror, perhaps during a hostile moment, suggest in words or substance that you were full of crap or that you were holding out in order to become a "star"?

AS: No. That came after. Those kinds of sentiments came after the deliberations.

JC: So in terms of your view of reasonable doubt, I assume you don't believe that Barack Obama was born outside of the United States.

AS: I do not.

JC: Do you have "reasonable doubt" ever about that? You've not seen his birth certificate. You were obviously not there. You weren't even born when he was born. So how are you so sure?

AS: I would think if I spent the amount of effort that I did on this trial to find out his exact place of birth I would be satisfied beyond a reasonable doubt. I haven't given it enough thought.

JC: Fair enough. So can you honestly say that you came to the *Hernandez* case with no preconception about the case?

AS: I can. I decided that if I get selected for the jury I will do it and I will try to find, as much as possible, the truth through the evidence.

JC: Did you get the sense that others on the jury had a preconception—based on things they said either before deliberations began or during deliberations?

AS: Yes. I won't mention names. But I would say if we had taken a vote within the first ten minutes of entering the deliberation room, the vote would have been eight or nine voting guilty, for sure.

JC: What led you to believe that?

AS: I do think there were a few people that came into the jury with a desire to see Hernandez convicted. I don't think it was a very large number. Maybe three or four people, but certainly people that were not going to be willing to render an unbiased opinion.

JC: Why do you think that?

AS: Part of it was their political views. And part of it is that there were some close-minded people on the jury.

JC: "Political"? What does that mean in this context?

AS: If I mention which views I was talking about, it would be obvious who it was. I'm not sure I want to do that.

JC: Fair enough. You don't mean "political" in the sense that they're Republican rather than Democrat, do you?

AS: No. Sort of societal/political views. It wasn't along party lines. Most people in there were Democrats, obviously. I would say a view towards humanity.

JC: Flesh that out.

AS: How to say it? There was one person in particular who struck me as very close-minded and said things that even made people who were obviously going to vote "guilty" cringe at some of the things he said.

JC: Like what?

AS: Off the top of my head? Well, here's a good one. This is not political so much—I don't know really how to describe it: Pedro Hernandez took three separate IQ tests and scored between 68 and 70 or something like that on each. And one juror said that he "faked" them; that he faked them because he was much more intelligent than that and much more manipulative. And everyone in the room just sort of gasped. Like—it's not possible. So even when we're trying to argue that Hernandez has low intelligence—we were trying to establish facts, things we could agree upon in the room. And we agreed upon a lot of things. We had a list of a 150 or so facts that we all agreed happened. And so we were, I was, trying to establish that Hernandez has low intelligence.

And it wasn't just this one juror. There were maybe four or five people that would not allow us as a group to say that this man had low intelligence. They thought he was manipulative. Because Hernandez did his own pro se divorce, they would say he's a "brilliant legal mind"; he can fill out a form and divorce his wife without a lawyer. Arguments like that that were straw-man arguments. Like just the most bizarre form of debate.

And the most bizarre use of information or misinformation to argue one side, simply because you think the person's guilty. I did try to open my mind to the other side. Like maybe if I accept that then I can get there. But there were too many, too many of those arguments being thrown around. Like his phone calls home made from prison demonstrated that he was this crafty mastermind that was totally manipulating his 22-year-old daughter and wife. But it was obvious; she has a high-pitched laugh and she was laughing at half of what he said.

It was just obvious that they were completely buying into the story line that the prosecutor was saying—Ms. [Joan] Illuzzi-Orbon—hook, line, and sinker. And I was baffled. I was like—how can you think that, how can you? Granted, he's intelligent enough to get through life, but he's not some manipulating strongman who was able to withstand the police interrogation.

According to them, it had nothing to do with the fact that he was low intelligence, had mental health issues, was on pain killers and that he wasn't allowed—well he was allowed to leave, but he wasn't really, I would say, given the right. He wanted to go home several times during his interrogation and the police truly didn't let him. They said, "You can, but just stay longer."

JC: Do you think that the prosecution of Pedro Hernandez which will lead, as we know, to a new trial, is an injustice?

AS: I think it's an injustice that a man who has no violent criminal history before or after May 25, 1979—zero, none—is still in jail now. I think that's a travesty.

JC: But do you think the prosecution of Pedro Hernandez and now a retrial of Pedro Hernandez is an injustice?

AS: Yes.

JC: Injustice because you think he's innocent?

AS: Injustice because I think that the authorities have latched onto a scapegoat that they want to prosecute, and they want to make this the reality.

JC: And they're doing that for what reason? Saying that they have "scapegoated" him is a pretty extreme statement, you'd have to agree.

AS: Yes. Well, I mean, if you look at what's going around the country; there's a lot of abuse of power that's going on by the police. I wasn't sure that's what happened in this case, but I wanted to see if that was part of it.

JC: You're saying that the district attorney is prosecuting this case for an untoward purpose?

AS: I think the state has a very weak case. But they knew that the city wants closure and Pedro Hernandez is a very good candidate to bring closure to New York. That's what I think now; going into the trial I had no idea. I need to make that very clear. That's not a pretrial feeling. That's after three months of listening to testimony and figuring out what the actual evidence was that the state had.

JC: So you think because the district attorney had a weak case going in and since you've not been persuaded otherwise that it has been an injustice to prosecute him?

AS: [Pause.] I mean obviously, if the police really believe that this is the person that should be prosecuted, he should be prosecuted. I think the prosecution thought he should be prosecuted. But seeing what the case was and seeing who the eyewitnesses were and how they were brought to testify caused me a lot of doubt as to whether the story was authentic.

JC: I read in some article that one of the things that bothered you is that there was an interview by the police of Pedro Hernandez going on for some period of time, maybe seven hours, before the interview began to be recorded.

AS: Yes.

JC: I take it you're suspicious that something that may have happened before it was recorded, or in the way in which Hernandez may have been moved to confess—by virtue of something that was said to him, right?

AS: Yes, a lot of us had a very big concern about that. We spent days going back and forth about this. We also sent out a note to the judge asking if New Jersey State law requires video recording, which the judge did not answer. All he said was that that's not part of this case for us to consider. But yes, that was a very difficult hurdle to get over for at least five or six of us.

JC: Well five of you, however, did get over that.

AS: Yes.

JC: I assume what helped the others to get over it was that he confessed several times; not only then, but also to an assistant district attorney in New York County, his then-wife, and also to a charismatic Christian group years earlier. But that didn't help you to get over your concern?

AS: No, because each time I saw him "confess," it was never "I killed the boy and here's how I did it." The first time we see it on video he says "I choked the boy." And the way he describes it was very inauthentic to me. It felt contrived every time he said it and even in his so-called confessions when he was in jail, speaking with mental health experts, he never says, "I killed the boy and here's what I did." He embellishes it; he adds different facts around it. I truly think that mental health is a huge part of this case.

JC: Did you believe that these were all false confessions?

AS: It's hard. Here's where we get into the mental health aspects of the case which, I think, again were nuanced and misunderstood by some of the jurors. I believe that it was a false confession to begin with and what happened later is that Pedro Hernandez formed sort of a belief that he was involved in this, and he truly felt guilty over it. We heard testimony from mental health experts on both sides describe how someone with mental health problems, low intelligence, poor memory, and a suggestible nature is more likely to make a false confession. The mental health expert for the prosecution even told us that some people who are innocent can form fixed false beliefs about something they did not do. As someone with a master's degree in public health and based on my experience working with mentally disabled children, the other jurors actually asked me to take the lead on explaining the mental health issues involved in the case so they could try to understand how Mr. Hernandez could confess to something he did not do and then stick to it.

So I was trying to argue that false confessions do happen and that a person like Pedro Hernandez perfectly fits the description of someone capable of forming a fixed false belief. We spent five days just discussing whether or not Mr. Hernandez had mental health problems—something I thought was obviously proven in court—that it's really too bad we didn't have the first seven hours of questioning; that Pedro wasn't read his rights, I think, at the appropriate time; that anyone with any kind of level of intelligence would say, "I'd like a lawyer." If that had happened, the case would never have gone to trial. The only thing the authorities could go on in this case was if Hernandez confessed that first day. So they had to get that confession. And I do feel, in retrospect, that that is a huge part of this case.

JC: One of the things you said is that the district attorney or the police may have brought this case because they wanted closure in part for the City of New York. I don't know if that's so. I mean I hadn't thought about this case in a hundred years. I think parents, needless to say, may have changed their lives in terms of leaving young kids alone on the street even for a couple of seconds. But I don't think the city requires the kind of closure it may have required 35 years ago when the events happened.

AS: Yes. I don't think I'm exactly saying the police wanted closure for the City of New York, or society as a whole. I'm trying to say is that when they reopened the case by doing the dig at Othneil Miller's house, looking for anything they could find, they were obviously still interested in the case and they wanted to find the killer. And we all wanted that.

But you find out that Etan Patz used to be close to a pedophile, Jose Ramos. We don't know how many people called and said I think this person did it. We only know about Pedro Hernandez. And I just think the way that the police went about pursuing the case—and this was laid out in painstaking detail by both prosecution and the defense teams—about how he was picked up, who picked him up, how many police officers picked him up, the attack plan the night before, the walking him through the police building so he could see every exit sign . . .

It was painstaking to listen to that for days and days. The police trying to show that they gave Hernandez every opportunity to know that he was free to go at any time, and the defense team trying to show that this is a low-intelligence person who really didn't know his rights and didn't know that he could walk out at any time.

Especially given the way they brought him in to the police station through the backdoor, through barbed wire fence, with a card keyed door. They didn't walk him through the front in a very nice manner, making him feel like he could leave. I feel they knew that if they could get Hernandez to crack under pressure and get him to stay in that room, it would be enough for them to bring to trial.

And I really think that the police were on the fence whether he was the real perpetrator, but that they knew they could get him to crack under pressure.

JC: I asked you about injustice before. I'll ask it differently now. I'll let you say anything you want, but please first answer "yes" or "no": Do you think Pedro Hernandez is innocent?

AS: I told this to my fellow jury members. I don't know he's innocent. I don't. But I'm much closer to believing 100 percent that he's not guilty. And I know it's a nuanced way of looking at it, but I think that's what our criminal system is predicated on. You don't vote "guilty" and "innocent." You vote "guilty" or "not guilty."

JC: But as you sit here, right now, many months after the hung jury, do you think Hernandez had nothing to do with this?

AS: I *do* think he had nothing to do with it.

I'm much more convinced that he had nothing to do with it than that he had anything to do with it. Especially when you introduce Jose Ramos into the story. Ramos was dating Etan's babysitter, Susan Harrington, and walked him home from school on a regular basis with her. Susan was hired by Julie Patz to walk Etan to and from the bus stop during a school bus strike.

JC: Before you do that, if you can go on percentages: by what percentage do you think he's innocent? 95 percent innocent?

AS: Yes, vastly close to . . .

JC: 95 percent is pretty strong. To my mind there is indeed an injustice if the defendant is pretty much innocent in your view. So why are you talking about possibly mixed motives on the part of the prosecution? Or about the tape not having started until late into the police interrogation. Shouldn't it be "end of story" for you that you believe by 95 percent that he's innocent?

AS: I didn't feel that way until close to the trial's end. Throughout the trial I was back and forth on what I thought, how I felt—as new evidence came in. When you add up everything that the prosecution did, especially given the Jose Ramos aspect of the story . . . we were not allowed to know the most important ones. We didn't know that there was a civil suit in 2004–5.[2] We didn't know that Stan Patz won a $2 million judgment. We didn't know that there was a schism between Julie and Stan over that issue of who was responsible for Etan's death. It's one of the things that I hope will be admissible at the next trial.

Ramos was a huge issue for several jurors besides me. I think there would have been at least three or four more people to vote not guilty with me if that had been admitted in court. It's hard to say. I feel it was an injustice.

Look at what it is we're talking about. You have Hernandez's ex-wife who detests him, saying that maybe there was a picture of a boy who looked like Etan 33 years ago. You have a friend of his from high school, Mark Pike, who's lower intelligence than Pedro Hernandez. And you have

---

2. Author's note: Stan Patz, Etan's father, sued Jose Ramos in a civil suit for, essentially, murdering Etan. Ramos did not challenge a motion for judgment and Patz was awarded $2 million in damages, which was never collected. On July 15, 2016, after the date of this interview, a judge granted the Patz's request to vacate the judgment against Ramos.

three 79-year-old men from Puerto Rico who never went beyond first grade, all illiterate and all part of this charismatic church group. And they very happily admit that they speak to God in tongues and that God tells them what to do. And that's it. They're the five eye witnesses who were supposed to corroborate this confession.

And I'll tell you the truth; I don't trust any of them. Not one of them do I think was not motivated to do the wrong thing in this case for the wrong reasons. That's truly how I felt. So if I had been the prosecutor and I had been collecting those kind of stories from those people in advance of bringing Hernandez to the police station, I don't think I would have pursued him before the confession, before all that.

JC: Did that go into your thinking in voting—that if you were the prosecutor you would have done it differently, and not prosecuted him?

AS: I think part of the aspect is that this case should never have been brought to trial based on the evidence that they presented in court. The only reason it was brought to trial was that he confessed.

JC: Doesn't it mean a lot that he confessed?

AS: It would, if you don't believe that false confessions can happen.

JC: What did you know about false confessions before the trial ended?

AS: Only what I learned in court during the trial. Only what three or four defense experts said and one prosecution expert. But the prosecution expert was also obviously biased in the case. It seemed like the defense mental health experts were a lot less biased. They weren't really trying to show that he was innocent, or not guilty.

JC: When did you first decide that you were going to vote to acquit?

AS: [Pause.] A hard question.

We first took our first vote on the fourth day. When we came into the deliberation room, someone asked if we could do a vote right away. But we didn't.

There was a juror who joined me in voting for acquittal the last week. But at the time we began deliberating, he said we should just wait and think, and I and several people agreed with him. And we decided to wait. So the first day we just went through our notes. Second day and third day we looked at videos—the different confessions. Jose Ramos's video confession with the assistant district attorney in 1982. It's chilling the way he described Etan.

And that was the video I forced them to watch multiple times. During the viewing of that video, that's when we got to six-six at one point.

So did I formulate my opinion before the end of trial? No. I think I went into the deliberation room closer to 50/50—I don't know which way I'm going to go. I need to talk to the people I had become friends with—about eight of them. And I was really excited to see what they had to say. I was open to seeing what they had to say. I was totally shocked when we started talking on day four because I thought more people would be closer to thinking he was innocent.

But I myself didn't rule out that he's guilty. I could have been persuaded by my peers. But I was the only one that was as close as I was to a not guilty verdict. It was a nonofficial vote. We didn't send it to the judge. I think it was eight–four actually. That really showed me a lot—that I wasn't the only one. But when we started talking and I saw the level of vehemence against Hernandez and some of the asinine comments being made by some of the jurors—like that he's a brilliant man faking his IQ test, or that has no mental health problems.

It was really frustrating.

JC: How much after day four were you yourself doing the talking in the jury room?

AS: I was doing most of the talking for the not guilty side. But it shifted. For the first nine days or so it was myself, it was me and two other gentlemen who were arguing more on the not guilty side and trying to throw out arguments or suggestions that this was a complex case and that we needed to think about it.

JC: After you determined that the vote strongly favored conviction, were you trying to convince other jurors to move in your direction? In other words, were you trying to persuade them to change their vote and maybe gain an acquittal for Hernandez, or were you just saying, "Look I've got my position, I think it's rational and reasonable for the following reasons"?

AS: At least four people, I knew, were never going to change. Never.

JC: Like you were never going to change, right?

AS: No, and I told them that. I could have changed, if someone helped me see, helped connect the dots in a more clear-cut way. But we started going through the evidence with a fine tooth comb. We had every piece of evidence on the table. We looked at everything. We made list after list of every possible thing. Every fact. We made time lines.

All that did, over time, was to make me feel more confident in my position, not less. And if I had started feeling less confident I could have changed my mind. But everything pointed more and more strongly for me, and this is why one of the jurors who was originally arguing more on the guilty side was sort of in the middle and then switched to guilty. And then he came over to my side for the last four days. And that's when I could shut up. Because from day 10 to 15, let's say, I did all the talking for the not guilty side, because everyone else who was talking had shifted to the guilty side. You see, one juror who seemed to favor the not guilty side simply did not talk very much.

JC: Did you ever tell them, "You can say anything, I'll listen to everything you have to say but I just want you to know I'm voting to acquit. If you want to vote with me, fine, but I'm voting to acquit"?

AS: It was obvious—we voted multiple times throughout the 18 days and every time I was the only one who actually wrote not guilty. Others were "leaning towards guilt," which we counted as a non-guilty vote, because I convinced them that that's a not guilty vote. I maintained my position that they could convince me, up until about day 15 or something. The last week I made it clear that I was really not going to change my mind.

I told them that I'd gotten to the point where I'm not comfortable voting guilty. I can't do it. And I'm really hoping that some of you will see what I see.

JC: You recognized that if you voted to acquit there was going to be a hung jury anyway, right?

AS: We all knew that, right.

JC: So what was the advantage of others joining you?

AS: I wanted as many people, because I knew that the number would be known to the judge or someone. This case was bizarre in the amount of attention focused on the jury.

JC: To be very direct, you felt that if you got enough votes in your favor—even though you weren't going to get the four who were definitely going to convict—you might influence whether there would be a retrial?

AS: I did think that. I thought I'd get four people.

JC: So you had a view beyond this trial, didn't you? You had a view about the prosecution itself and wanted to accomplish ending the prosecution of Hernandez, even though you weren't going to be able to get him acquitted at the trial. In other words, you wanted the district attorney to conclude that it would be foolhardy for him to prosecute the case again, correct?

AS: I'm not a legal eagle or anything like that. I don't know how any of this works, actually. It was kind of eye-opening to see—but I knew that if we had a larger number than one on the acquittal side that it would make people hesitate about retrying the case. Maybe it wouldn't. Maybe if it was eleven-one the other way they still would have retried it. I don't know. But I just felt that there would be a better chance if there were more not guilty votes than just one.

That's why I was really saddened—for the last four days the juror came over to my side, and the silent guy came over to my side, so I thought it was going to be nine to three. I was almost sure of it. And for four days that man argued very eloquently; he's a very intelligent man. He added points that I didn't think to argue, because I was already exhausted. And then at the last day we voted he made a 90-minute talk, not a speech but he just said what his final feeling were. And he said "but I'm going to vote guilty," and I couldn't believe it.

JC: Returning to the issue of "injustice," we now know this case will go back to trial. Let's assume the exact same evidence that the judge makes the same rulings about the Ramos confession evidence and the other things you learned about after the trial. Assume also the jury comes in quickly with a unanimous vote to convict. Would you still see this as an injustice?

AS: I do feel that it's an injustice. I do. I feel ashamed of our country for not admitting evidence that could be exculpatory or could lead to a not guilty verdict . . .

JC: So you think it's an injustice on the part of the system. But what about the jury in concluding on the same facts that you voted to acquit? Now 23 jurors will have voted to convict. What about that?

AS: I would feel they're all wrong. Not because I'm some megalomaniac. Based on what I saw in the jury room, the level and type of argument that was being proposed by the "guilty" side was irrational, and often brought in irrelevant thinking to the case. It was thinking which suggested a willingness to accept anything to make the jurors feel comfortable voting guilty.

JC: But let's assume that the jurors in the next case are 12 people that you went to school with, or know from work.

AS: Most of these people did not have advanced degrees. Most were not well educated.

JC: Okay. Let's assume that all 12 people on the new jury are people that you've gone to school with, or know from work or your neighborhood. Or people you have great respect for in terms of intelligence, sensitivity, and a willingness to look at different ethnic groups with complete fairness.

AS: Then they won't vote guilty.

JC: You're so confident that they won't vote guilty?

AS: Absolutely. I'm so confident in my position I can't express it enough. I wish we could have—well obviously we couldn't videotape it—to listen in on the type of argumentation that was going on by, especially by the people who were convinced from day one. Especially this one gentleman who said things about Hernandez faking the IQ test and purposely answering questions to make himself have a low IQ. You can't do it. It's not possible.

JC: Me being the devil's advocate: you might be viewed in some of your comments just now as a bit of an elitist in how you see yourself vis-à-vis the other jurors, and your ability to assess what was before you. I see, for example, you attended Johns Hopkins.

AS: I don't agree with your characterization at all.

JC: Ok, but I assume there were likely some in the jury room who felt that way, right?

AS: Yeah, probably. I mean if they thought "elitist"—sort of like there were a few people in the room that said almost nothing the entire time, who were obviously uncomfortable speaking in public or speaking about this. So we all tried to make them feel very comfortable, but they didn't. And that was . . .

JC: There are of course justices on the Supreme Court who never ask questions.

AS: Yes that's true, one really—Clarence Thomas.

JC: Thurgood Marshall was well known for not asking a lot of questions too, and was the total opposite of what people think of Clarence Thomas.

AS: I don't mean that being quiet means you're not contributing. The person who didn't speak much was there listening every day, and he did sort of blow up one time and say, "All you guys talk so much and say nothing."

Look, there was another gentleman who was very quiet about the trial but was voting not guilty with me. He wasn't saying much but what he said and when he said it was very eloquent, very well put, and very meaningful at different times. And when it came to voting he was one of the people voting not guilty most of the time. But at the end, he raised his hand and voted guilty.

But it's not a matter of schooling for whether you can make a good decision. I think he would have been more than capable of making a good decision. I think there was a lot of pressure on this jury because we all knew that if we voted not guilty, only some of us, we'd be exposed—that the public and the press would know who we were.

JC: But you don't mind the media scrutiny.

AS: I didn't enjoy it. But I wasn't going to be scared of it.

JC: Hold on. Wait a minute. You went on CNN. You wrote an article. So it's not as if you're in any way shunning the publicity, correct?

AS: Well, no because it's there. I didn't seek it.

JC: Well, when you're giving interviews and writing an article you can't say . . .

AS: That's for a different reason. I do believe that the story of this case and how the jury worked in this case has to be out there. As much as possible. That's why I'm speaking with you about how this happened. I'm certainly not trying to seek fame and glory through doing this, but I do think the story needs to be told, and I think it's an important thing in America at this time. And if I have a soapbox for whatever reason to scream about this, what I saw . . .

JC: Would you still have the soapbox if you actually thought he was guilty, even though the prosecution was a poor prosecution?

AS: No. If I thought he was guilty I would have voted guilty.

JC: Well, if you thought Hernandez was guilty but there were still problems with the proof, would you say he was guilty but there was an injustice? In other words, if hypothetically the police beat a confession out of Hernandez but he's guilty because you all decided that it was nonetheless a true confession, it would have been an injustice even though he's guilty, right? So there can be an injustice even though a defendant is guilty. I'm not suggesting that they beat a confession out of Hernandez.

AS: It was much more nuanced.

JC: By the way, do you think that they obtained a confession from him through misconduct—getting him to confess to something that they knew he was not in fact guilty of?

AS: I'll answer it this way. They sent in a team of two detectives with a very good track record of interviewing people in New York. They brought in their best, basically. And I don't think that they shouldn't do that. But based on what the police said they said, and based on what the defense said was said in the room, I could see someone cracking under that kind of pressure.

They did nothing illegal. They're allowed to use any tactic that they can. They can lie and say we have this information, we know this. That's all fine. I'm not against any of that. But I do certainly question not videotaping it. It would have been very nice to have had that. I do question believing what a person says when they fit every possible characteristic of being more prone to make a false confession. I wouldn't crack under that questioning. I wouldn't be there in the first place. I would have said "call my lawyer, Joel Cohen, and he'll handle this." And so would 99 percent of Americans. So I think the police got very lucky with this suspect. I think they got very lucky.

JC: Why do you think he confessed several times?

AS: Well the ones that are most important to me are the first confessions. That first day. That first 24-hour period where they basically have him in custody. Well, maybe not officially in custody because he wasn't arraigned yet or whatever, or in handcuffs. Custody was an important issue for all of us, not just me.

JC: Why did he confess?

AS: Why? During that first confession in New Jersey, there were multiple times that he asked to go home. And that's not on tape. And multiple times they told him, "You can go any time you want, but we just have a few more questions for you," and he stayed. And then when they switch on the videotape, when they got 35 or so minutes of video, it's obvious to me that he thinks that after he's confessed he can go home. He actually asks, after signing what they wrote—the police wrote, he did not write his statement. Or he didn't sign it, he just initialed it. He asks at the end of that whole process, "Can I go home now?" Who asks that in their right mind after signing such an incriminating statement?

They read him his rights. They read each one on tape. He initials each one. Then the police write down his statement, to which they add in the first line "I am here voluntarily." He never says that. The police officer adds that line. That wasn't a doubt just for me. These are very contentious issues that went back and forth among us for a long time.

Was the police pickup of Pedro Hernandez done based on the law? When was custody established? Should they have read him his rights earlier? Things like that. Should they have said something like, "You're welcome to get a lawyer if you want before you talk to us." Police don't operate like that but when you're dealing with someone with low intelligence and mental health issues—and I think the police knew that he was low intelligence and had mental health issues before going into this whole thing—that weighed a lot on most of us in the room. Some of us, not at all.

That's why it seemed like a very disingenuous confession. I just think he wanted to get the hell out of there, go home, and be with his family and get back to his simple, very simple little life.

JC: So you need to suspend your disbelief for this question. Let's assume the police dug up the bag and the box tomorrow and found Hernandez's DNA on the bag. That would change everything?

AS: Well, of course, that would change everything.

JC: What would that make you think about this experience that you went through on this jury?

AS: Obviously in that case, I'd feel awful. I'd feel terrible. But, and this may sound strange to you, I'd also feel awful for the family that he wasn't convicted earlier. But I still don't think the case as it was presented was a very strong case against Pedro Hernandez based on the evidence.

JC: Well "very strong" is not really the issue, is it?

AS: Well, yeah it is the issue.

JC: No, the issue is whether it was proven beyond a reasonable doubt, right?

AS: Exactly. But that means the burden is on the prosecution to prove guilt beyond reasonable doubt. That, for me, is very high. Without any shred of physical evidence; I mean there was only circumstantial evidence and the inference can go either way. And, for me, my thought process just to dig into my head a little bit, for it to have been Pedro, every single fact that has an inference that you can take this way or that way, every single one had to point to Pedro Hernandez. Everything had to line up perfectly. It basically had to be the perfect crime, committed by this person.

A key thing that prevented me from voting guilty, other than the Jose Ramos introduction into the case, was that—and the prosecution made a big point of this—that Etan was carrying this bag to school that morning, and that Pedro threw it over the walk-in refrigerator and that his toys and everything must have been scattered on top and behind the fridge. And yet nothing was ever found; that bag was never found, never recovered. None of the toys, nothing.

It's bizarre; it's unbelievable to me that a police search team in 1979 would not have searched the bodega. Now there's no search documents that state that it was searched. There's also no search documents that say that a lot of places, because they lost a lot of the search documents. So we didn't have all the search documents for where they searched.

JC: Did it bother you that Hernandez didn't testify?

AS: No.

JC: Did it bother any of the jurors that he didn't testify?

AS: No. But the one thing that bothered jurors—and this was a point of contention too—was that they were saying that he never countered his confession. He never said, "I didn't do it." On tape. And I said what do you think this trial is? He's entered a plea of not guilty. That is as blatant as you can get that he is . . .

JC: Why didn't it bother you that he didn't testify?

AS: Because you're not . . . most people in a criminal case don't testify, as far as I've learned on TV and stuff like that. And obviously, you're not required to.

JC: Then didn't it bother you that, if Hernandez is innocent, then these confessions are false and testifying would have given him an opportunity to make a clean breast of it. Why didn't that bother you as a human being, if not as a juror?

AS: That's a non-issue. I saw his statements to different mental health providers on video. He was not all there. I'm not saying that he shouldn't stand trial. I don't think he's like insane or criminally insane, or whatever would be the standard to have him not go to a criminal court. But he's not reliable to talk about his own life. I think the defense did a good job in making it clear to me at least that he has poor memory and he can't remember dates, facts, events.

JC: Well memory has nothing to do with it. This man says he choked a little child. Memory is not the issue in this case.

AS: Yes, he said he choked a little child. He never said he "killed" a little child.

JC: If he choked a little child, he'd be convicted by you, too, if you felt that was a truthful statement, right?

AS: Absolutely, yes. But even that is a bizarre way of confessing. To me, it's just very strange. All his confessions were very strange to me. I'm no expert. I haven't seen other confessions, but I tend to think that most people who admit to doing a crime own up to it and can describe it in much more detail and with much more accuracy than did Pedro Hernandez on tape.

JC: Let me ask you this by way of comparison: Although it wasn't a confession case, did you follow at all the O.J. Simpson case?

AS: I was overseas, but I did a bit.

JC: Did you think there was an injustice there?

AS: I haven't thought about the O.J. Simpson case for a long time—in the sense that O.J. was innocent? In that case, this is as a bystander who is just watching TV, I find it hard to believe that he didn't do the crime.

JC: So you do recognize it's fair for an outsider to look at some other jury and have some view of how that jury acted in that case, don't you?

AS: Absolutely. His defense team was excellent.

JC: As it would be fair for outsiders to judge what happened in the Pedro Hernandez case.

AS: I'm very open to judgment. I've received a lot of it.

JC: Do you get negative judgments about your role in the case? Perhaps, from people who are friends?

AS: Not from one friend or one person that I've met on the street that comes up and talks to me or whatever. Not that it happens all the time, but I've gotten a huge amount of support from friends, from high school people I haven't talked to for years on Facebook so actually [I got] a lot of comments on the articles and stuff. A majority were positive.

There was a lot of negative too—*The New York Post*—and I'm fine with that. People are welcome to their opinion. No problem with that whatsoever. Obviously it's a gut reaction. I get that. Not many people followed the case, maybe as closely, of course, as I did. But it's a free country—you can have your opinion on whatever you want.

JC: What do you hope to accomplish with the articles you've written and blogs you plan to write?

AS: It's cathartic for me to write. It always has been. It was cathartic to write the article I wrote for CNN. I just wrote it and I decided to put it out there.

JC: Cathartic in order to accomplish what?

AS: In that it helped to sort of make me clear that what I did was right—that it was the right thing. I was clear that it was right, but as I jot down more ideas, more things I remember about the case, I know that I was right. Because the first few days after the case was rough. It was rough—there was a lot of *The New York Post, The New York Daily News*. I mean they wrote some pretty nasty articles, and hearing what a few of the other jurors said was tough, and it's not great to hear that from people that you got so close with over time.

I also wanted to counter a little bit what was being said by the others; not 11, maybe five or six of them. Like holding a vigil for Etan. I have nothing but love for the Patz family—but jurors holding a vigil on the anniversary of his death at the alleged scene of the crime, seemed much more "tabloidy" for me than my little piece in CNN.

JC: But you did attend the next court appearance, didn't you?

AS: I did, yes.

JC: Why?

AS: Well, I do plan on going to some of the court hearings for the retrial as well. I wasn't alone. There were seven other jurors there too.

JC: Yes, but you're the only juror who held out for acquittal. So why did *you* go?

AS: I wanted to. The case was—and still is—very important to me. It has been a very deep part of my life now.

JC: But you say you intend to go to court appearances during the upcoming trial? For what reason?

AS: One reason is that I'm assisting in formulating their defense. I've been sending them certain ideas I have that could help them to counter the kind of thinking that happened in the jury room. I want to be very active in doing whatever I can to assist in the acquittal of Pedro Hernandez—now with the defense side. In terms of going to court—I have the freedom to go to court whenever I want.

JC: I'm not saying you can or can't, I'm just saying that is unusual in my experience, virtually unprecedented.

AS: This was an unusual jury issue. I don't think I've ever seen a jury followed like this. How many acquittals have there been recently with the police in Baltimore, in Ferguson, or whatever is going on around the country? And you don't hear thing one about which jury members held out. I'm not familiar with the process, but having a press conference right after the trial was also bizarre, very bizarre. So it's not *me* seeking the press. It's the press seeking me. I mean, on Saturday morning the day after the trial, I was at my friend's apartment, and there were reporters ringing the intercom all day long. That's why I decided to talk to them. Because I didn't think they'd go away. I asked some lawyer friends if there was anything I could do, and was told they can stay there all day.

JC: Whether in the wake of the hung jury it was you seeking the press or vice versa, there could be a fair debate on that subject. But you going to the trial?

AS: I won't be the only one. There will be plenty of jurors there from the guilty side too.

JC: Yeah but you're *the* guy.

AS: Yes, and I don't mind bringing more attention to it so that my views on the case can be spread to the public more.

JC: That's a little cute, isn't it? It'll be about you, right?

AS: For a long time I've been a social activist, an NGO worker, someone who's trying to make the world better. I'm not trying to say that I've accomplished it, but I'm not like a corporate lawyer or something like that. Or someone who's trying to get rich from the jobs I've had. I believe in social justice. I believe that in this case—now looking back on it in retrospect—that an injustice has been done. And if there is not an acquittal in the next round, it will be an even deeper injustice, especially if they leave out the Ramos story. I feel Ramos should testify as well. And the Ramos civil judgment. I feel that is something very, very important to include in the case. I can't understand why it wouldn't be.

JC: Last question: Do you think Jose Ramos is guilty of the murder of Etan Patz?

AS: He wasn't on trial.

JC: And we're not in a courtroom.

AS: I know—but here we go to likelihood. If I look at Jose Ramos and I think about all of the evidence that the defense presented about him and his predatory nature, his connection to the Patz family, and his connection even to Etan Patz through Etan's babysitter, why does that not line up much more closely with him? Why isn't he the guilty one rather than some bodega clerk who, without any criminal history, would have had to suddenly just go psycho and kill a child and then commit the most amazing job of getting rid of the evidence? And then just go about his day, then live his life and have two families and three kids, never have any abuse record, murder or anything.

But Ramos walks around until the early '80s abusing more children, is found with a wallet full of photos looking like Etan, and admits on camera when talking to the district attorney that he knows what Etan looks like and describes him physically. He says the babysitter describes him so that's how he knows him. And he saw him on the news or something like that, but the way he physically describes him is much more intimate. It's chilling.

JC: So, if Jose Ramos had been seated as the defendant rather than Pedro Hernandez, would your jury have voted the same way, 11 to 1 to convict?

AS: No, I think *he* would have been found guilty unanimously.

JC: Thank you.

8

Operation Merlin

Jeffrey Sterling

*. . . some individuals just sat and watched me
burn when they could have done something.*

—Jeffrey Sterling, July 28, 2016. [1]

You may view this story as different from the others, at least when considering the issue of injustice. Jeffrey Sterling, a former CIA operative, says he is
innocent of violating the Espionage Act—that he did not give confidential,
secret information to a reporter for *The New York Times*. The government
successfully proved to a jury that he did—but did it solely through circumstantial evidence. There were no witnesses to conversations, no recordings,
no emails transmitting classified information, no smoking gun, as it were.
Jeffrey Sterling did not have to prove his innocence—it was (and always is)
the prosecutor's burden to prove that a defendant is guilty beyond a reasonable doubt. Such is the law—at least in theory.

---

1. Jeffrey Sterling was interviewed by telephone for the reasons described in the interview.

So, as you think about Jeffrey Alexander Sterling, Inmate #38338-004 at Federal Correctional Institution, Englewood, Colorado, think about whether an injustice was done. While there is technically no higher legal standard, think about whether a prosecution for espionage should ever rest solely on circumstantial evidence. To put the issue into context, think about the fact that the government—at Sterling's trial—put into the public record far more "confidential" information than Sterling himself was accused of releasing. Think about whether, if Sterling did disclose confidential information, he was treated differently (perhaps, made an example) given that most "whistleblowers" are merely slapped on the wrist (some, frankly are thanked). And think about whether Sterling, a black man who likely embarrassed the CIA when he sued claiming he was discriminated against because he is black, was treated differently from others who—again, even if Sterling did what he was accused of—delivered far more compelling "secrets" to the press.

With those thoughts in mind, let's begin at the beginning.

Jeffrey Sterling grew up in a small town in Missouri. He went to college, then law school. He wanted to do nothing more than serve his country; to protect Americans. So he joined the CIA in 1993 and worked on missions we—the public—will never know about. Such is the "deal" one makes when working for "the Agency." In fact, Sterling signed a standard secrecy agreement (yes, that's what it is called)—he could never disclose information without the prior consent of the CIA. The ultimate agreement to "take it to the grave," and probably rightly so.

Sterling was an operations officer, assigned to the Iranian Task Force. He spent endless hours learning the language, the customs, and the culture. But he was not being given any new cases. When he approached his superiors, they told Sterling that he "stuck out" and would draw attention as a "big black man speaking Farsi." Sterling's response—"when did you realize I was black?"

As his assignment ended, Sterling filed a complaint with the CIA's Equal Opportunity Employment Office, charging that the agency engaged in racial discrimination. He tried to settle—demanding $75,000. The agency refused to pay and the Employment Office denied his complaint. When the agency refused to negotiate, Sterling sued, as was his right. The CIA's defense—the "state secrets doctrine." Meaning, the agency said, the case must be dismissed because, in order to proceed (court being a public forum), military and state secrets would necessarily be disclosed. Yes, the court noted, when the doctrine is asserted, the result is unfair. Still, Sterling's case was dismissed—to protect the "greater good."

We will never actually know what "state secrets" could not be told in that courtroom, but at least one was the operation called "Merlin," which ran from 1998 through 2000. Merlin is no longer a secret, by virtue of a reporter for *The New York Times*—James Risen. Risen's book, *State of War: The Secret History of the CIA and the Bush Administration,* was published in 2006. More to the point, perhaps, it is no longer a secret because the government decided to prosecute Sterling and put forward public testimony about the operation.

Why did the government believe Sterling was Risen's source?[2] That he breached his secrecy agreement? You see, Sterling—who was a case officer on the Merlin project—was concerned that the operation would fail. And "failure" in this context was serious—that, perhaps, Iran would acquire the means to build a firing switch that could be used in a nuclear bomb. Serious consequences, indeed.

Sterling knew Risen. In fact, Risen had written an article, published in March 2002, about Sterling's publically filed discrimination suit against the CIA. The article quoted Sterling and described his position, as set forth in court papers. Still, did Sterling tell Risen about Merlin? Would Sterling have compromised the security of the United States, particularly after 9/11, by telling Risen—who would effectively be telling the world—about a secret project involving Iran and a nuclear bomb firing mechanism?

What exactly was Merlin? Well, the answer depends on whom you ask. All agree that a Russian nuclear scientist (code-named Merlin), who had defected to the U.S., was dispatched by the CIA in an undercover role to give plans for a nuclear firing switch to the Iranians and that the plans were intentionally flawed. The flaws would be hidden so—the theory went—Iran would not realize there was a problem and would spend years trying to build the unbuildable. "Disinformation" at its best.

---

2. Author's note: I attempted to reach James Risen on July 31, 2016. He did not respond.

From that point forward, there are two versions. Turning first to *State of War*, Merlin reviewed the plans with the Agency and noted immediately that they were wrong. However, Merlin should not have been able to detect the errors. The Agency told Merlin not to worry, and sent him to deliver the plans to the Iranians through a subterfuge. Nonetheless, Merlin was worried and, without the Agency's knowledge or authority, he inserted a letter addressed to the Iranian scientists, in essence telling them that the information was good, but that in order to create the switch they would have to ask questions—which the Russian (Merlin) would answer, but for a price. He later gave a copy of his letter to the Agency. Such was the story as released to the world in 2006, perhaps embarrassing to the Agency.

The CIA told a somewhat different story—in open court, to the public—at Sterling's trial. When Merlin reviewed the plans, he noted several missing components, but the Agency told him that was intentional. The plan was for Merlin to give the Iranians an incomplete schematic and offer to fill in the blanks for a fee. Other flaws existed, but the Agency never told Merlin about them and Merlin never noticed them. Merlin gave the Iranians the plans and a letter, as above, but the CIA edited and approved the letter—it was all part of the ruse. The operation was a success. A far different ending than the story told by Risen. Was that a motivation to prosecute Sterling; to give the government a public forum to tell its version of Merlin—one that did not make the government look, shall we say, ineffective?

Let's look at the timeline. All of these events took place in early 2000. By midyear, Sterling formally sued the Agency for discrimination. By the end of 2001, Sterling had been fired. Risen's article about Sterling's claims of discrimination was published in March 2002. Sterling wrote his memoir, which the Agency would not permit him to publish (more state secrets). And as Sterling became increasingly uncomfortable with the prospect that Iran had plans for a nuclear firing switch at its disposal, he did what he believed he was supposed to do—he alerted the inspector general of the CIA and, when that failed, the Senate and House Intelligence Committees. Through all of this, Risen and Sterling kept in touch. And Risen? He was preparing an article about Merlin, which the Agency successfully convinced *The New York Times* not to publish in 2003. He was also writing *State of War*.

Now, the government investigated Risen and Sterling and knew that they spoke. Yet, it did not charge Sterling until 2010, four years after Risen's book was published and seven years after the Agency knew about Risen's never-published article. Why did it take so long? When did the government decide it had enough evidence to indict Sterling, and why did it decide to pursue him criminally then?

What happened at Sterling's trial? Risen was ordered to testify, but he never did. He was never prosecuted nor compelled to take the stand—even though other reporters, e.g., *The New York Times* reporter Judith Miller in the Scooter Libby case, had been held in contempt and jailed for similar refusals. What does Sterling think about Risen's silence, his failure to tell the world: "Jeffrey Sterling was not my source!" What does he think about the government's failure to pursue Risen, as it did Miller? And, as an aside, does Sterling know Risen's source?

Does Sterling believe he was prosecuted to be made an example, as a whistleblower, a troublemaker and one who just did not fit the Agency's mold of an operative? And on that note, does he think whistleblowers serve a need—that if all else fails one can, indeed, take their "to-the-grave" secrets to the press?

Sterling, a black man, was prosecuted at the time an African-American president and attorney general were at the helm. But was he nonetheless targeted because of his discrimination suit? He was also an "outsider," and at about the same time an Agency "insider"—former CIA director David Petraeus—gave his mistress confidential materials while she wrote his biography. He was "punished" too—he pleaded to a misdemeanor and was given probation. Now, it is not quite apples-to-apples; Sterling vehemently maintains his innocence while Petraeus conceded his guilt. Still, was Sterling offered a plea that would have avoided a jail sentence? And would he have taken a plea?

At the time of this interview, Jeffrey Sterling is serving his three-and-one-half year sentence while appealing his conviction (the government, by the way, asked the judge to sentence him to 19 to 24 years). Is Sterling angry? And at who—Risen?; the person or persons who actually gave Risen the information?; the government for prosecuting him, but not others?

And so we return to the underlying question. Even if the reader concludes, after reading this interview, that Sterling was indeed Risen's source despite his vociferous denials, was Sterling nonetheless the victim of injustice? And perhaps a better question: if you believe Sterling is in fact guilty of having been Risen's source, would you be more inclined to see him as a victim of an injustice if he simply bit the bullet and admitted that he was the source—that he took it upon himself to, as he saw it, protect America? And what would that say about the role of honestly acknowledging one's own actions in assessing the existence of an injustice?[3]

The Dialogue

JC: Mr. Sterling, you and I have never spoken before, have we?

JS: No, we have not.

JC: I am conducting this interview of you by telephone from New York to the Federal Correctional Institution in Englewood, Colorado. Warden Denham declined my request for an in-person interview supposedly because of "safety and security concerns of the orderly running of the institution." As I understand it, we have an hour to speak. You are sitting in the office of Englewood's public information officer, and while he's not on this call he's within earshot of your side of the interview, correct? We'll have to deal with that.

JS: Yes.

JC: Ok. How old were you when you first joined the CIA?

JS: That was in '93. So I was 26 or 27.

JC: When joining the CIA you were aware, were you not, that it is extremely controversial—it engages in provocative conduct that generally isn't in the public domain, correct?

JS: Certainly, I come from a small town in the Midwest, and secretive information about what the CIA says and it doesn't say has always created a mystique about it. But to the issue of whether it was an "evil" organiza-

---

3. Shortly before this book went to print, on January 17, 2017, President Obama commuted the sentence of Chelsea (nee Bradley) Manning, who leaked military and diplomatic activities and served 7 years of her 35-year sentence. President Obama also pardoned former General (and former Vice Chair of the Joint Chiefs of Staff) James Cartwright, who had pleaded guilty to lying to the FBI about his discussions with reporters about Iran's nuclear program. Cartwright had not yet been sentenced, although the government requested that he serve two years. Do these facts change the reader's thoughts as to whether Sterling suffered an injustice?

tion or anything like that—certainly I had a view and opinion that there was some dubious things about it—but to me, it was an organization there to protect the interests of the United States. That's what I joined.

JC: That said, I wonder if this comparison to the movie *A Few Good Men* with Jack Nicholson playing Colonel Jessup applies. The film, of course, involved the killing of a marine in Guantanamo Bay by fellow marines as a means to discipline him. During his testimony at the marines' criminal trial, Colonel Jessup (Nicholson) said: "My existence, while grotesque and incomprehensible to you, saves lives. You don't want the truth. Because deep down in places you don't talk about at parties, you want me on that wall; you need me on that wall." Basically, he was saying that Americans want the type of security accorded to them by the CIA, but they don't really want to know the details of how it accomplishes that security. Is that how you see how most Americans view the CIA?

JS: That certainly wasn't *my* view. I joined with the view that, yes—some things that we do should not be publicized. But that there must be a level of trust which comes with a level of transparency. Security can't be accomplished in a vacuum, employing one's own self-serving view that he serves the better good.

I didn't sign up with the CIA with that viewpoint. I joined because it was a unique opportunity to serve my country. Yes, I knew that there was the backdrop of things like that—but I had no inclination, no purpose, no desire, if you will, to compromise my principles nor ethics, going in. I certainly know about ethics. I was also a member of the New York Bar. But to me, it wasn't so much that "I'm going to be doing something to help place me on a pedestal," ostensibly doing good regardless of who's going to get hurt. That wasn't my purpose in joining.

JC: But you did know going in that utmost confidentiality was required of you for classified information that came into your possession. That being a CIA case officer you would be banned, literally for life, from public disclosure of any such information?

JS: Absolutely, and I willingly signed that pledge. I understood—going in—the obligation of total confidentiality in the handling of classified information. My view was always that this agency wasn't for wildcards simply doing what they want to do. There would have to be a check and balance on whatever I would do. Yes there would be the balance between keeping things confidential or classified; but there's also the overall mission of the organization. Maybe my viewpoint has been a little tainted given the experiences I've had—but certainly, going in, I clearly understood that you don't work for the country by working against it.

So maybe I was a bit naïve going in, but I certainly didn't go in thinking, "Well, we're going to be doing bad things." We're going to be doing *necessary* things was my viewpoint. Necessary things. I couldn't tell people what I was doing, but I certainly wasn't going in with the view that I would be doing anything that might be considered illegal.

JC: Still, you're sitting in jail doing a three-and-a-half year stretch—actually far less than the government had requested—convicted of having been *the* source or *a* source to James Risen of *The New York Times* for chapter nine of his book, *State of War*. The chapter dealt with an undercover operative code-named "Merlin" who was given nuclear plans deliberately containing disinformation to be given to Iranian officials—intended to cause the Iranian government to be distracted and slowed down in creating nuclear weaponry. And a jury basically found that you were that source or at least *a* source of Risen's book.

JS: Certainly during the trial and the so-called investigation leading to it, I have maintained my innocence always. I am innocent of those charges. I never divulged any classified information to anyone! And that's why I'm appealing that decision.

JC: Okay. So you say you're innocent—that you didn't disclose classified information to Risen that enabled him to write that chapter. Let's put aside Operation Merlin. Let's assume that you're a CIA case handler for an undercover agent whose goal is to provide disinformation to, say, Syrian or, say, North Korean weapons personnel. In the process you conclude that what the CIA is doing is ill-conceived. That it is inimical to the interests of the United States, and might actually aid those enemies of the United States to better develop a nuclear stockpile. Armed with that knowledge, what would you do?

JS: I would do just what I did. I went to the House Intelligence Committee. I went to the Senate Intelligence Committee. I was permitted and supposedly encouraged to do both. I reported my information, and my fears.

JC: Before that, did you go up the chain within the CIA itself?

JS: I went to my supervisor. I went to the inspector general. I made my rounds complaining that the Merlin operation in practice was not the way it had been presented to me. I explained that it could pose a danger, based on the meeting with Merlin (and as disclosed in the trial).

JC: What was your concern?

JS: Again, as disclosed in the trial, it was presented to me from the outset of my involvement that Merlin would not know about the flaws placed into the plan—that he would never know those flaws because we didn't want him to potentially jeopardize the mission by knowing that something was wrong. The moment he saw the plans—also as disclosed during the trial—he immediately saw that there was something wrong with the plans and that they wouldn't work. To me, he was not supposed to know, so there was something wrong. And if Merlin was able to see it so quickly, the Iranians could figure it out quickly and fix it.

I made it known to my supervisor who assured me that he would talk to others. Soon after, I learned of the disparate treatment I was receiving at the hands of my supervisor in New York, and I was taken off the project. I made the rounds and made my complaints about Merlin—I was the only one voicing those concerns.

JC: But you struck out, both internally within the CIA and at Congress.

JS: Yes I did.

JC: Okay. So let's turn back to my hypothetical—dealing with Syria. What would you do? You've concluded that this program was flawed, actually dangerous to the United States, and the CIA didn't recognize it or want to. The Congress didn't recognize, or also didn't want to. What do you do?

JS: I thought I was answering that. I would have gone through the legal chain that I was I was authorized to pursue.

JC: Okay, but you strike out with the "legal" chain. What do you do then?

JS: Well then, it's up to them. There's nothing more I could do. That's what I was permitted to do. I signed my commitment to not disclose classified information in an unauthorized manner. I follow the rules. And that's all I could do—bring it to those who are supposed to be the check and balance on such operations and such actions. Whether it had been with your

Syria hypothetical, or even my actual experience with Merlin and Iran. You go through the proper channels, and that's exactly what I did.

JC: What would you think of a CIA officer who concluded "Look, I just can't let this go. I've gone through proper CIA channels. I've gone through proper channels at the Congress. To allow this to go forward is just too dangerous." And so, he gives it confidentially to *The New York Times*, or *The Wall Street Journal*, or *The Washington Post*—because, he figures, that's the only way to stop the CIA from doing something so potentially harmful to the United States.

JS: I guess there may be, and certainly have been, those who feel that if they take action and nothing happens they need to go further and even compromise the pledge that they willingly signed on for. Each individual must answer to his own motivations. But for me, that was not the case. I did what I was allowed and supposedly encouraged to do. And I think it is borne out through the trial that each step I took demonstrated that I did not disclose classified information. A good example was Risen's article about my discrimination suit for *The New York Times*. The government conceded that no classified information was divulged in that article.

JC: But as the Justice Department sees it, you were a "disgruntled" CIA case officer—and being disgruntled led you to stray beyond the permissible.

JS: And they contradicted themselves in their own investigation. Even the FBI admitted that it would make no sense for me, in the middle of my discrimination suit, which was underway, to take such an action. They even dropped their investigation at one point. Of course, they'll say that I was disgruntled. One of their more vociferous objections at trial was when my attorneys pointed out that my contacts with Mr. Risen were while my discrimination action was proceeding. They wanted no allusion to that. They wanted to give the impression that I had already lost that action, while, technically, I had not. It was dismissed on the grounds that if it went forward, it would be a danger to national security. Of course they were going to do that.

And they portrayed me as disgruntled—I should make this point as well—mine was the only black face involved in the operation. The only black man in that courtroom with a jury without one black face on it—how easy and convenient for them to portray me as a disgruntled man trying to play the race card. Never mind the fact that I had moved on with my life at that point. It was just an easy avenue for the government to take. And they played it for all it was worth.

JC: Do you think the Justice Department was out to get you for some untoward reason?

JS: I think the Justice Department was certainly motivated by what seems the unspoken purpose (or whatever) of the Obama Administration to go after what they considered leakers or whistleblowers. Mine was a part of that. The FBI had dropped the investigation of me in 2006, as they admitted on the stand. They decided to reopen it when the Obama Administration came in. Another point—there's no way that the Justice Department could have accomplished what they did at trial with their witnesses without the full cooperation, if not full motivation, of the CIA. The CIA certainly had an axe to grind with me, and that really came out with every witness.

JC: Whether they had an axe to grind with you and whether they wanted to punish you more severely than any other (alleged) leakers, do you think that the Justice Department didn't believe in their heart of hearts that you were actually Risen's source?

JS: I really don't think they did. They didn't start coming after me until the Obama Administration—look at how long this took. I don't think they thought I would turn down a plea deal. I don't think they wanted to go forward with this. I think, to them, I was just an easy target—some lowly nobody. No political connections or anything like that. And how easy is this going to be? He'll either plead or we can play the race card with him.

I don't think they were really interested in actually doing anything except to use me as an opportunity for the CIA to get its reputation back. Again, this was a full tag-team effort between the CIA and the Justice Department. There was no way the Justice Department could have conducted that trial without the full unremitting cooperation, if not direction, by the CIA. I don't think there's ever been an instance with that amount of classified information being disclosed in an open court.

JC: But it sounds almost like, pardon the expression, you're making a big deal out of yourself. Why were you such a big deal to the CIA and the Justice Department—because the Obama Administration wanted to go after leakers?

JS: That's part of it. But, also, I think, from the CIA's standpoint, I had the colossal nerve to sue it for racial discrimination. The CIA is all about setting examples for its personnel.

JC: You think that the CIA was discriminating against you in giving you poor assignments—for example, you being a black man would stand out like a sore thumb in your assignments?

JS: Yes, and that's exactly what they told me. That I wasn't receiving better assignments because I stuck out as a big black guy speaking Farsi. That's not what I thought, that's exactly what I was told.

JC: What position did your counsel take with respect to the government's extensive effort to compel Risen to testify against you. Did they support Risen's motion to quash his subpoena from the government or did they oppose it?

JS: The government's going to do whatever they're going to do. Our attitude was that I'm not Risen's source. So whoever they want to call, let them call him. That was our position at trial.

JC: The devil's advocate in me would say that since you're innocent, Risen, of course, knew it couldn't be you. It would have been in your interest for Risen to testify at the trial because if compelled to testify, he would unmistakably tell the jury "Ladies and gentlemen, Jeffrey Sterling was not my source." So, it seems, you would have wanted to encourage Risen as strongly as possible to testify.

JS: Absolutely, but that runs headlong into a reporter's requirement that he can't reveal his source. It would absolutely have been to my benefit had he gotten up there and told the truth. The government had the opportunity to compel that, and they won in the appellate decision to do that. But yet, they chose not to. What does that say?

JC: I imagine, you've never been asked this question before—Who do you think the source was?

JS: I think you have to add plural. I think it's sources.

JC: Fair enough. Who?

JS: Hard to say; I was so far out of it. There were so many people involved in that operation by the time I was out of it. So maybe there were other developments that came about. There could have been any number of people. But, look at the investigation. I was the only person investigated, over so many years. They interviewed no one else.

JC: Well, they did have information suggesting a relationship between you and Risen over your discrimination case. They had emails and phone records showing that you had contacts with Risen. Wouldn't it make sense for them to look at you?

JS: Certainly. But I never hid my contact with Risen. He did the article, and I hoped he would do a follow-up. I let him know along the way what was going on with my discrimination case. The phone calls, the contacts, the emails—there was nothing classified in the email. I think the longest phone call was maybe 90 seconds.

But if I'm the only person investigated then, of course, that's going to be spun into making me the most nefarious person out there, who'll damage what the CIA and the government touted as the most important and crucial operation in a generation.

JC: Let's talk about Risen's chapter about Merlin. What damage, if any, could making the Merlin story public have done to United States security?

JS: No idea. I didn't follow any of that—that was for the government to say.

JC: So your view, stripped to its bare bones, is that you were investigated and prosecuted because you're a black man who had sued the CIA for racial discrimination, correct?

JS: Absolutely. Think about it. One point we certainly weren't allowed to bring out at trial was that my discrimination suit was dismissed because it posed a danger to national security. The government turned right around, however: same person, same subject matter, same facts, same details were readily thrown around in open court to prosecute me. At what point was national security no longer an issue? And the fact that I was the only person investigated. Also look at the evidence at trial. Not one shred of evidence presented to say when or how I supposedly did this. All they proved was that I had contact with Jim Risen. I look at the whole tenor and the whole history of the investigation. I mean there was a search warrant done, conducted at my home in Missouri in 2006. I wasn't indicted until December 2010. That's not the typical sort of warrant that we had a revolution about in this country many years ago. I don't know how else you can define it.

JC: In connection with the race discrimination issue—obviously, you were prosecuted during the administration of America's first black president, and a black attorney general well known for pursuing civil rights issues. But yet you think they allowed the Justice Department to pursue you vigorously because you brought, in their view, an unwarranted race discrimination case against the CIA?

JS: At one point, I was an easy target—so the Justice Department would jump on that at any opportunity they get. It's easier to get someone to cop a plea to something. I mean look at [former National Security Advisor Thomas] Drake and others. And, again, the FBI admitted on the stand they dropped the investigation in 2006, with no indication of any new evidence brought forward.

So I think there was a combination of this almost McCarthy-like witch hunt by the Obama Administration which spurred the Justice Department to find any and all leak cases they could get their hands on. Obama comes in, black or otherwise, and, I guess, I was still on their minds. The CIA certainly still would have brought it up to them.

And look at the disparate treatment comparing what was done with General Petraeus, director of the CIA, who intentionally gave information to his paramour as she was writing a book about him. And, as my wife said in the letter she wrote to the president—I'm paraphrasing—if you strip away the real differences here, the real difference is the color of his skin and his status to this administration. I don't have worth. I didn't have worth to this Obama Administration and its Justice Department.

JC: But you're not bugged because you got a stiffer sentence than others, including Petraeus. You're bugged because, you maintain, you were framed—that you're a total innocent, unlike Petraeus, who got a lenient plea for something he admittedly did. You say you were prosecuted for something you simply didn't do.

JS: Absolutely. And again, the activity, the length of time, and in some ways the aggressiveness of the FBI and DOJ coming after me, you can't say that matched up in any way with what happened to Petraeus. And I'm going to throw in Hillary Clinton. For the FBI director to say there was no intent on her part. The Espionage Act is a strict liability statute—intent is not required. Tons of evidence with Petraeus and Hillary Clinton. But with me, there's a trial disclosing tons of classified information and, yes, I happen to be black. A Class A misdemeanor for Petraeus? Insulting!

JC: Are you saying you would have accepted a misdemeanor plea?

JS: No, absolutely not. I wouldn't have taken any plea. But for them to settle on just a misdemeanor with Petraeus when he had obviously lied to the FBI about the information that he turned over. Why didn't they do the same thing with him that they did with me? And why hasn't the same thing been done with Hillary Clinton?

JC: I don't want to get into any conversation between you and your lawyers, but you didn't testify at your trial. One would think, given how you've dealt with this entire episode, you would have wanted to rush to the witness stand to testify that "This is wrong. It wasn't me. I don't know who Risen's source was, but it wasn't me. It just wasn't me." And one would think that you would have wanted to shout from the highest rooftops that Risen should come forward and testify—because his testimony would exonerate you.

JS: Okay, I understand. A couple of points on that. One, I certainly believe, having gone to law school and become an attorney that you're innocent until proven guilty, and there is no adverse inference to be drawn from someone not taking the stand. That the government would have the burden to prove my guilt beyond a reasonable doubt. There was nothing for me to testify about. The trial turned out to be nothing more than a "he said, she said."

JC: Yes, but the jury didn't hear *you* say anything. But what about Risen?

JS: As I said in the article in *The Washington Post*, it would have been nice if he had gotten up there and told the truth, but I have to respect him for his position. I can't speak for others.

JC: Mr. Sterling, that astonishes me. You respect him, but he's the guy who had the keys to your cell and kept them in his pocket.

JS: *He* didn't create the situation. *He* didn't create that investigation, this ordeal, that has lasted since 1999.

JC: He created the situation by his book, didn't he?

JS: If I was the source, maybe I could then say that he created the situation and left me hanging. But I wasn't.

JC: Well, in a way he left you hanging—and I don't mean it in a negative way toward him. But he wasn't prosecuted ultimately for contempt.

You were prosecuted and you're paying the price for it. What do you think when the government didn't bring a contempt action against him or force him to testify?

JS: That was amazing. Another ridiculousness. From when the case was taken off the calendar and the government appealed, it was three-and-a-half years of waiting, wondering what was going on. I became a side show. It wasn't even the *United States vs. Jeffrey Sterling* anymore. It became the "Risen case" or the "Risen trial" to the mainstream media. I became an observer at my own trial.

With regard to Risen, at one point I considered him a friend because he listened to me. He allowed me to talk to him about my discrimination problems at the CIA. That's why I say I have respect for him. He was one of the few that had any belief, or even took the time to hear me out. And he wrote an article about it. After that, I can say it would have been nice if he had gotten up there and told the truth, that I was not his source. Yet he didn't. But, obviously, that wasn't stopping the government from doing what they were doing to me.

JC: He could certainly have written an article saying the government's got it wrong—"Sterling is not my source on this!"

JS: A lot of people could have done a lot of things on my behalf. There could have been people at the CIA who could have come forward and said this was wrong. There could have been individuals in the Senate Intelligence Committee and the House Intelligence Committee to come forward and assist me, but they too didn't.

JC: Assume that the Risen sources were actually CIA officials, and the United States government was able to prove that. What should happen to them?

JS: You've seen what's happened to me.

JC: I've seen what's happened to you, but you believe it shouldn't have happened to you. What do you think should happen to them?

JS: If they are the sources and it is proven, they should face the same prosecution that I have. Absolutely.

JC: In other words, they violated the law and they belong in jail?

JS: Absolutely.

JC: With a stiff sentence given the potential of the harm they did to the United States.

JS: Of course, my view is colored by the fact that I'm sitting in prison, taken away from my wife, and with the fact that I've had to endure this situation for so long. There is certainly value to whistleblowers. My view is certainly tainted by my (admitted) bitterness over what has happened to me, and that there are others out there who have done far more than I was accused of and received either a slap on the wrist or nothing at all. Petraeus, Clinton. The hypocrisy of it all.[4]

JC: But it's not the hypocrisy that bothers you so much. You see it as a straight out injustice—you've been convicted for something you simply didn't do.

JS: Absolutely.

JC: Let me wrap it up with this. For a young CIA case officer, what should be his or her takeaway from what has happened to you?

JS: The odd thing is that I was absolutely proud of my service in the CIA. I entered the CIA with the pride that I would be serving my country. And I still believe it's a valuable resource for America and for our national defense. Any young officer coming in—don't ever compromise your principles. You're there, at the forefront of our national defense. Don't compromise your principles—just because someone tells you something, you don't have to accept it if it doesn't feel right. My favorite writer is Shakespeare. "To thine own self be true." That's what I would tell anyone at the CIA. Don't drink the Kool-Aid. That's not what you're about. Your service is valuable, but don't be a lemming. If something is wrong, stand up and say something within the parameters that are available to you.

JC: What about whistleblowers?

JS: There is a value, certainly, in whistleblowers, and there should be some protections for them. Look at Edward Snowden. Everyone is all up in arms that he should return and face prosecution. At the same time, he started a conversation that needed to take place. So there's a value there.

JC: Let me get this straight. I thought I heard you say earlier that if someone was responsible for leaking the Merlin operation to Risen he belongs in jail.

---

4. Author's note: In an email sent immediately following the interview, Sterling wrote: "I do apologize if what I had to say, or how I spoke to you had a modicum of hurt in it. This has been an incredibly difficult ordeal I have endured for quite a long time now. I wouldn't want what has happened to me to happen to anyone."

JS: Again, what I said before is also tainted by the bitterness I feel over what has happened to me. If someone had the guts to come forward and disclose that information, should there be a cost paid for going to unauthorized destinations with that information? Yes. But I also think that should be weighed against the value of that information to the security of this country. I'm still in the midst of this, and there is residual bitterness there. And knowing that others within the CIA had to have been the source while the CIA threw me to the wolves, certainly taints my viewpoint. So, for me, should they face some punishment? Yes, and it should be weighed against the best interests of the United States.

Usually any leak will provide something that the United States and its citizens should know about. Where is the balance? Where is the check? If Snowden had not come forward would there have been any discussion about the things he has uncovered? No. So, yes, there must be a balance there. Should there be harsh punishment for doing such a thing? No. Again my viewpoint, right now, is based in part on bitterness. There's a level of frustration I'm certainly going through.

Should they automatically be jailed? No. My view is that there may be value in what is disclosed, and it must be weighed and considered. It takes a lot for anyone to come forward. Look at me. You have a certain level of trust in an institution, and when that trust is betrayed, it hurt.

I don't want to be heard to say that anyone except me who goes outside should go to jail. No. That comes out of my anger right now, because some individuals just sat and watched me burn when they could have done something.

9

A White House Invitation

A. Ashley Tabaddor[1]

The decision to fight—I never had second thoughts. . . .
Everywhere I go, I always say "You have to stand up for
what you believe in. You have to protect these rights. . . .
We stand on the shoulders of people before us who've
had to protect our rights." So for me it would have been
absolutely contrary to everything I believe in to let it go.

—A. Ashley Tabaddor, July 6, 2016[2]

When we discuss Immigration Judge Afsaneh Ashley Tabaddor, we must explore the issue of when and whether judges can be removed from hear-

---

1. A. Ashley Tabaddor is an immigration judge with the Los Angeles Immigration Court, Executive Office for Immigration Review (EOIR), U.S. Department of Justice (DOJ). The responses made by A. Ashley Tabaddor in this publication were made in her personal capacity, and the views expressed herein are solely hers and do not necessarily represent the positions of EOIR, DOJ, or the United States.

2. Judge Tabaddor was interviewed at the author's offices in New York, New York.

ing cases before them ("recused," in legal terminology). As a general matter, judges who sit in state and federal courts should *not* recuse themselves unless they believe their personal prejudices would get in the way of rendering a decision, or their rulings demonstrate bias or prejudice. In the federal recusal world, there is actually a "duty to sit." Thus, judges who are staunch, practicing Catholics routinely decide cases about abortion; judges who are African-American decide civil rights issues; and it was actually a gay judge who decided the California same-sex marriage case that made its way to the U.S. Supreme Court. In other words, judges are understood and expected to have personal lives and interests—as Justice Benjamin Cardozo articulated it, "a stream or tendency"—and those interests do not alter their ability to make decisions within the bounds of the law.

Should an immigration judge—one who decides whether someone is deported, or given asylum—be treated differently? Should the judge's country of birth, or her ancestry, dictate whether she can hear cases concerning those born in that country? What if the judge belongs, for example, to an organization that seeks to bolster British-American economic relations? Or his or her religious beliefs are steeped in the Greek Orthodox Church? Should a judge—any judge—be required to become a hermit, a recluse, when they take the bench? Or should they be permitted to participate in events they believe in, as long as it does not prejudice those who appear before them?

As we look at these questions in the context of Immigration Judge Tabaddor, we should note that immigration judges are required to get permission before issuing written remarks. This chapter is included in the form in which it exists because the Department of Justice (DOJ) vetted this chapter, and allowed it to be published. Without that process, you would not be reading this!

And this is perhaps a good place to insert the required advisal (also footnoted above at the request of the DOJ) that the responses Judge Tabaddor has provided in the interview questions here are in her personal capacity; that, while she is an employee of the DOJ and the Executive Office for Immigration Review (EOIR), anything she has shared in this publication is her personal opinion and is not necessarily shared by her employer.

Immigration Judge Tabaddor was born in Iran before the 1979 Iranian revolution, and left shortly thereafter. She has lived in the U.S. since she was 11 years old. She spent her entire career working for the U.S. government, and, in particular, in the area of immigration. She worked her way to assistant U.S. attorney in Los Angeles, where she advanced the government's immigration positions. She worked without incident or complaint that she was not fully and forcefully advocating for the government. Indeed, in one notable case, potentially at risk to her personal safety, the Iranian-American community chastised her aggressive defense of a government policy it believed was fundamentally wrong.

In 2005, Alberto Gonzales, attorney general during President George W. Bush's administration, appointed Tabaddor as an immigration judge—one who decides whether the government is correct when it demands that someone not born in the United States should be deported or removed. They also rule on asylum requests—whether people should receive U.S. protection after having left their home country. They do not, it should be noted, decide who gets a visa or who becomes a U.S. citizen.

Tabaddor served her country well in each of her government positions. So much so apparently that, in 2012, she was invited—without solicitation on her part—to attend a White House event entitled "Roundtable with Iranian-American Community Leaders." A White House event—it is an honor to be invited and no one could possibly object. How could they? And to add to the mix, Tabaddor was (and remains) actually employed by the DOJ. Since the head of the DOJ is the attorney general, and the attorney general is a member of the president's cabinet—what possible issues could Tabaddor face were she to receive an invitation to attend this Roundtable?

Well, things are never simple. The EOIR is a division of the DOJ. And when the Office of General Counsel (OGC) of the EOIR received word that she would be attending this event, its line ethics officer had questions. He wanted to know precisely why Tabaddor was invited. She told him she didn't know, that the invitation came out of the blue, but that she was active in the Iranian-American community. Was that a mistake? Did the OGC believe that immigration judges should not have outside interests or causes?

Certainly, Judge Tabaddor was not the first immigration judge to have been born in another country. In fact, she is not the only immigration judge to have been born in Iran. But she helped form the Los Angeles chapter of the Iranian-American Bar Association, and accepted invitations to speak at conferences sponsored by Iranian-American organizations, in each case obtaining the prior approval of the OGC and the EOIR. She also spoke at non-Iranian related events and taught law school classes. And, one more thing—Immigration Judge Tabaddor is a Muslim.

So returning to our question, was OGC's concern that immigration judges should not have outside interests? Was it that Tabaddor's outside interests had to do with Iran, and Iranian-American relations given that Iran may be the least favorite nation to the United States, particularly to its State Department? Or was it that Tabaddor was participating in a White House program, raising questions or suggesting that the United States immigration authorities treat Iranians or Iran-Americans poorly?

Shortly after Tabaddor was told that she could take the day off to attend the White House Roundtable (we cannot say that enough—she was invited by *the White House*, not to a fringe group preaching some politically divisive rhetoric), EOIR "recommended" that she recuse herself from any cases where a party was from Iran. The recommendation became an order, and for three years, Judge Tabaddor was not permitted to hear cases that involved someone from Iran.

Now, truth be told, immigration cases involving Iranian nationals comprise less than 1 percent of the court's docket. And at the time she was ordered to recuse herself, she had only eight cases involving ten Iranians before her out of approximately 2,000 cases pending. So why did she object to the order? Were other judges subjected to the same standard—would they be recused if they appeared at conferences hosted by organizations celebrating Mexican-Americans or Chinese-Americans? Would they be removed from hearing cases if they were born in that country? Or had Tabaddor shown some bias, some prejudice toward Iranians?

Maybe EOIR was concerned about how Tabaddor and her parents came to America. More to the point, did or would that journey—one she would certainly remember as she was ten years old when it began—impact her rulings in any way? Would she be—was she—more sympathetic to those who traveled a similar path?

What was the EOIR actually concerned about when it ordered Tabaddor to remove herself from Iranian cases? Tabaddor courageously decided to find out, to take the bull by the horns and challenge that decision ultimately in federal court. Tabaddor filed a complaint with another government agency, the Equal Employment Opportunity Commission (EEOC), demanding that the DOJ and EOIR lift the recusal order.

Rather than concede—rather than have the issue go away quietly—DOJ and EOIR fought the case for three years. What did the government claim as the basis for denying Tabaddor the right to hear these cases—requiring her to abrogate her responsibilities as an immigration judge? Was Tabaddor, in fact, more lenient to Iranians than those from other countries, or more lenient to Iranians than other immigration judges?

How did the EEOC rule? And what did the court say? Ultimately, Tabaddor and the government settled their differences. The DOJ acknowledged that, to their best "knowledge, information and belief there has not been any allegation or finding of any bias, partiality or misconduct by [Tabaddor] in her capacity as an EOIR Immigration Judge." The government agencies also agreed to review their policies for issuing recusal orders, and pay Tabaddor's attorney's fees and damages. In other words, Tabaddor was cleared. Did that satisfy her and was it enough?

Indeed, when talking to Immigration Judge Tabaddor, one must ask—was it worth the three-year fight? And why did she agree to this interview, particularly as she knew that, when she sat and spoke to the author, her every word would be reviewed, vetted, parsed, considered, and passed upon by the DOJ and EOIR before this chapter could be published?

Sometimes, we have to look at the context of what is going on in the world. At the time of this interview, Donald Trump was the presumptive Republican nominee for president of the United States. Since he began his campaign, he called for a "total and complete shutdown of Muslims entering the United States" and announced that he would build a "great wall" between Mexico and the U.S. because the people who come from Mexico are criminals. He "called out" U.S. District Judge Gonzalo Curiel, who ruled against Trump University in a case pending before him, charging that the judge ruled as he did because he was (to Trump) "Mexican" and was offended by Trump's stated plan to build that wall. Indeed, while he was a prosecutor, Judge Curiel led a joint task force to bring down a

Tijuana drug cartel and had to be relocated from his home by U.S. marshals because of credible death threats. Did concerns about events such as these prompt Immigration Judge Tabaddor to talk about what happened to *her* at the hands of the *Obama* Justice Department, and how she handled it?

Ending where we began, judges do have personal lives—they must. They have causes and projects; they teach; they vote. Should judges—in particular, immigration judges—sit by and simply "follow orders" without challenging them if they are held by their superiors to a standard that demands too much? Or, is it better to question one's fealty to a department that bears the name "Justice"?

The Dialogue

JC: Judge Tabaddor, we haven't spoken substantively about this. But I'm going to ask you some probing questions. If I ask a question that goes over the line, please object and sustain your own objection. And we shall move on.

So today in particular, there is great controversy around Hillary Clinton, the FBI director having cleared her just yesterday and it is expected that the attorney general will adopt that finding. If I were to make a statement critical of the attorney general, it would be a poor idea, but nothing could happen to me. It's my First Amendment right to offer that kind of criticism. You, however, are an immigration judge, and as such you are also an employee of the Justice Department. What consequence would flow if you were to make that kind of statement?

AAT: Well, if I understand you correctly you're really trying to understand the role that immigration judges play in relation to the attorney general as the person who appoints us. Where does her influence or status as our ultimate employer end, and where does our independent judicial decision making begin.

It's a complicated issue, but essentially we act in two different capacities. One is as a judge who has taken an oath of office to act independently and impartially in upholding the Constitution and the laws of the United States. The other is as an employee of the Department of Justice. There is inherent tension between the two capacities. As a judge you always want to be mindful of what you say and how it reflects on your position and the court. On the other hand, as the employee of the attorney general . . .

JC: I see you are very slowly and carefully choosing your words.

AAT: You began with a very tough question, which I'm not surprised at—but perhaps it goes to the very heart of the issue.

JC: Let me ask it another way. We are having this interview where I'll be asking you questions about you actually having sued the Justice Department over its decision that required that you disqualify yourself from certain cases. And we both understand that you are required to seek Justice Department approval before this interview can be published—so that it can vet what you say in response to my questions. Indeed, I have agreed that, unless you receive that approval from the department, this book chapter won't be published.

AAT: Correct. One of the restrictions of the job is that we are held to the requirement that whenever we engage in any public speaking or writing engagement, it has to be cleared. For regular speaking engagements it's generally cleared before—you let them know that you've been asked to come and speak. For written materials, generally you write it up and you let them review it. So yes, that's part of the job.

JC: And, although this is not really the subject of this interview, what does that requirement say, or should it say, to those who appear before you to seek asylum—that the judges themselves are employees of the Justice Department?

AAT: I think it goes back to that tension that exists—that immigration judges are given independent decision-making authority by statute and regulations, and they are expected to honor that and act consistent with that and with their oath of office. But, still, at the end of the day, we are still the delegates of the attorney general and as such have to be mindful of that.

JC: There's probably a sense of people who are immigration lawyers, or those seeking asylum or to not be removed, that immigration judges—because they're employed by the Justice Department—are somewhat in the hip pocket of the Justice Department. Much as lawyers who practice before the SEC come to think that SEC administrative judges are in the hip pocket of the SEC. What do you think about that?[3]

---

3. Author's note: This question and answer were given via email after the interview.

AAT: I can only speak for myself. I take the responsibility to make independent judgments on the individual cases before me very seriously, and as you can see, if I feel that my authority in that realm has been unjustly compromised, I will challenge it. Having said that, however, I have no control over how and if the department issues regulations or operating policies that bind me or prevent me from ruling in certain ways.

JC: So let's turn to the case you brought against the Justice Department. When did you come to the United States?

AAT: I believe, December 24, 1982. I was born in Iran.

JC: As were your parents—your father, I believe, is a semi-retired orthopedic surgeon in California?

AAT: Yes.

JC: Why, if I might ask, did they decide to come to America?

AAT: Well, after the revolution in Iran, we initially thought that things would improve—it was supposed to be a revolution which would bring in democracy. But soon thereafter it became pretty clear that it wouldn't be what was anticipated. Things became progressively more difficult. Now, I was too young to know the details, but I do know that my father came to the United States with my grandfather for his open heart surgery and within a few months, I believe, my mother contacted him and said, "Don't come back. Things have gotten worse. We're coming to you." So she made arrangements for us to flee. We were aided by smugglers who helped us cross the border to Pakistan and then from Pakistan to Spain and then, while we were in Spain my father was able to hire attorneys in New York. He was staying with my uncle (a neurosurgeon) here, and secured visas for us to come out here.

JC: If I can ask, since I really don't know the immigration system, what was the basis for those visas?

AAT: I believe it was initially a visitor's visa to come here. At the time my uncle had petitioned for my father, because my uncle had been here for decades and he was a United States citizen. While we were waiting for the visa to become available my father wanted to make sure we were reunited. And so initially we came in on a visitor's visa and then waited for that immigrant visa to become available so we could then change our status.

JC: Would an immigration judge back then have had any authority over one's ability to come to the United States?

AAT: When you're outside the United States, the decision is made by the consular office, not an immigration judge. An immigration judge is only involved when the government seeks one's removal from the United States.

JC: So, for example, had the U.S. government decided that activities of your parents were antithetical to the interests of the United States, an immigration judge would have presided over the removal or deportation process?

AAT: Yes.

JC: Do you think that if, today, your parents had sought to emigrate to the United States and bring you, their child, they would be able to accomplish that, given the current tension with Iran?

AAT: No. Or I should say it would be incomparably more difficult.

JC: What is different now than under the Ayatollah in terms of an Iranian's ability to gain access to the United States?

AAT: When we came, the Ayatollah was in power, and there were many problems between the two countries. Still, the processes and the procedures in place to secure a visa were not as difficult as they are now.

JC: And that's because of the tension involving the nuclear capacity issue?

AAT: I think it's 9/11, the nuclear issue, and over 30 years of really bad relationships.

JC: In looking at court papers you filed, it says you are a first generation Iranian-American and that you are "culturally Muslim." What does that mean?

AAT: I'm an American of Iranian descent. When I was in Iran, obviously, the primary religion was Muslim. So, I was very much surrounded by it, and I had many family members who were practicing Muslims. My parents never imposed any particular religious practices on us but we grew up in a culture and community where Muslim practices were prevalent. So, I'm very comfortable with those practices—similar to friends who say, "I'm culturally Jewish." It means you are familiar with many of the practices, but you are not necessarily self-identified as a religious Muslim.

JC: But your religious practices aside, in terms of your career, you identify yourself as deeply involved in the American legal system.

AAT: Absolutely.

JC: You were actually an assistant United States attorney, in Los Angeles?

AAT: Yes. I worked for the civil division, which was structured so that all the assistant U.S. attorneys were expected to handle all types of cases. So we were general practitioners, but each of us came in with a certain experience enabling each of us to assist one another when it comes to the particulars of a special case. Some were more experienced in employment discrimination. Others with tort claims. I came with immigration experience, so after 9/11 and the explosion of litigation, immigration came to the forefront of the Justice Department's interest—the U.S. attorney's office wanted to be sure it had people on staff who were familiar with the law.

JC: Did you handle any cases while an assistant U.S. attorney that involved Iranians, or Iranian-Americans?

AAT: Yes.

JC: Did you take positions adverse to Iranians or Iranian-Americans?

AAT: Yes.

JC: Was there any suggestion that you lacked sufficient aggressiveness in representing the United States in such cases?

AAT: No. The case that comes to mind is a case that was filed as a potential class action by males from certain Muslim countries of a certain range of age—19 to 35 or something like that. It required them to come in and register. This resulted in a lot of pushback from the community because it was forcing people to come in and self-report, and men were detained and put in custody. It was obviously done based on nationality—very targeted. The lawsuit was filed the day before Christmas and I was the only one at the office. So I ended up working 48 hours straight to put together the government's response. We went in to argue, and we prevailed on our motion to dismiss the case. So, I didn't have anyone question my defense of the government in terms of what you characterize as . . .

JC: Aggressiveness?

AAT: Aggressiveness. In fact, there were people from the community who were essentially threatening me or were unhappy with me for what I was doing as an attorney for the United States. There was even some discussion about having to send the U.S. marshals to some people to tell them to stand down.

JC: So, while you were in the U.S. attorney's office and thereafter, you've obviously associated with the Iranian-American community in terms of your legal work?

AAT: Yes, in fact, when I was at the U.S. attorney's office, I was one of the founding members of the Los Angeles chapter of the Iranian-American Bar Association.

JC: Have you had speaking engagements in connection with that bar association or other places in terms of promoting the Iranian-American community in Los Angeles?

AAT: When I was involved with the bar association, while I was an AUSA, I did what was very common for any bar association. I was trying to encourage people to become members; to give back to the community; to try to present continuing legal education programs; to basically help the chapter get on its feet. So we would reach out—we put together a speaking engagement, bringing the first Iranian-American judge to speak. We would bring influential Iranian-American attorneys to speak. It was a lot to deal with trying to help law students or recent graduates gain access to mentors, because there's very limited opportunities for mentorship—people who would understand the cultural and ethnic issues presented to Iranian-Americans here in America.

JC: Did you do anything to promote greater rights for Iranian nationals in terms of the immigration process?

AAT: No. Neither as an AUSA or as a judge.

JC: So there came a time when you were invited to participate in a roundtable discussion at the White House.

AAT: That was many years later, after I became an immigration judge.

JC: What caused you to be invited, if you know?

AAT: It was an unsolicited invitation and I tried to find out how I was invited. My understanding is that the White House had reached out to some community leaders and expressed their interest in doing this event. I think it was the first of its kind, and they had asked for people who their contacts would recommend as invitees. They had been given dozens and dozens of names.

JC: Were you slated to give a speech or give a talk?

AAT: No. It wasn't a speaking engagement. We actually had no idea really what it was going to be about. I had done a fair amount of speaking engagements. This wasn't like that at all. This was more, "Come to the White House." That's all I knew about it.

JC: Did you seek permission from the Justice Department to attend that program?

AAT: I sought permission from my supervisor to take the day off to attend the event. The reason I even mentioned it was because, at the time, I was supposed to be on "detail," and when you're on detail, generally it's very difficult to take time off because you're being sent somewhere else to take care of another docket. So, before I made the request, I contacted the other court and made sure it wouldn't have an impact on the calendar. I went to my supervisor and said, "I know it's unusual to request time off during a detail, but this is the reason that I'm requesting it and I just want one day. I'll make all the arrangements on my own." Otherwise, generally speaking, when you take a day off you don't owe an explanation as to why.

JC: I take it that the response you received was uneventful—"that's fine"?

AAT: No, actually he was reluctant to give me the day off. He wasn't very clear why. He wavered back and forth, and sort of said, "Well I don't know, I'm not sure—and you're on detail." I said, "Well I've taken care of everything. I'm going to address all my cases; there'll be no impact." So that's when he said, "Why don't you just put it in writing and I'll send it up to the deputy chief immigration judge or the chief immigration judge." So I put it in writing, and forwarded the email invitation I had received.

I didn't hear back for several days and it was getting very close to the event. I was in New York on vacation and I started calling to get a final decision. I was routed to Jeff Rosenblum who, at the time, was the chief counsel of the Employee/Labor Relations Unit and the duty attorney for the ethics office of the Office of the General Counsel (OGC). He left a message saying he wanted to talk to me about it. So I called him. He asked whether I would be appearing on behalf of any organization. I said, "No." He explained, "Well, if you're going on behalf of an organization and are lobbying another government agency when you are an employee of the government, that can trigger severe consequences, some criminal." Again, I said, "No, I'm not appearing on behalf of any organization. This is the first time this event is being held. I don't even know what's going to happen at it. Most importantly, though, this is not a lobbying event, at least as far as I know." And he said "Okay." I think he also asked why I was invited, and I told him I wasn't sure, but that I was active in the Iranian-American community.

JC: This was an invitation to the White House. This is not an invitation to the Iranian consul's office, or to a controversial organization, something like "Black Lives Matter" as applied to Iranian-Americans, was it?

AAT: Correct. That's why I was very confused. When I spoke to him, he said, "Yes." We had no conversations other than those from what I remember. He reminded me that I was going in my personal capacity and that I wouldn't use my title as judge. Of course I agreed with all of that and I thought it was all put it to rest. Later on, when I received the official email approval, I noticed at the bottom—almost like a postscript—a recommendation that I should consider recusing myself from all cases involving Iranian nationals.

JC: You received this before you went to the White House?

AAT: Yes.

JC: Did that deter you from going?

AAT: No.

JC: Give me a ballpark—what percentage of cases on your docket at any given time are those of Iranians or Iranian-Americans? Two percent? Twenty percent?

AAT: For the past two years I've been on the juvenile docket, so we don't really see any Iranian nationals on the juvenile docket. Back then, it was a handful of cases—not even one percent. When the order came down I had eight Iran-related cases involving ten individuals. And maybe a total of some 2,000 cases on my docket. So eight out of 2,000. A very negligible sum.

JC: Were any of those eight cases controversial?

AAT: No.

JC: Could you estimate approximately how many Iranian-Americans or Iranians appeared in front of you since you were appointed as an immigration judge?

AAT: I honestly don't know, but I don't think it was unusual to have maybe a dozen cases pending out of about 2,000 cases. I've been on the bench close to 11 years now. This was four years ago.

JC: Would you say that over the course of your judgeship you were more lenient toward Iranians than you were toward other ethnic groups or nationals coming before you?

AAT: Absolutely not.

JC: The mild smirk on your face just now tells me that you do not—and that you may wonder how I could even ask such a question. What conduct is typically at issue in the case of Iranians or Iranian-Americans that motivated the Justice Department to seek removal?

AAT: Very similar to other cases. Generally speaking, we hear cases predominantly from individuals from Central America, Mexico, and China. Those are the top three regions. In all of the areas, you see people who have either overstayed their visas or seek asylum, or people who have engaged in activities that trigger removal after receiving their green card or lawful permanent resident status. Criminal conduct, that kind of thing.

JC: How long was the event at the White House?

AAT: It was a day-long event with about two dozen people. They gave us the itinerary, with six to eight representatives from different offices who gave presentations about different programs that impact the Iranian-American community. There were health care issues, OFAC, student visas, some consulate issues relating to visas, business development. An Iranian-American in the Treasury Department came and spoke generally about his position. It was very varied.

JC: Was there anything discussed suggesting that the U.S. immigration judges were too harsh or not fair to Iranians or Iranian-Americans when the Justice Department sought their removal?

AAT: No discussion of that at all.

JC: You said earlier that there was a notation on the memo approving your day off "recommending" that you recuse yourself from Iranian-American cases. Do you view it now as a recommendation or as an order from a superior that you recuse yourself?

AAT: At the time it was a recommendation.

JC: Did that change?

AAT: Yes. Under our current setup the OGC is supposed to act in just an advisory capacity. So the ethics clearance is really their way of saying, "Okay, you've given us the information. We've done our review. No one can raise an issue with you regarding this activity." I interpreted the postscript as nothing other than a recommendation; and it wasn't even contingent upon whether I attended the White House event or not. It was just something like, "Now that this has come up, I recommend that you recuse yourself." As I said, all of this was happening quickly. It didn't sit well with me from the beginning. It just sort of stewed and ultimately after several weeks I just said to myself, "This was just not right." Even as a recommendation it wasn't right. I didn't know what the ethics officer was basing it on.

So I asked what facts or analysis was used as the basis for this recommendation. That's what triggered the recommendation becoming an order. Through the next couple of emails back and forth, the associate attorney at the OGC became more and more persistent with this position, and it escalated to an order. Because I knew that, technically, he was not my direct supervisor, the only way it could become an order was if my supervisory judge adopted it. So I went back to the supervisory judge to verify. From the emails it became very clear that they were in contact with each other, that the OGC was essentially speaking on behalf of both of them—that the OGC associate attorney was the messenger.

But just to be certain, because I felt that it was so wrong and indefensible, I went back to the supervising judge and verified it for myself. This was important for me because now I was thinking that if it's an order, as much as I think that it is absolutely wrong and outside of their authority, I would be facing potential claims of insubordination should I refuse to follow it.

JC: So when you say it morphed into an order, did he ever say, or did anybody in your direct chain say "I order you" or "I direct you" or words to that effect?

AAT: Yes. It went from "I recommend" to "You should." And the "You should" went to Assistant Chief Immigration Judge Thomas Fong and I said, "Am I being ordered?" and he said, "Yes." It was very clear, at least to me, that Judge Fong's "yes" was because he felt that he had to do it based on OGC's recommendation. Also, no cases concerning Iranians were going to be assigned to me.

JC: When Judge Fong communicated that to you in writing, what did you decide to do?

AAT: I had to think about how to fight this, because this was just wrong. I reached out to my contacts at the National Association of Immigration Judges. At the same time I spoke to Judge Fong saying, "Okay, you're telling me to recuse myself and I have to issue these recusal orders on my pending cases. If you're telling me to recuse myself give me the order." Then he started backing off a bit, saying, "Well, these are orders under your signature. You write it the way you want." I kept saying, "But this is not my order. I would never issue this order." So we went back and forth a bit, and I ultimately felt that it was very important to make very clear why I was being ordered to recuse myself.

So I gave him a draft of the order that I would issue. I don't remember the specifics, but I believe it was something along the lines of, "I'm being ordered to recuse myself from these cases because I am involved with the Iranian-American community." I was making very clear that this was not my order. He was somewhat surprised, saying, "Why are you putting all of that in there? Why are you airing our dirty laundry?"

JC: So where did it end up. Did you maintain the "dirty laundry" language in your order?

AAT: It's online. I honestly don't remember. You know, I don't know if he used those words, but the subtext was, "Why do you want to be so specific. You can just put a very generic recusal order and just forget about all of this." And I kept telling Judge Fong that this is not something you forget.

JC: Obviously, the Justice Department did not complain when you recused yourself from these cases. But did any of the respondents complain about your having recused yourself from their cases and they then get a non-Iranian American judge?

AAT: I never heard from any of the respondents. They knew I had been recused, written orders were issued to all parties, but they never asked why.

JC: Did you take any steps to vindicate your rights as a result of the Justice Department's actions?

AAT: Through the National Association of Immigration Judges' president and vice president, I tried to reach out to the powers that be at our headquarters, because after back and forth emails with the associate attorney at OGC, he basically cut off any other review. I later learned that this was quite incorrect, and that he had not even contacted the deputy designated ethics officer in charge. However, I was trying, in a more informal way, to reach people who might be able to just set this straight, because everyone I spoke to agreed that this was an indefensible position for the agency. And so, I really felt that if we just talked to the right person at headquarters, they would step in.

JC: How many other Iranian-American immigration judges are there in the United States?

AAT: At the time there were three of us. Since then I think there's one or two more.

JC: Did either of the other two at the time say, "Why don't you just stand down? We're subordinates in the Justice Department hierarchy. You shouldn't pursue this. It's going to hurt us too."

AAT: Every judge that I spoke with was outraged and supported challenging it. I don't remember any immigration judge telling me to stand down. There were people who would say, "Well, you do realize if you do challenge this you're going to be targeted—that this will have a pretty negative consequence for you regardless of what happens?"

JC: How about your family?

AAT: They were very supportive. My parents have always supported my professional and personal goals. They've been pretty progressive for people of Iranian descent [laughter].

JC: What was your next move?

AAT: My lawyer and I had to make a decision. Under my collective bargaining agreement I could have raised it as a grievance, but if I did, if the deputy chief judge didn't agree with me, the only thing we could have done is go to arbitration. Our other alternative was to go to the EEOC. But it was going to be a much longer and more arduous process.

JC: Not only arduous, but controversial.

AAT: Correct. But we felt that if the system doesn't work, at least we have the option to go to U.S. district court. It should have taken six months under the rules, but it took a year-and-a-half or two years just for the administrative part.

JC: At any point, did the EOIR come up with anything suggesting that by virtue of just your ethnicity you would have been too favorable to Iranian-Americans whom the government sought to deport or remove?

AAT: No. Their entire position from day one was: We don't deny that there is absolutely no basis to question your impartiality. There is no allegation or claim that you're biased. They relied on an argument that there was an "appearance of impropriety." Something along the lines of—she is an Iranian-American advocate for the Iranian-American community, or a high-profile Iranian-American.

JC: Who is the highest profile Iranian-American in the legal community in Los Angeles? Or in the country?

AAT: I have no idea.

JC: You're right up there?

AAT: Maybe.

JC: Are there any Iranian-American Article III judges?[4]

AAT: No.

JC: What was the result of the EEOC process?

AAT: When you file an EEO complaint with the government, the agency has 180 days to complete an internal investigation and issue a final decision. You have to exhaust that administrative remedy before you can pursue your claim before the district court. Here, the agency failed to complete the process within the allotted 180 days. Therefore, the EEOC issued what's called a "right to sue" letter. However, we decided to wait to let the department complete its internal process, which took about one-and-a-half or two years. At some point, the agency decision-maker issued an interim order to EOIR, stating that, assuming Judge Tabaddor has shown the basics of a case of discrimination, "Why don't you give us your basis for this decision?" I can't remember all the details, but the agency's response was something like, "Because we never intended to discriminate, therefore it is not discrimination." And that became essentially the final agency decision after the entire administrative process.

JC: Did you have any reticence about suing?

AAT: The decision to fight—I never had second thoughts. I always knew that it was something I had to do. Otherwise it would be contrary

---

4. Author's note: Article III judges are appointed by the president of the United States with the approval of the Senate. They sit in federal district courts, courts of appeals, and the U.S. Supreme Court and exercise, what Article III of the U.S. Constitution terms, "the judicial power of the United States." In September 2016, President Obama nominated Abid Riaz Qureshi, a Muslim, to the district court bench.

to *everything* I've ever stood for my entire life. Everywhere I go, I always say, "You have to stand up for what you believe in. You have to protect these rights. These are so important. We stand on the shoulders of people before us who've had to protect our rights." So for me it would have been absolutely contrary to everything I believe in to let it go.

JC: And you were willing to do this even though it might have resulted in your termination?

AAT: I didn't think it would result in my termination. There is no term to my appointment. They can remove me from an immigration judge position and place me . . .

JC: So when you brought the lawsuit in federal court—Ali Mojdehi, Esq., of Cooley, LLP filed it on your behalf—did you first have communication with the government, saying you were about to file a lawsuit, "Do you really want us to do that?"

AAT: We submitted a notice of intent to sue with the U.S. attorney's office, and to the attorney general's office. The wrinkle in all of this . . .

JC: You're an alumna of the U.S. attorney's office?

AAT: That's the wrinkle. I had worked for the civil division. And I went to the chief of the civil division because he's a good friend of mine and said, "This is what's coming down the pike. I don't want you to be surprised. This is what happened." So he did exactly what I expected, which was to say, he was really sorry, but they were going to recuse the office.

JC: You ultimately filed a complaint in federal court?

AAT: Yes, against the DOJ, the EOIR, related government agencies, Eric Holder, as he was the attorney general at the time, and the individuals involved. They filed a motion to dismiss. The court granted it in part and denied it in part, keeping the core of our claim. The claim of discrimination survived.

JC: How long was the case pending?

AAT: Maybe six months. The district court judge ordered the department to engage in settlement discussion and attempt to resolve this case without a trial. With that, we were able to settle. The DOJ lifted the order that I recuse myself and that I not be assigned any cases where the respondents were Iranian nationals. It agreed to pay attorneys' fees as well as damages. It issued a letter confirming that I had done nothing wrong—that at no point was the decision based on any claim or finding or allegation of wrongdoing on my part. It agreed to go back and review their interpretation of the regulations.

JC: What were the damages you received?

AAT: It was $200,000 of which $194,200 was designated as attorneys' fees and the $5,800 as damages. I choose to allocate the $5,800 for damages because that is the amount I was precluded from being paid, after I filed my complaint, for the classes I taught at UCLA Law School, even though I had been paid for them for years before.

When you're an employee of the DOJ, you can't work anywhere else without prior authorization, and generally speaking you can't get paid for "speaking engagements" unless you're teaching as part of a regular curriculum at a university or a similar institution. So for years, I had been teaching at local law schools and I was paid for teaching the classes. Right after bringing my lawsuit, when I sought reauthorization for the next year, I was denied the right to be paid.

JC: You weren't in this for the money, right?

AAT: Exactly. I was not in it for money at all. To be honest with you, if they had come to me and said, "We are sorry. We are reversing this order"—that's all I wanted. I would have been happy with that.

JC: So I originally contacted you to interview you in January [2016]— it's now July 6—so about six months ago. You were very reticent to do so, and I spoke to Mr. Mojdehi about it without much success. Then, totally out of the blue, three weeks ago, I received an email from him in which he said that you would be willing to do it now.

Did something happen in the last month to trigger the thought that you now needed to make the statement you are making by giving this interview?

AAT: Oh yes. I started getting lots of inquiries and people coming to me saying that my case was just like the controversy in all the headlines concerning Donald Trump's attack on the district judge presiding over his federal case in San Diego.

JC: Judge Curiel?

AAT: Exactly. It's the same type of "injustice" for lack of a better word. But the comments to me were: "Isn't it interesting that that gets such immediate recognition for how wrong it was?" I believe the quote in the headlines about the comments on the district court judge is that they are "textbook examples of discrimination." So many people commented to me that they thought my case presented the same issues. So when the parallel was drawn and people kept saying that I should speak up about it, my attorney raised it as well and I said, "Well, okay."

JC: So to refresh the readers' minds, because they won't read this until 2017—Donald Trump has a lawsuit relating to Trump University. The case is pending before U.S. District Judge Gonzalo Curiel who sits in San Diego. The judge, like yourself, is a former assistant United States attorney. In fact, although he was born in the United States, because he's of Mexican descent, Trump says he's Mexican. Trump says that, because Trump has very publicly promised during his presidential campaign that, if elected, he'll build a wall to keep Mexicans out of the United States, Judge Curiel has made biased rulings against Trump. That the basis of those rulings is that the judge associates himself with the Mexican community. That's what your friends and supporters are talking about by comparing the Curiel case to yours?

AAT: Correct. That since Judge Curiel is known as being Mexican-American, he's being challenged just on that alone.

JC: What's different in that case—although, I guess, the possibility exists that Trump will be president one day—Trump really can't do anything in that litigation besides make public complaints and maybe seek recusal of Judge Curiel, which I suspect would not succeed. Your situation is actually far more imposing because you're an employee of the Justice Department.

AAT: Yes, that was the big challenge for us—instead of allowing the regular procedures to address a claim or perception, the department took this unprecedented, preemptive step outside the regular recusal procedures and jurisprudence to issue the order against me. In contrast, when an Article III judge, such as Judge Curiel, is challenged based on ethnic or religious background, the department actually supports the judge in opposing his or her recusal request by the litigant. When we raised that and asked why the department was taking a completely contrary position in my case, the basic response was, "You're not an Article III judge."

JC: To ask a very hard question—obviously, with the possible exceptions of Syria and North Korea, Iran is likely the most unpopular country in the United States today. Would you agree?

AAT: Probably.

JC: Do you think that if an immigration judge of Mexican-American, French-American, or Japanese-American descent had been invited to the White House to participate in programs not involving immigration but involving representatives of their respective communities, the same thing would have happened?

AAT: I should clarify. There were discussions about immigration at the event. But they had nothing to do with immigration court or immigration judges and I didn't participate in those discussions. Deliberately, because I'm a judge.

JC: But let's assume it was a Mexican-American judge invited to a Mexican-American program at the White House. Do you think there would have been the same fallout in the Justice Department involving recusal?

AAT: I'm confident that it would not. I've always felt that it's because of the word "Iran." And, honestly, that's one of the reasons that I felt it was so important to challenge the decision because other minority groups would probably not receive this treatment. Perhaps if it was a Syrian-American, or something similar; yes I wouldn't be surprised. But I really believe it was the word "Iran."

JC: Are Iranian-Americans in Los Angeles, for example, subject to a unique discrimination by law enforcement? Or are they put upon by American society?

AAT: I wasn't in the U.S. during the hostage crisis. Still, in talking to friends and family who were here at the time, there is no question that there was a fallout based on the negative relationship between the two countries. They speak of many instances in which they were told to go home, or were beaten up. They were clearly targeted because of America's frustration with what was happening between the two countries. I will not speak about any current particular cases, but there is no question that being an American of Iranian descent won't win you any favors!

JC: Did you run into that problem when you were an assistant United States attorney?

AAT: No. My colleagues there were some of the best people I have ever worked with. I have some of my fondest memories from my time there. I still look back and really miss those days with them.

JC: If an experienced attorney were to go to a federal district court he could probably pick out which judge he'd want to appear before for sentencing—some more lenient, because there's obviously a continuum there. How about that continuum on your court—where do you stand in terms of how people might perceive you as along the continuum of leniency toward respondents? Harsh? Soft? Middle of the road?

AAT: I honestly don't know how I'm perceived.

JC: Given your family's experience in immigrating from Iran and the circumstances under which you and they came, would you be more empathetic toward an asylum case coming from Iran?

AAT: I'm asked that a lot. I tell people my judicial philosophy is formed by my past experiences. I come from a country where I saw the consequences of nepotism, of failure to follow the rule of law. So for me, one of the greatest attractions of our system here was this separation of powers—the commitment to the rule of law and recognition that unless you really play by the rule of law, the whole system falls apart. So first and foremost, rule of law, and then to the extent that the rule of law allows me to exercise the discretion and consider the human side of it. Of course, you are human. You recognize that people have had to go through amazing and difficult times.

JC: Judge Tabaddor, in our line of work there's a saying: "There's a question pending." Do you think you'd be more lenient than others or more empathetic to an Iranian seeking asylum in the United States?

AAT: I don't think so. I'm empathetic to people who come to the United States; but I'm also very empathetic to preserving this system that we have in making sure that we all play by the same rules. So I think it's important not to lose your humanity because it's easy, sometimes, with the sheer volume of cases and number of people you deal with. So it's really important to remember that every person coming before you is probably facing some of the most difficult challenges of their life. That this is the most significant decision that you can make for them. So whether they're from Iran or Mexico or China or Russia or anywhere else, one has to be mindful of that, but first and foremost it really is about keeping to the rule of law.

JC: You said at the outset of this interview that your mother told your father to stay in the United States. It's hard to accept that if you heard that story from a current Iranian looking for asylum in the United States that that wouldn't pull on your heartstrings likely harder than a judge of non-Iranian descent down the hall from you. That would be natural, wouldn't it be?

AAT: It really isn't. I don't know how else to explain it. I've always been very interested in human rights. Period. I'm part of an organization called the Pacific Council on International Policy. I joined because I'm very much interested in what's happening to people around the world, and the challenges that they're facing. So I care about what's happening to people in Syria, what's happening to people in Europe, etc. To me, their background doesn't matter.

I don't know how else to really emphasize it. When I look at someone coming from Afghanistan and hear their stories knowing what the Taliban does to women, of course that's going to have an impact. Or hearing the people struggling with what's happening in Central America. People struggling with what's happening in China. It's just recognizing that people are struggling around the world. And I have to balance that to make sure that I'm mindful of that humanity within the construct of our system. So you really have to first and foremost put aside the emotional part. Focus on the rules; focus on the facts; and then be mindful that you're dealing with a human being.

JC: So you're saying you wouldn't be more empathetic or favorably inclined to an Iranian or Iranian-American seeking relief before you by virtue of your ancestry and your family's narrative?[5]

AAT: No. I would not.

JC: Would you go back to Iran today, to visit?

AAT: I don't see how I could, safely. The Iranian government would easily know I work for the U.S. government. They would probably think I worked for the CIA. It would not be safe given today's climate.

JC: What do you think will be the result of your case and the publicity that surrounded it?

AAT: I'm hopeful that pursuant to our agreement, they will review their procedures and regulations, so that something like this doesn't happen again in either the Department of Justice, where they do have some amazing and extraordinary people, or anywhere else. Not just to someone of Iranian-American background, but anyone who is in sort of a non-favored status. Because it's very easy to scapegoat, and very easy to project onto others whatever fears, apprehensions, or anxiety one might have.

---

5. Author's note: This question and answer were given via email after the interview.

So I just want to make sure that to the extent I can, I always level the playing field—that everyone is treated the same.

JC: Last question, Judge Tabaddor:[6] Thurgood Marshall was probably the most important civil rights attorney in United States history. His rulings on the Second Circuit and later on the Supreme Court were generally consistent with the positions he had advocated previously as an attorney in courts. And certainly as a private citizen, he clearly empathized with the "Black Experience." Would you have wanted to be a litigant or litigator before him advocating *against* the positions he personally held?

AAT: Many people believe that "the law" is some sort of tangible, objectively verifiable information that a judge, in almost a robot-like manner "discovers" and delivers to the litigants. That is often not the case, which is why it is absolutely critical to have judges of diverse backgrounds and experiences on the bench. Whether you are facing Justice Marshall or Justice Clarence Thomas, you are before a human being who has sworn to administer the law in an impartial manner. And if you know that a particular judge is well-versed on the issue, then you better be well-informed as well.

JC: An extremely judicious answer, Your Honor!

---

6. Author's note: This question and answer were given via email after the interview.

10

Refusal to Bow to Popular Opinion

Marsha Ternus

When you vote against judges because they make an
unpopular decision, you are sending a message. You
are telling judges that next time there is a controversial
decision, the judge should consult the latest poll
in the Des Moines Register *to determine what the*
people want, or like this case, consult the Bible to
determine what God wants. That's the message
you're sending judges—look to public opinion polls
or the Bible rather than to the Iowa Constitution.

—Marsha Ternus, March 7, 2016.[1]

Our federal and state systems of government are comprised of three branches—the executive, the legislative and the judicial. The system works because of checks and balances—no one branch can make laws, or

---

1. Justice Ternus was interviewed at her offices in Des Moines, Iowa.

enforce them, without the input of the others. The judiciary interprets the laws enacted by the other two branches—and it should interpret them, uninfluenced by the executive branch, that may really want the law, and not because the legislature has passed it, and certainly not because popular opinion demands a particular outcome.

And that's the point—executives (presidents or governors, as the case may be) and legislators can—in fact, should—be voted in, or out, of office largely depending on the views of their constituents. But not judges. Judges must interpret the law in accordance with the Constitution, statute, and precedent. Yes, there are nuances to that statement but, at bottom, competent judges will tell you that they have had to make decisions that go against everything they believe in—which may pick at that judge's personal ideology to the core—because the Constitution, statutes, and precedents require the outcome. They will similarly tell you—when faced with a particularly controversial issue—that they have had to ignore the media, ignore shouts from the citizenry as they walk up the courthouse steps, and ignore pleas that they make the "right" decision, whatever that particular side of the aisle believes "right" is, all to decide in accordance with the Constitution, statute, and precedent.

In the federal system, judges are appointed for life. If citizens (even the litigants themselves) don't like a judge's decision, they can challenge it. They can encourage a higher court to reverse it. They can rally, protest, blog, and maybe even get their point across on the 24-hour news cycle. But people cannot, in the federal system, remove the judge from the bench for an opinion that some segment of the populace may believe is objectionable.

States are different, as are state judges. Many states have adopted the "Missouri Plan"—a committee vets judicial candidates and the governor appoints one of them based on the committee's nominations. The judge is then essentially appointed until retirement—except that every X years (depending on the state), the judge comes up for "retention." "Retention elections," as they are known, are historically pro forma. So much so that no one, even the judges themselves and the lawyers who appear before them, pays the vote much attention. Judges are retained by rote and many even forget that it is their year to come up for a retention vote. They don't campaign or solicit campaign funds—it is, except under extreme circumstances, a "done deal."

And when judges are not retained, it is historically based on things such as the judge's failure to apply the law or his poor judicial temperament. The popularity of a judge's opinion was *never* a basis for removal. Indeed, it is the opposite—one of the criteria to determine whether a judge should be retained, at least in Iowa where our story takes place, is whether judges decide "cases on the basis of applicable law and fact, not affected by outside influence." It is a fundamental principle of our independent judiciary—judges are to decide cases based on applicable law *not affected by outside influence.*

Turning to Iowa in 2009—not so long ago, but remember how the country then thought about whether gay and lesbian couples could marry. Massachusetts and Connecticut were the only states to have struck down a law requiring that a marriage be between a man and a woman. California banned a similar law but its now infamous Proposition 8 (which was ultimately before the U.S. Supreme Court) had been passed by voters so that—notwithstanding some 18,000 gay marriages until the passage of Prop 8—California again permitted only heterosexuals to marry. So two northeast states and California (but only briefly) allowed same-sex marriage. Pretty much to be expected.

But then the issue came to the fore in Iowa. Not a Bible Belt state, and it does mostly vote Democratic, but Iowa is still in the Midwest—a ruling there allowing same-sex marriage could not be chalked up to those northeast liberal-elite enclaves. Also, even though Iowa might be Democratic-leaning, as of 2010, the majority of Iowans opposed same-sex marriage.

Justice Marsha Ternus was, then, the chief justice of Iowa's highest court—the Supreme Court. She had been appointed to the court in 1993 by the Republican then-Governor (and now governor again) Terry Branstad. Her colleagues later selected her to serve as chief justice in 2006. When the seven-member court learned that they would have before it *Varnum v. Brien*—to decide whether Iowa's Constitution allowed marriage to be limited to a union between a man and a woman—they of course knew it would be controversial. They knew they were the first high court in the Midwest to address the issue, and that there would be an outcry across the electorate.

Yet, these seven justices looked at the information before them, interpreted the Iowa State Constitution, the statute, and precedent and *unan-*

imously concluded that Iowa's Constitution did not permit a limitation that allowed only heterosexual couples to marry.

Beginning on April 3, 2009, as a result of the court's decision, gay and lesbian couples had the right to marry in Iowa. But as a result of that decision, the three justices of the Iowa Supreme Court who were scheduled for a retention election in 2010—Marsha Ternus, David Baker, and Michael Streit—were in for a fight. Because even though judges should not make decisions based on popular opinion, in fact, many Iowans— and, importantly here, non-Iowans as well—were upset by this decision. They couldn't understand how Iowa's Supreme Court could decide that gay and lesbian couples could marry.

"Iowa for Freedom" sprang into action—calling for the removal of these justices who had, in its parlance, done so much harm to Iowa, to families, to family values, to our children. But Iowa for Freedom had little to do with Iowa. It received most of its support and funding not from Iowans, but from out-of-state groups like the American Family Association (based in Mississippi) and the National Organization for Marriage (New Jersey). It was supported by (actually, one could say it was a platform for) former Pennsylvania Senator Rick Santorum and former Arkansas Governor Mike Huckabee. Newt Gingrich chimed in—some reports say he loaned financial support—calling for all seven judges to step down: "If they have any sense of integrity about protecting the court, they'll step down."

To be clear—this should be unsurprising reading the names of Iowa for Freedom's affiliates and supporters—the ruling was seen as an abomination because same-sex marriage is against "the very will of God." This was an argument—*the* argument—the state in *Varnum* never made. Yet the justices—having little doubt that religion was the real source of objection to same-sex marriage—addressed the issue head-on. They explained what the state, and what lawyers generally, already knew—that the Iowa Constitution, like the U.S. Constitution, ensures that government not make laws based on religious beliefs, and similarly, that the court's decision did not force religious denominations to perform same-sex marriages. And, while Iowa for Freedom never outright said *Varnum* was wrongly decided on the law, the group also never acknowledged any legal precedent or constitutional limitation when it fought to ensure these three justices were removed from the bench.

Iowa for Freedom, with its more than $1 million war chest funded mostly by out-of-state concerns, went on a 20-city bus tour, demanding that Justices Ternus, Baker, and Streit be removed. The bus exterior contained photos of the three judges with a slash through their faces. There were robocalls and billboards. There were also TV ads—using all of the right buzzwords to make sure the populace understood that the apocalypse was near unless these judges were removed: "*When activist judges on Iowa's Supreme Court imposed gay marriage, they were the only judges within 1,200 miles to reach such a radical conclusion. If they can redefine marriage, none of the freedoms we hold dear are safe from judicial activism.*"

Iowa for Freedom campaigned and electioneered to ensure these judges were not retained. But why? The decision was final—it wasn't going away. Gay and lesbian couples in Iowa would be free to marry even if the three justices were removed.

But that was no longer the point. By spending the money it did—by excoriating these judges for what they had done—these organizations intended (beyond punishing these three judges) to send a message. Not to Iowa—that damage had already been done. But to the judges in the many other states who had yet to rule on the issue of same-sex marriage. Iowa for Freedom—but really, the American Family Association and the National Organization for Marriage—made clear that they were sending a message across the country that "*judges ignore the will of the people at their peril.*"

And if that worked—if the Iowa retention vote made a single judge anywhere in the United States reconsider whether to act in accordance with the Constitution, statute, and precedent—then Iowa For Freedom and its out-of-state contributors will have caused great harm. The Brennan Center for Justice has shown us that trial judges impose significantly longer sentences in violent criminal cases the closer the judge is to running for re-election. In one study, sentences were 10 percent longer at the end of a trial judge's political cycle than at the beginning. In one state, because of popular opinion supporting the death penalty, trial judges are more likely to impose the death penalty during election years. And the studies show that because of the huge amount of money spent to oust judges who make unpopular decisions—even if those decisions are well within the law—criminal defendants (and perhaps civil parties as well) are being hurt because some judges (by no means all) consciously or unconsciously may accede to public opinion.

Justices Ternus, Baker, and Streit made a decision to not campaign on their own behalf. They spoke publicly about the *Varnum* decision, and about judicial independence, and they directly took on some of the more outrageous things being said by Iowa for Freedom. But they did not run ads nor raise money—their thought was how could they hear cases argued by attorneys who contributed money to their retention campaign? Still, what about others who certainly supported what the justices had done? Did the Iowa State Bar Association come to their aid and educate the public? What about Governor Branstad, who had appointed Justice Ternus in the first place? Did any out-of-state organization *support* these three justices who participated in an unpopular—but legally defensible—decision? Could the justices have saved their jobs had they directly—and unashamedly—campaigned for retention?

The Iowa retention vote was a success for Iowa for Freedom—only 45 percent of the voters favored retaining these judges. Did the vote chill other judges in other states from voting with the law? One can't be sure. We will never truly know the answer.

Now, six years later, Justice Ternus has no regrets about *Varnum* and its afterlife. She says she could not "live with myself" had she decided the case any differently. Even in retrospect, she would not have campaigned or asked for contributions to enable herself to campaign to keep her job. Marsha Ternus, however, is also adamant that she is not a "victim" of Iowa for Freedom and its supporters. Nonetheless, she recognizes the dangers and injustices caused when groups demand that the judiciary take action based on their beliefs (religious or otherwise), rather than consistent with the Constitution, statute, and precedent.

The Dialogue

JC: Judge Ternus, before I ask my questions, I'll ask you two hypotheticals to gauge your thinking: Suppose there's an Iowa state legislator who is particularly interested in a piece of legislation. He knows that it will be unpopular. But yet, committed to it, he persuades his colleagues to vote with him for it. The governor signs the bill shortly before leaving office. Some wealthy voters are so offended by the legislation that they throw a lot of money against the legislator's reelection campaign to ensure that he's not reelected—they don't like the legislation, and therefore they don't like him. He's defeated. Would you say that that's an "undeserved outcome"?

MT: Well it *might* be undeserved. The more appropriate question is whether that's an abuse of the process or an outcome that's inconsistent with the role of a legislator and the place that the legislative process takes in our society. So, to answer my own question, I think that legislators are elected to represent their constituents, and that each legislator must strike a balance between what they think is appropriate and wise legislation and what their constituents want. If they vote contrary to what their constituents want, they run the risk that they'll lose their office, and I think that's the way the legislative system is intended to work because legislators sit in a *representative* capacity. The legislator being voted out of office doesn't necessarily "deserve" to be voted out because maybe the legislator has indeed made a wise decision, but he or she still loses the election because the voters felt the legislator failed to represent them and their views.

JC: Okay, so consider another scenario. Assume an Iowa state legislator believes, perhaps not as ambitiously as Donald Trump, that Muslims should be outright banned from Iowa. He manages to get the Iowa legislature to pass such a bill and the governor signs it just before he leaves office. A lawsuit to declare the law unconstitutional comes before the Iowa Supreme Court, and the court upholds the statute's constitutionality.

Immediately, there's a campaign funded against her by several extremely wealthy liberals to accomplish throwing the chief justice off the court through an upcoming retention election. She is voted off, even though she believed in her heart of hearts that the statute is in fact constitutional. Is that an undeserved outcome—she's a judge, not a legislator?

MT: The distinction I'm going to make here—and maybe it's what you're getting at—is that there's a difference between judicial and legislative roles. Judges do not sit in a representative capacity. They sit to uphold the rule of law. So I don't think a judge should be removed because she makes an unpopular decision. If citizens believe that judges have abused their power and are unfit because of judicial temperament or because they refuse to recuse on cases where it appears that they should, those are examples of valid reasons to vote a judge out. But the fact that a judge makes a decision contrary to public opinion? That alone, to me, is no basis to remove a judge.

JC: So if the judge in the hypothetical I just presented truly believed, applying the law as she viewed it, that it was constitutionally permissible to ban Muslims from Iowa, which we can probably agree—of course, you're no longer a judge—would be unconstitutional, it would, or wouldn't, be an injustice to throw money at a campaign to remove her?

MT: The problem with your hypothetical is that it's so extreme. It would be like the Iowa Supreme Court ruling it acceptable to ban Catholics from coffee shops. You can theorize a decision so patently wrong that you would have to step back and ask yourself what is motivating these judges. For example, are they being caught up in some hysteria causing them to ignore the rule of law? Are they acting out of personal bias rather than being fair and impartial decision makers? In those circumstances, if you believe the judge is not upholding her oath of office or does not have the temperament to serve as a neutral decision maker, supporting the judge's removal is an appropriate response. That is something different than voting against a judge simply because you disagree with his decision. I don't think the same-sex marriage case in any sense approached the extreme example you have proposed.

JC: But you don't think there are many people in the United States, or at least there were many people in the United States six or seven years ago when *Varnum* was decided, that believed that same-sex marriage was antithetical to American values?

MT: There may have been people who believed that the *Varnum* decision was contrary to their personal values or even American values. That view is reflected in public opinion polls at the time. But the public opinion polls simply asked voters for *their opinion*: Do you think that same-sex marriage should be allowed? That question had nothing to do with what the Iowa Constitution required. I don't recall any criticism of our constitutional analysis, even by the people who sought our removal. They simply argued that judges shouldn't have the power to make this decision—the people should decide. I did not hear any criticism that our analysis of what the "equal protection" clause of the Iowa Constitution required was wrong.

JC: So let's get right to it. Do you think, under those circumstances, that there was an "injustice" perpetrated against you and your two colleagues who were removed from the bench basically because you reached a decision contrary to what the opponents of same-sex marriage believed?

MT: I did not experience it as an "injustice." I thought it was wrong to remove a judge who had upheld the rights granted by the Iowa Constitution simply because voters believed that same-sex marriage was contrary to their religion, or because they thought gay and lesbian people shouldn't have the same rights and privileges as opposite-sex couples. That's an inappropriate basis upon which to remove judges. If voters did not want to grant gay and lesbian couples equal protection of the law, then they should amend the Iowa Constitution. I'm just uncomfortable with this idea of personal injustice. When I took that job I had no promises, any more than anybody else in life has, that everything was always going to turn out rosy and that I was always going to be rewarded for doing "the right thing." Sometimes, you do the right thing and you're not rewarded. And the idea of calling it an "injustice"—yes, I think it was an unfortunate thing to happen to us. Yes, I think it was bad for the Supreme Court. Yes, I do think it was damaging for justice. I also think it was a negative reflection on the State of Iowa.

JC: I'm not saying it was necessarily an injustice perpetrated against you or your two colleagues personally. Was it an injustice that "the system" was abused by having seen three justices literally thrown off the court precisely because they decided a case in a way that some people didn't like?

MT: What do you mean by injustice?

JC: No, what do *you* think an injustice means? You believe that the system requires you to apply the law as you see it, correct?

MT: Well I think—when you say "as you see it" that implies to me a little more of personal option than I think . . .

JC: Let me say it differently. You believe that the precedents directed you to a particular place, and that place was that a statutory ban on same-sex marriage was unconstitutional.

MT: I agree with that.

JC: Okay. And you thought that was the case in *Varnum*—that those precedents led you directly to the decision that you and your colleagues reached, correct?

MT: Correct.

JC: And there was no alternative for you but to decide the case that way?

MT: Yes.

JC: And you decided the case that way.

MT: Yes.

JC: And you got thrown off the bench for having done so.

MT: That's right.

JC: And you don't see that as an injustice—an injustice to the system?

MT: I guess it is. It just sounds like I'm complaining.

JC: Well it sounds like you're complaining about my questions.

MT: I've always been reluctant to complain about it: "Woe is me, and it was such an injustice and it was so terrible." I'm too much of an optimist to view what happened *to me* in that way.

JC: When did you first realize that they were going to try to vote you off the court?

MT: It's hard to remember. But the closer it came to the election, the more I believed it would happen.

JC: So when you came close to the decision, what led you to believe that the ultimate result would be that if you decided in favor of same-sex marriage there would be a serious effort to vote you off in a retention election.

MT: I didn't think about it before the decision. But as we got closer to the retention election I became more convinced. I was aware before the decision that if we held the statute unconstitutional, many, many Iowans would be very unhappy—if not angry. In my mind, I knew that anger could come back on the judges when they were up for retention. But, honestly, when the case first reached our court, I wasn't even sure if I was on the next retention ballot. And I just didn't go there. It simply had nothing to do with my decision.

JC: Weren't people vocal, weren't people protesting before you and your colleagues wrote the decision? Wasn't there press and editorials that same-sex marriage should not—or, I suppose, should—be permitted? This wasn't a low profile case at the time.[2]

MT: It was certainly a high-profile case, but I had had a practice throughout my judicial career to avoid reading or listening to media that discussed a matter pending before the court. I did not want to be influenced in making my decision by information outside the record made in court. So I was aware there was a very public disagreement about the issue of same-sex marriage, but it was one to which I paid little attention.

JC: What about your two colleagues who were also up for a retention vote, Justices David Baker and Michael Streit—did they talk about the potential outcome if they supported the court's decision that same-sex marriage was permitted by the state's Constitution?

MT: I think they approached our decision the same way that I did. None of us ever talked about the potential consequences to members of the court. It may be hard to believe, but we never talked about it, in or out of the courtroom.

JC: Are you saying when you went to conference or to a cafeteria, or wherever you may have spent time off the bench with your colleagues, nobody mentioned that you all had a tiger by the tail here?

MT: I'm not sure what you mean by "a tiger by the tail." We certainly talked about the fact there were demonstrators in front of the building, how to accommodate the large crowd who would want to hear the oral arguments, and those kinds of things. We knew this case was no ordinary one. But we did not discuss the retention election or any personal consequences our decision might have on us until after the decision was made.

JC: You're telling me that, and of course I must believe you. But it's hard to believe; you understand that, don't you?

MT: There's actually a clear explanation for our approach. When I became the chief in 2006, the justices had a retreat. At that retreat, we had a discussion about what kind of court we wanted to be, how we wanted to be described as a court, and how we wanted to function internally. We had two or three new judges and a new chief and so we had an opportunity to create our own court culture. I thought we needed to be mindful about the kind of court we were going to be. I was certainly aware—I'd

---

2. Author's note: This question and answer were given via email after the interview.

been on the court for 14 years at that point—that some courts function well, and some courts don't. Some courts are known for not getting along and for always breaking down four-three on issues, or not talking to each other, and other unseemly descriptions of how some courts functioned. I wanted to enjoy going to work every day. I wanted to have a good working atmosphere. I'm devoting myself to this institution and I wanted to be proud of it, and the people I worked with. So the justices had a very frank discussion about what does it mean to be a judge. Some people came from plaintiffs' backgrounds and some from defense backgrounds. Some were prosecutors and some had defended criminals. So what meaning did that now have to us as judges?

You hear about courts where judges talk to each other privately and line up support for votes. Is that what we're going to do? Because if that's what we're going to do, let's be honest about it. Are we going to have this behind-closed-doors lobbying going on and enter the conference room with our minds made up? Are we going to vote along certain predictable lines, never listening to someone with a different view? So I just laid all that on the table, and we came to the conclusion as a consensus that our oath of office really meant something—that we didn't represent the trial lawyers or the defense bar or the county attorneys (as district attorneys are called here). I know I'm going way off topic, but it explains why we didn't talk about the possible personal consequences of our decision before we made it. At our retreat, we brought in a consultant who taught us how to listen to each other, because we were committed to making collective decisions where we didn't come into the conference room with our minds made up. We were going to be willing to listen to someone who disagreed, and we might even change our minds. We decided to be open to the idea that someone else might have some seed of wisdom that maybe we didn't have and that we weren't going to have these little side discussions. We would respect everyone's views and we would have our discussions in front of everyone. And including everyone—all seven of us.

So no, we didn't discuss this is "really dangerous," or this could come back to bite someone. To my knowledge, no one talked about the decision at all until we were in the conference room. And we never talked—in or out of the conference room—about what our decision might mean to our judicial careers until after the opinion had been written.

JC: So how was Justice Mark Cady chosen to author the *Varnum* opinion?

MT: Well, the chief—me—randomly assigns opinions to justices.

JC: You say randomly?

MT: Normally, my administrative assistant and I would agree on how the cases to be submitted in a particular month would be listed, for example, in alphabetical order based on the plaintiffs' first name. The cases would then be assigned in that order to the justices based on seniority. So the first case on the list would go to the chief justice, and the next case on the list to the justice who had been on the court the longest, and so on. Each month we changed the basis upon which we ordered the cases so lawyers wouldn't be able to figure out who had been assigned a particular case.

But this time, knowing of course that *Varnum* was going to be a controversial decision, I wanted it to be randomly assigned with the entire court present. So this time—and this is the only time we did this—we put seven slips of paper in a little cloth bag that my secretary had in her desk. We all drew numbers—like lots—to determine the order in which we would draw for case assignments. Then the cases to be submitted that month, including *Varnum,* were written on slips of paper, the slips of paper were put in the bag, and the members of the court drew a slip in the order that had just been determined. That's how *Varnum* went to Justice Cady to write—he drew the slip of paper that had *"Varnum v. Brien"* written on it.

JC: This kinda says you knew you were in for something depending on how the decision came out, doesn't it?

MT: As I said, we knew this decision was one in which there was a lot of public interest.

JC: Getting back to the word "injustice" that I used before, you're saying that your colleagues—in particular Justices Streit and Baker and you, yourself—weren't bothered by the prospect of a retention election after which you might be removed from the bench? Weren't you concerned in terms of "injustice" that there might be judges down the pike who might not be so conscientious or disciplined about applying the rule of law, no matter the consequences? You weren't concerned that *they* might be intimidated in how they might decide a case by the prospect of millions of dollars being thrown against them in a retention election? Weren't you concerned about an injustice in that sense—the kind of impact your removal might ultimately have on your successors on the court?

MT: Responding to your last question, the impact of our removal could certainly result in an injustice—an injustice to parties who are denied a fair and impartial decision maker because a judge is too weak or gutless or however you want to put it to follow the law.

JC: You're now doing better than I was!

MT: And certainly the biggest impact of the 2010 judicial retention election in Iowa was not on the three of us who lost our jobs. It was instead the message of intimidation that was sent to judges in other states—that if you have the audacity to do what these judges did in Iowa, you will suffer the same fate. Yes, again, that could result in an injustice.

JC: Finally, I hit pay dirt. So tell me how did they intimidate you and your colleagues?

MT: They didn't intimidate us.

JC: Sorry, how did they *try*?

MT: Well, all this happened *after* our decision, in connection with the retention election. The website of the organization that was formed in 2010—"Iowa for Freedom"—said: We're sending a message in Iowa and across the country that "the ruling class ignores the will of the people at their peril." But, as I said, that was after the *Varnum* decision.

JC: What did they do after the decision, besides their website? Did they put up advertisements?

MT: There were advertisements and billboards. They had a bus that went from the Missouri River to the Mississippi River, from one side of the state to the other, that had our pictures in circles on the side of the bus with a slash-mark across our faces. The bus stopped in towns where persons riding the bus and opposing our retention would rail against our decision—and us individually.

JC: Anything else?

MT: I think Rick Santorum and maybe Mike Huckabee joined in that. It became an opportunity for potential 2012 presidential candidates to come to Iowa and show their faces to Iowans. The people working against our retention also did a lot of outreach to churches and ministers, asking them to preach to their congregations that they needed to get out and vote against us.

JC: Did it get back to you that people were listening to all that?

MT: I don't remember precisely, but I became resigned—prepared—to the fact that I would lose my job. Whether it was polling or just the sense that I was getting from what people were saying. It's been long enough now I don't really remember, but I was prepared for the outcome.

JC: Did you do anything in opposition to Huckabee and Santorum and "Iowa for Freedom" trying to get you off the court?

MT: The three of us talked among ourselves about "What are you going to do?" "What do you think we should do?" because we had great respect for each other and the others' assessments of the situation. We decided that we were not going to form campaign committees, we were not going to fundraise, and we were not going to campaign even though our code of judicial ethics would have allowed it. We hoped the bar association or other citizens who found value in the rule of law and/or our decision would come to our aid.

JC: And what happened?

MT: The bar association didn't. The bar association effort was too little, too late.

JC: Why? Weren't you what was considered a popular judge at the time?

MT: I don't know about "popularity."

JC: Popular in the sense that you're balanced in your judging. Good demeanor. Your decision-making wasn't aberrant.

MT: Yes, I think all three of us were respected jurists. A couple of years earlier we had had the same budget crisis that most states experienced at the time, and our budget had been cut. So the Supreme Court implemented cost-saving measures, such as reduced hours in some of the rural counties for their clerk of court offices and layoffs. Many of those measures were extremely unpopular. Lawyers were mad about that. And, as chief justice, I was the face of those decisions. It wasn't that they weren't mad at the whole court, they were, but they were really mad at me because I was the chief. So I think there was an underlying current of, "Well, the supreme court didn't care about keeping our courthouse open so why should we care about them." There was some of that.

I think the primary reason, however, that the bar association was so slow to respond to attacks on the justices was lawyers' inexperience with judicial campaigns. Judges hadn't gone out and raised money before, and lawyers hadn't had to open their pocketbooks to support judges before. I think there was a little bit of "We don't know how to go about this" and "We're not used to spending money." There was also some naïveté: "Iowans would never vote justices off the court!" And finally, bar leadership at that particular time was not very strong or decisive.

JC: Was the bar's leadership opposed to your decision?

MT: I don't think so. I'm sure there were members of the bar who were. There were a lot of letters to the editor by lawyers across the state explaining the *Varnum* decision and how the court applied a well-established equal protection analysis—saying it was the right decision under the law, that judges are not supposed to decide cases based on public opinion polls. There were letters from attorneys saying that a judge's role is to uphold the Constitution; uphold the rights of minorities. There was that kind of support for us. But active, organized, and large-scale support was very late in coming.

JC: What was the breakdown of the vote when they voted against you? Ballpark.

MT: Lower 50s against upper 40s.

JC: Close.

MT: Yes, roughly the same for the three of us.

JC: Have you ever, in your reverie, thought that perhaps you should have waged a more active campaign?

MT: It's interesting, but occasionally I'll come across some article on judicial independence where the authors say that if we would have campaigned, we would have kept our jobs—kind of saying that it was our own fault that we lost our jobs.

I don't know. Maybe if we had formed campaign committees and campaigned, we would have kept our jobs. We discussed at the time that perhaps the only way to save our jobs was to just get out there and campaign. But we also decided that campaigning like politicians is not what judges ought to be doing notwithstanding the situation in which we found ourselves. I still believe that. We were being accused of being liberal agenda-driven people in robes.

JC: Activists?

MT: Activists! Yes, "activists" was the word used. As if we had just waited for the opportunity to do something really liberal like throwing out the prohibition against same-sex marriage. Our feeling was that if we started *acting* like politicians then we were only giving the public reason to believe that the Supreme Court *voted* like politicians. We didn't vote like politicians, so we weren't going to act like politicians to save our jobs. We decided we would protect the institution of the Iowa Supreme Court by not campaigning, by not forming campaign committees and by not raising money. And if that meant we would lose our jobs, then we would lose our jobs.

JC: And nobody like a law professor, TV anchor, or journalist was willing to come forward and say, "This is an outrage, I'm going to lead the campaign to do the right thing—to make sure that people trying to do the right thing as they perceive it, aren't getting thrown out of office for doing that"?

MT: Every Iowa newspaper that addressed our retention in an editorial—save one small paper in northwest Iowa—strongly supported our retention. Of course, Iowa for Freedom's response to the overwhelming journalistic support for our retention was to the effect that of course the media would support our retention, newspapers are part of the ruling elite. There was also an organization—it's now known as Justice Not Politics—that advocated for our retention. It was led by two former lieutenant governors—one Democrat and one Republican. That group raised money, ran radio ads, and did other things. I wasn't privy to exactly everything they did. I think in the end there was around $1.2 million dollars spent by the people who opposed us and maybe $400,000 spent by individuals or groups who supported us. Yes, Justice Not Politics tried.

JC: Did you spend time with them?

MT: No.

JC: Why?

MT: It wasn't our organization. I don't even know if it would have been ethical for me to coordinate with them.

JC: What sort of surprises me, if I might say it like this, is the passivity that you and your colleagues exhibited. I'm not blaming you for letting yourselves get voted out of office. But in some sense, you didn't defend the rule of law—that, in deciding the case as they saw it, seven judges were doing what they should have been doing.

MT: Let me say this: We didn't campaign. We didn't have campaign committees. We didn't raise money. We didn't have any media blitz. I took every opportunity, though, and so did my colleagues, to go out to Kiwanis Clubs and breakfast clubs and any kind of community organization or college campus that would have us. We spoke about the decision and what it meant to have an independent judiciary—what the rule of law meant. I never said "and vote for me in the retention election." Still, I did considerable public education in that year-and-a-half about the necessity of having a judiciary that made decisions based on the rule of law, and not based on public opinion polls, intimidation or the judge's own self-interest. I spoke myself blue in the face. I understand why you say we were passive, but that's not totally accurate.

JC: So, some years have passed. Let's assume there's a vacancy on the Supreme Court and Governor Branstad says, "You're my gal. I want to reappoint you to the Supreme Court." Would you accept?

MT: No.

JC: Why?

MT: I spent 17 years there. It was a wonderful 17 years, but I enjoy my life now. I don't think the experience would ever be as good now as it was back then.

JC: Why?

MT: I loved the people I served with. It was so good when I was there, and you don't recapture that.

JC: Maybe you could bring back that consultant of yours.

MT: I don't really have any desire to go back. I really don't. First of all, it's not my nature to look back. That part of my life is done. It's over.

JC: I'm not saying look back. I'm saying look forward.

MT: Exactly and I have looked forward. I've looked forward for five years now. I have a very fulfilling life. I'm doing a lot of fun things in this new chapter of my life. When I left the court I didn't go back to my old law firm or any law firm or even a law practice like I had before, so my professional life now is different than ever before. It's fresh and exciting. I experienced the Supreme Court for 17 years. I don't want to go back and do it again.

JC: But you do, albeit begrudgingly, acknowledge that there was in fact an injustice perpetrated against judges . . .

MT: Why do you think that's so important?

JC: That there was a potential impact on the elected judiciary generally across the United States.

MT: This is how I see it. An injustice was done to the American people because what happened to us threatens their access to justice—to fair and impartial judges. So yes, there was an injustice—but it wasn't to judges. When we take our oath we have to have the fortitude to uphold it and not worry about what's going to happen to us. And if something bad happens to us, that's what happens. We have to realize that can happen and not complain about it. I doubt most people care that a judge loses his or her job—lots of people lose their jobs for reasons they consider unfair. What's bad about what happened in Iowa is that it threatens the ability of citizens to access fair and impartial justice in the future. That's the injustice.

JC: So wouldn't you be making a greater statement in going back to the court? They knocked down the World Trade Center and now the World Trade Center is being built up again. Isn't that the greatest statement to make to those who try to tear things down?

MT: No, because it's not about me. It's not about restoring me to the court.

JC: You said before that the decision you made was unavoidable; the precedents clearly led you directly to where you came out.

MT: In my mind, it was an easy legal decision.

JC: You say it was easy. Your decision was, yes, unanimous. But the Supreme Court of the United States didn't see it as so easy. Theirs' was a five-four decision. A different statute, but basically the same thing. So why was it so easy for your court but not for the Supreme Court of the United States? You're smiling. It seems you want to tell me something but you're reluctant to. Try your best.

MT: It was interesting the way the majority wrote the decision in the U.S. Supreme Court. I think our decision was much better. I'm just going to say that.

JC: Better than the majority's decision in the U.S. Supreme Court?

MT: Yes, because the U.S. Supreme Court's decision focused on policy and not on well-established equal protection analysis. That focus made it appear they were making a policy decision—deciding what they thought was the best policy rather than what the Constitution required, and I don't think it was a policy decision. I don't know why they approached it that way; but when the majority talks like they're making a policy decision, I can see why that approach would draw dissent.

JC: Well, you recognize that there was no chance of getting a unanimous decision in the Supreme Court on that case.

MT: Well, maybe that says something more about the judges than the issue.

JC: Tell me what it says about the judges.

MT: Well, I will say that the decision for the seven of us, given the approach we took as jurists, was easy, and it was unanimous for a reason because none of us believed the statute could be upheld under an equal protection analysis. Substantive due process, ok there are arguments for and against that theory, but focusing on equal protection, honestly, I don't see how the result could be anything other than what the Iowa Supreme Court reached. Justices on the U.S. Supreme Court appear to be more committed to a predetermined view of the law than were the justices on our court. Yes, there are justices on the U.S. Supreme Court whom, I think, no one in the world expected them to vote any way other than the way they voted.

JC: You mean split the way they did.

MT: Yes. But as jurists, the seven of us came into that conference room, not having discussed the case at all . . .

JC: That is not hard to believe but, frankly, hard to accept, if there's a distinction.

MT: Why?

JC: It just seems that it's such a controversial case that you face. You knew there were going to be consequences to it. You have a collegial relationship with your colleagues and yet you say, "We didn't talk about it at all."

MT: No, because our approach was that we would educate ourselves on each decision that we were considering and come to conference with our own independent judgment.

JC: So having gone through this experience and assuming you wanted to keep your chief justiceship after you decided the *Varnum* case, what would you do differently today?

MT: I certainly wouldn't have made a different decision. If I had it to do over again, I still wouldn't campaign. I think it's unseemly. I think it would have presented judges in a light to Iowans that would not be helpful to a perception of the judiciary as a fair and impartial branch of government. I don't want to act like I did everything perfectly, that there's nothing I would change. But those two big things I wouldn't change in any way.

JC: If it was yours to change, would you get rid of the retention system?

MT: If a state has a robust judicial performance evaluation system, one with integrity, and a judicial disciplinary system that functions well, I think I might get rid of retention elections. There is no perfect system for choosing judges, and any system is only as good as the people who implement it and their commitment to operating within the system in a way that maximizes the opportunity to get judges who are open minded, neutral, fair, and impartial.

But if the nominating commissions aren't committed to that or if the governor is not committed to that or if the voters are not committed to that, then it's not going to happen. So you can take the voters out of the equation and you still don't have any guarantee that the process won't be politicized. I mention judicial performance evaluations because I think that is one of the weaknesses of the retention election system: voters don't have information about performance and so they vote on the basis of other reasons.

JC: Well, in this case they voted for only one reason, right? Do you think the voters let down the system?

MT: Yes. The message voters sent to judges does not support the rule of law. I said when I was out speaking before the retention election that if citizens want a fair and impartial judiciary then they have to remember that the Constitution protects the rights of minorities. It protects the rights of people who do not have a voice and who do not have power. And so judges at times, when they uphold the Constitution, will make decisions that the majority of citizens don't like. And when judges do that, they need the support of the public, because some day you might be in the minority and you will expect the courts to protect your rights. I didn't say it exactly that way, but I made the point that the only way to have a fair and impartial judiciary is to recognize that voters have to support the judiciary even when they make a decision that voters don't like.

I did say this: "When you vote against judges because they make an unpopular decision, you are sending a message. You are telling judges that next time there is a controversial decision, the judge should consult the latest poll in the *Des Moines Register* to determine what the people want, or like this case, consult the Bible to determine what God wants. That's the message you're sending judges—look to public opinion polls or the Bible rather than to the Iowa Constitution."

JC: Do you think the populace let the system down because they didn't understand the role of judges, or rather because they were narrow-minded in terms of what your decision represented?

MT: I think that the judiciary suffers from the same skepticism and cynicism that all branches of government suffer from. *You* even expressed disbelief about how we approached decision making. How do you think people on the street saw it? They believed that we were activist judges and that we voted for same-sex marriage because we were liberals and thought that Iowa ought to have same-sex marriage. I think voters are skeptical that judges are anything but politicians in robes. Many have the perception that the court's decision making is just like the legislative process—that judges vote the way the judges think it ought to be, rather than in a principled manner. I think that's part of it. I also think that some voters were angry and they felt threatened by the decision—that there was something going wrong here with society; that something they thought was so against God's will could happen. And it's hard to fight against the Bible. When people think they're on God's mission, they don't care what the Constitution says.

JC: So I saw you said in some speech or article that you weren't "angry," you were "sad" as a result of what happened here.

MT: I was sad, yes.

JC: Still sad?

MT: I am sad about it because I think it's just another example of what's happening to our society. It's an example of us losing our inclusiveness and our compassion and our willingness to see things from the viewpoint of someone that we don't understand or that doesn't look like us. We're not tolerant.

JC: Did you start to feel better about the whole thing when other courts started agreeing with the decision that your court made?

MT: Well, I don't know what you mean by whole thing. It didn't change anything that I just said about how I feel about how our society is evolving.

JC: But that basically your decision was followed by many other courts?

MT: Absolutely, of course I did.

JC: Governor Branstad appointed you, right? And he's governor now?

MT: He is. He was governor, and then decided not to run. And then he ran again.

JC: Did he come out and say anything about the *Varnum* decision and the fallout?

MT: He said the retention election was up to the voters.

JC: He punted.

MT: Yes. And that does make me angry—because he knows better.

JC: Was it an issue in his campaign when he was reelected, "You appointed these people to the bench and look what they did?"

MT: I'm not sure; it might have come up. But he wanted to be reelected, so he chose to . . . he didn't care what happened to the judiciary, or what it might mean for the Iowa Supreme Court or that the three of us would lose our jobs as long as he got elected. And I guess that's how many politicians are.

But, fortunately, not the way my colleagues and I thought judges should be. I'm proud of that. The three of us are all very proud of that.

Epilogue

During the writing of this book, a number of friends and colleagues would musingly comment to me on the breadth of the subject—the so many instances of injustice. They would typically, however, see injustice as depicted in *mass* atrocities: the Holocaust, slavery, Saddam Hussein gassing the Kurds. Those events are incredibly easy to characterize as "injustices," because they are objectively so. Probably only Nazis, ante-bellum slave owners, or Saddam-loyalists might have seen them otherwise.

But what are individual "injustices," the subject of this book, and how is injustice determinable in the individual scenario? When, today, we speak of individual injustices, we are spoiled enough by modern science to believe that the existence of an injustice typically can be determined objectively: that DNA can exonerate the wrongly accused, and so injustices may—virtually always—be scientifically proven. Such *objectivity*—the ability, for example, to squarely establish innocence notwithstanding a conviction—however, is rare.

The stories that were selected for this book represent a cross-section—some are such that (almost) every reader will have seen and acknowledged the wrong, the injustice. And some may leave the reader scratching his head asking, "what was the author thinking." As individuals with idiosyncratic views about the law, and as people whose blamelessness (versus blameworthiness) is tested daily, we certainly have our own views in deciding—for ourselves—whether these cases represent true injustices. Although in certain stories, there will be little doubt. Some readers will wonder why other cases, perhaps more notable cases (if that word should ever apply to the question of injustice), weren't selected for inclusion here. My colleague, Dale Degenshein, and I plead guilty to the selections made.

I am hopeful that these interviews—the stories told and the lives led—will give the reader insight into the challenges of dispensing and even commenting on, justice. Perhaps insight into what happens when one is

247

thrust into injustice. Yes, injustice often cannot be predicted—yet it is there, and the way people deal with it is just as important as the injustice itself. You may read this and think about those questions I failed to ask; or how the other figures in the story—those not interviewed—felt and whether they believed an injustice was done.

Is there an injustice when the game seems to have been played fairly, but the system still got it wrong? Or can there never be a level playing field because even good cops and prosecutors don't always ask the right or follow-up questions; they don't always follow the right road, even if through no fault of their own. And, of course, there are those who follow their own road—making sure the things they do take them exactly where they want to go; to the confession they know or feel they must have. Indeed, should law enforcement be required to follow *every* lead, as they failed to do in Kenneth Ireland's case?

Is it an injustice when a jury, properly charged with the evidence fairly presented, still gets it wrong? Or when people—so passionately positive in their own point of view—use over-the-top tactics to persuade others of their position, just as those who clamored for Justice Ternus's removal from the bench did? Should Jeffrey Sterling be sitting in a cell? Even if he was the *Times*' James Risen's source (which he flatly denies), was he punished for failing to conform to the CIA's imprint of what an agent should be?

Can one truly fault the FBI, in the wake of the horror of 9/11, for using (perhaps) questionable law enforcement techniques to get Abdallah Higazy to confess, particularly at a time when so much was at stake for the safety of America? Or, maybe, one could argue—would you?—that by using those tactics to obtain a confession, the FBI betrayed the very justice that America stands for.

Is Marty Stroud a "bad guy" for having tried to convict a man whom he truly believed to be guilty? Was he obliged to look inwardly at his own biases before prosecuting a man to death row on slim evidence? Was Ted Cruz doing the devil's work in insisting that a defendant he knew should have been released stay in jail even though, as he saw it, he was upholding an important court precedent? Ashley Tabaddor and Marsha Ternus, both judges—did the system they work within betray them? Is Steven Pagones truly a victim of an injustice—after all, no charges were brought and there is an official report of his exoneration available for all to see. And should Miriam Moskowitz have been exonerated now, 60 years later, because, even though the prosecutors followed the rules, the rules have since changed?

I doubt I can satisfactorily answer many of the questions I raise, even those that I pose as "devil's advocate." Nonetheless, I am hopeful that the interviews, and these questions, add spark to a continuing and important conversation about injustice in America.

Selected Materials

Glenn Ford discussed by A. Martin Stroud, III

State of Louisiana v. Ford, 489 So. 2d 1250 (Sup. Ct., La., 1986).

State of Louisiana v. Ford, 10-KP-1151, 02/04/11 decision.

Ford v. State of Louisiana, Docket 126,005, 3/11/14 motion.

Ford v. State of Louisiana, Docket 126,005, 2/5/15 order.

Emily Bazelon, "If We Can't Prevent Wrongful Convictions, Can We at Least Pay for Them?," *The New York Times Magazine*, April 9, 2015.

Ford v. Caddo Parish District Attorney's Office, U.S.D.C., W.D. La., 15-CV 00544 (SMH-KLH).

Vickie Welborn, "In the Wake of an Apology, Ex Prosecutor Calls For Abolishment Of Death Penalty," *Shreveport Times*, March 27, 2015.

Vickie Welborn, "ADA on Death Penalty: 'We Need to Kill More People'," *Shreveport Times*, March 27, 2015.

Dana Spiotta, "All Alone," *The New York Times Magazine*, December 27, 2015.

60 Minutes, "30 Years on Death Row," October 11, 2015. http://www.cbsnews.com/news/30-years-on-death-row-exoneration-60-minutes/?authenticated=1

University of Pennsylvania, Quattrone Center, Spring Symposium 2015, "Defining Quality in Criminal Justice." https://www.law.upenn.edu/institutes/quattronecenter/conference/springsymposium2015/videos.php

Berger v. U.S., 295 U.S. 78 (1935).

Michael Wayne Haley discussed by Eric M. Albritton

Haley v. Cockrell, U.S.D.C., E.D.Tx., Civil Action 6:00cv518.

Haley v. Cockrell, 306 F. 3d 257 (2002).

Dretke v. Haley, Argument, U.S. Supreme Court, March 2, 2004, No. 02-1824, found at https://www.oyez.org/cases/2003/02-1824.

Dretke v. Haley, 541 U.S. 386 (2004).

Edward Lazarus, "A Little Noticed Supreme Court Case Represents a Huge Injustice," CNN.com, June 15, 2004.

David Brooks, "The Brutalism of Ted Cruz," *The New York Times*, January 12, 2016.

Aman Batheja, "In Nine Trips to Supreme Court, Ted Cruz Saw Mixed Results," *The Texas Tribune,* January 24, 2016.

Adam Liptak and Matt Flegenheimer, "After a Rocky Start, Ted Cruz Had Success Before the Supreme Court," *The New York Times*, February 16, 2016.

Abdallah Higazy

In re Application for Material Witness Warrant, 214 F. Supp. 2d 356 (S.D.N.Y. 2002).

U.S. v. Ferry, Southern District of New York, 02 Cr. 221.

Benjamin Weiser, *The New York Times,* "Worker Is Sentenced for Lie That Jailed Egyptian Student," May 31, 2002.

Higazy v Millennium Hotel, 346 F. Supp. 2d 430 (S.D.N.Y. 2004).

Higazy v Millennium Hotel, 505 F. 3d 161 (2d Cir. 2007).

Certain public records from the proceedings before Judge Rakoff can be found at https://cryptome.org/usa-v-higazy.htm.

Kenneth F. Ireland Jr.

Archives regarding the murder and arrest, https://issuu.com/recordjournal/docs/ireland_pelkey.

State v. Ireland, 218 Conn. 447 (1991).

The National Registry of Exonerations, Kenneth Ireland.

The Innocence Project, Kenneth Ireland.

Alison Leigh Cowan, "Ex-Inmate on Connecticut Parole Board Brings an Insider's View to Hearings," *The New York Times*, December 19, 2014.

Generally, State of Connecticut, Claim of Kenneth Ireland, Claim Number 22457, including hearing at www.ct-n.com.

60 Minutes, "Life After Death Row," January 10, 2016. http://www .cbsnews.com/news/60-minutes-life-after-death-row-exoneration.

Alaine Griffin, "Wrongfully Imprisoned Man Describes Perspective He'd Bring to Parole Board," *Hartford Courant*, January 23, 2015.

"Kenneth Ireland, Wrongfully Convicted of Rape and Murder, Awarded $6 Million," *The Huffington Post*, January 29, 2015.

Miriam Moskowitz

Miriam Moskowitz, *Phantom Spies, Phantom Justice: How I Survived McCarthyism and My Prosecution That Was the Rehearsal for the Rosenberg Trial*, The Justice Institute, © 2010, 2012.

U.S. v. Brothman, 191 F. 2d 70 (2d Cir. 1951).

Testimony of Harry Gold, found at https://catalog.archives.gov/id/2538316.

In re National Security Archive, 2008 WL 8985358.

Rebecca Mead, *Setting It Straight*, The New Yorker, November 29, 2010.

Generally, Moskowitz v. U.S.A., S.D.N.Y., 14 Civ. 6389 (AKH).

Moskowitz v. U.S., 64 F. Supp 3d 574 (S.D.N.Y. 2014).

Steven Pagones

"State Probes Klan Attack," *New Amsterdam News*, December 12, 1987.

"Ku Klux Klan Abduct, Sexually Abuse Girl, 15," *New Amsterdam News*, December 5, 1987.

"Race-Sex Attack Enrages a Town," *Newsday*, December 20, 1987.

"Black Leaders Plan to Protest Violence," *Newsday*, December 6, 1987.

"Bias Cases Fuel Anger of Blacks," *The New York Times*, December 14, 1987.

"Attack Puts Quiet Hudson Area in Civil-Rights Fight," *The New York Times*, January 28, 1988.

Pagones v. Maddox, et. al., Sup. Ct., Dutchess Co., Index No. 4595/88.

Tawana Brawley Grand Jury Report, October 1988, https://archive.org/details/TawanaBrawleyGrandJuryReport.

In the Matter of Alton H. Maddox, 201 A.D.2d 24 (2d Dept. 1994).

In the Matter of C. Vernon Mason, 208 A.D. 1 (1st Dept. 1995).

"Sharpton Admits Rape Claim Wasn't Firsthand," *Chicago Tribune*, February 10, 1998.

Morning Joe, MSNBC, October 8, 2013, found at "Sharpton Can't Admit Tawana Brawly Hoax," freebeacon.com.

Adam Sirois

"Police and Neighbors Join in a SoHo Search for Missing Schoolboy," *The New York Times*, May 27, 1979.

"New Lead is Reported in Etan Patz Mystery," *The New York Times*, November 4, 1989.

Katherine E. Finkelstein, "Death Declaration Ends Hunt for Etan Patz," *The New York Times*, June 20, 2001.

Susan Saulny, "Judge Rules That a Convicted Molester, Now in Prison, Is Responsible for Etan Patz's Death," *The New York Times*, May 5, 2004.

James Barron and William K. Rashbaum, "In Basement, Hopes to Solve '79 Case of Missing Boy," *The New York Times*, April 19, 2012.

Joseph Goldstein and William K. Rashbaum, "After 33 Years, Police Make Arrest in Case of Etan Patz," *The New York Times*, May 24, 2012.

James C. McKinley, Jr., "Ex-Wife of Suspect in Patz Case Testifies That He Confessed to 'Something Terrible'," *The New York Times*, February 9, 2015.

"Defense Expert Says Pedro Hernandez More Vulnerable to False Confession," CBS, March 20, 2015.

James C. McKinley, Jr., "Etan Patz Jurors, on Anniversary, Meet at Scene of Boy's Disappearance," *The New York Times*, May 25, 2015.

"Former Informant: Convicted Pedophile Jose Ramos Admitted Molesting Etan Patz," *CBS New York*, March 26, 2015.

Adam Sirois, "Why I Said Not Guilty: Etan Patz Jury's Lone Holdout Speaks," *New York Post*, May 10, 2015.

Adam Sirois, "Why I Voted Not Guilty in the Etan Patz Court Case," *CNN*, May 28, 2015.

Adam Sirois, "Holdout Juror in Etan Patz case: Prosecution Has No Evidence," *New York Post*, October 19, 2016.

Confessions:

https://www.youtube.com/watch?v=GdIUFGZg3Z8

https://www.youtube.com/watch?v=2DmysyADXXc

Jeffrey Sterling

James Risen, *State of War: The Secret History of the CIA and the Bush Administration*, Free Press © 2006.

James Risen, "A Nation Challenged: The Intelligence Agency," *The New York Times*, November 4, 2001.

James Risen, "Fired by the CIA, He Says Agency Practiced Bias," *The New York Times*, March 2, 2002.

Sterling v. Tenet, 416 F. 3d 338 (4th Cir. 2005).

Generally, U.S. v. Sterling, U.S.D.C., E.D. Va., 1:10cr485 (LMB).

U.S. v. Sterling, 724 F. 3d 482 (4th Cir. 2013).

Peter Maass, "The Whistleblower's Tale," *The Intercept*, June 18, 2015.

A. Ashley Tabaddor

Materials can be found at www.cooley.com/Tabaddor.

Marsha Ternus

Varnum v. Brien, 763 N.W.2d 862 (2009).

A. G. Sulzberger, "Ouster of Iowa Judges Sends Signal to the Bench," *The New York Times*, November 3, 2010.

A. G. Sulzberger, "In Iowa, Voters Oust Judges Over Marriage Issue," *The New York Times*, November 3, 2010.

Mark Curriden, "Judging the Judges: Landmark Iowa Elections Send Tremor Through the Judicial Retention System," *ABA Journal*, January 1, 1011.

Editorial Board, "Money and Judges, a Bad Mix," *The New York Times*, November 2, 2014.

Kate Berry, Brennan Center, "How Judicial Elections Impact Criminal Cases" at http://www.brennancenter.org/sites/default/files/publications/How_Judicial_Elections_Impact_Criminal_Cases.pdf.

Joanna Shepherd and Michael S. King, "Skewed Justice," at http://www.brennancenter.org/sites/default/files/publications/How_Judicial_Elections_Impact_Criminal_Cases.pdf.

Index